"I can't express how refreshing I have found this book to be. I've been studying these themes of union with Christ, dying and rising with him, and growing in likeness to him for many years in Scripture and in academic writings. What I've been missing is a book with the practical, real-world focus that Paul Miller has captured so powerfully. The examples he uses from everyday life, from the lives of 'ordinary saints,' and from his own life make it so easy to envision what these gospel truths look like in practice. More than once I thought to myself, 'This one sentence will be worth the price of the book!' I can't wait for this book to come out because I would like my whole church to read it."

C. D. "Jimmy" Agan III, Senior Pastor, Intown Community Church, Atlanta, Georgia

"I love this book. I feast on Miller's emphasis on resurrection. I'm enthusiastic about his stress on union with Christ; there's more to the gospel than justification. But the J-Curve community (part 5) seems best to me. This is a wonderful, bigger, more Jesus gospel! It's much needed, and Miller's style is just right, building on scholarly contributions but with personal experience and examples of others. It's just what you need to equip you for gospel living in our crumbling Christian culture."

D. Clair Davis, Emeritus Professor of Church History, Westminster Theological Seminary

"This wise and readable book shows how the beloved doctrines of justification and union with Christ shape the thoughts, words, emotions, and actions of believers. I highly recommend this book for everyone who pursues gospel-driven discipleship."

Dan Doriani, Professor of Theology, Covenant Theological Seminary

"A masterly treatment of the Christian life from a biblical perspective. It takes full account of the absorption with self, the preoccupation with appearance, and the individualism that characterize our age to present a biblical model of living that is both liberating and joy generating. I hope this desperately needed, countercultural approach to life will begin to impact worldwide Christianity more and more."

Ajith Fernando, Teaching Director, Youth for Christ, Sri Lanka; author, *Discipling in a Multicultural World*

"Paul Miller's earlier book on prayer, *A Praying Life*, had a profound impact on how I understood prayer and reshaped how I taught it. To date I consider it the most important book written in our generation on the subject! I am delighted to see him turn his attention to another misunderstood and forgotten subject—the power of new life that comes from reckoning ourselves dead to sin and alive to God in Christ. Paul has a way of taking profound truths and making them accessible, and in this book you'll see why—because he lives them. This is not a book of theological posturing, it is simply a guide written by someone who has walked the path and wants to show you how you can also."

J. D. Grear, President, Southern Baptist Convention; author, *Not God Enough*; Pastor, The Summit Church, Raleigh-Durham, North Carolina

"I enjoyed this book on many levels. The apostle Paul tells us that believers have died and been raised with Jesus. Paul Miller helps us discover what this looks like in everyday life. His teaching rings true and will be helpful to many."

John M. Frame, Emeritus Professor of Systematic Theology and Philosophy, Reformed Theological Seminary

"Nothing is more important for the gospel and for our lives as Christians than the reality of our union with Christ as Scripture teaches us about that union. Paul Miller is to be commended for seeking to apply that teaching to issues of discipleship."

Richard B. Gaffin Jr., Emeritus Professor of Biblical and Systematic Theology, Westminster Theological Seminary

"Paul Miller has carefully observed Jesus. He has carefully observed how the work of grace unfolds in the apostle Paul's life and in his own life. Take time with this book. You will become a deeper, wiser, truer person. You will become more humble, more joyous, more purposeful. And you will walk more steadily in the light."

David Powlison, Executive Director, Christian Counseling & Educational Foundation

"I own my prejudice with respect to my excitement about Paul Miller's new book, *J-Curve*. Written with the glory and grace of Philippians 2:5–11 at its core, Miller has given us a most accessible, timely, and theologically sound introduction to life in Christ. Miller has always been known as a great lover of the gospel and a master illustrator, and both are on display in copious measures in *J-Curve*. This book shows us how to live by the rhythms of the gospel at the pace of grace. A life of union and communion with Jesus has never seemed more beautiful and practical."

Scotty Ward Smith, Pastor Emeritus, Christ Community Church, Franklin, Tennessee; Teacher in Residence, West End Community Church, Nashville, Tennessee

"'Take up your cross and follow me.' What was Jesus asking us to do—or be? How does it play out in everyday life? These questions are intensely practical from the moment I wake up in the morning. And that's why I love Paul Miller's new book, *J-Curve: Dying and Rising with Jesus in Everyday Life*. Never have I read a more practical work on how a Christian can flourish through deep affliction. This book will revolutionize the way you look at your sufferings and your relationship to Christ. If you're craving a life with your Savior that utterly transforms, this book is your best hands-on guide."

Joni Eareckson Tada, Founder, Joni and Friends

"The footnotes and shrewdness of this book point to an author who has read widely and pondered deeply. The stories and real-life focus of this book reveal an author who has paid a high price—the laceration of his ego—to begin to learn not only the power of Christ's resurrection but the fellowship of his sufferings. And a healing, fruitful, even joyful fellowship it is! In just three dozen brief and engrossing chapters, Paul Miller helps the reader see what's missing in many of our Christian lives—namely, they are sub-Christian! This book demonstrates how faith in Christ can more nearly attain its God-intended goal of a 24/7 immersion in Christ and expression of Christ-like love. Integrating the cross with the resurrection in an unusually graphic and encouraging fashion, this book is sure to not only challenge but also change many lives."

Robert W. Yarbrough, Professor of New Testament, Covenant Theological Seminary

J-CURVE

J-CURVE

Dying and Rising with Jesus
in Everyday Life

Paul E. Miller

::: CROSSWAY®

WHEATON, ILLINOIS

J-Curve: Dying and Rising with Jesus in Everyday Life

Copyright © 2019 by Paul E. Miller

Published by Crossway
          1300 Crescent Street
          Wheaton, Illinois 60187

Cover design: Kevin Lipp

First printing 2019

Printed in the United States of America

Unless otherwise indicated, Scripture quotations are from the ESV® Bible (The Holy Bible, English Standard Version®), copyright © 2001 by Crossway, a publishing ministry of Good News Publishers. Used by permission. All rights reserved.

Scripture quotations marked AT are the author's translation.

Scripture quotations marked MESSAGE are from *The Message*. Copyright © by Eugene H. Peterson 1993, 1994, 1995, 1996, 2000, 2001, 2002. Used by permission of NavPress Publishing Group.

Scripture references marked NRSV are from *The New Revised Standard Version*. Copyright © 1989 by the Division of Christian Education of the National Council of the Churches of Christ in the U.S.A. Published by Thomas Nelson, Inc. Used by permission of the National Council of the Churches of Christ in the U.S.A.

All emphases in Scripture quotations have been added by the author.

Some names and details of the stories have been altered.

Trade paperback ISBN: 978-1-4335-6156-6
ePub ISBN: 978-1-4335-6159-7
PDF ISBN: 978-1-4335-6157-3
Mobipocket ISBN: 978-1-4335-6158-0

Library of Congress Cataloging-in-Publication Data

Names: Miller, Paul E., 1953- author.
Title: J-curve: dying and rising with Jesus in everyday life / Paul E. Miller.
Description: Wheaton, Illinois: Crossway, 2019. | Includes bibliographical references and index.
Identifiers: LCCN 2018029012 (print) | LCCN 2018046291 (ebook) | ISBN 9781433561573 (pdf) | ISBN 9781433561580 (mobi) | ISBN 9781433561597 (epub) | ISBN 9781433561566 (tp) | ISBN 9781433561597 (ePub) | ISBN 9781433561580 (Mobipocket)
Subjects: LCSH: Christian life. | Jesus Christ—Crucifixion. | Jesus Christ—Resurrection.
Classification: LCC BV4509.5 (ebook) | LCC BV4509.5 .M555 2019 (print) | DDC 248.4—dc23
LC record available at https://lccn.loc.gov/2018029012

Crossway is a publishing ministry of Good News Publishers.

LB		27	26	25	24	23	22	21	20	19
14	13	12	11	10	9	8	7	6	5	4	3	2	1

To our beloved daughter Ashley M. Frearson
(November 16, 1975, to September 9, 2018).
We can't wait to see you again!

Thank you to
Tina Harrell and Catharine Grigsby,
whose generosity make this book possible.

Contents

PART 3: THE DESCENT OF LOVE

PART 4: RISING WITH JESUS

PART 5: FORMING A J-CURVE COMMUNITY

Illustrations

DISCOVERING THE J-CURVE

What Is the J-Curve?

What Is the Larger Theological
Framework of the J-Curve?

What Is the Connection between the
J-Curve and Justification by Faith?

"I Will Never Do This Again"

The J-Curve and How It Helps

Caring for someone affected by multiple disabilities is never boring. Life is generally pleasant, but at any given moment, you are seconds away from disaster—a part of your brain is always on. So to give my wife, Jill, a break, I decided to take our disabled daughter Kim with me on a speaking trip.

On a Friday in January 2001, Kim and I headed to the Philadelphia airport for a trip to Florida. We had two suitcases and a large box with "seeJesus" written on the side. As soon as we parked, Kim rummaged through the carry-on bag, only to discover that Jill had not packed the recorded book that Kim wanted. She began a low-level whine, one we've considered patenting and selling to CIA interrogators. Forget water torture; just play this tape of Kim and your prisoner will be putty in your hands.

When we got to the bus stall, I told Kim we had to wait for the bus, and her whining grew louder and more irritating. Everyone was looking at us. I glanced down at my box, wondering if there was any way I could hide the big "seeJesus" sign. I looked like a religious nut.

When the bus arrived, I had a horrible thought: "How will I get all this luggage and Kim on the bus at the same time?" I decided to help her on first, then return for the luggage. As I was getting on with the luggage, much to Kim's delight, the back door closed on me. Her well-honed sense of humor kicked in, and she grinned broadly as she watched me shouting at the bus driver while being crushed by the door.

The ride to the terminal was uneventful—Kim is fine as long as she is moving. But when we got to the check-in area, we found a line that wrapped around the terminal. Knowing we'd never make our flight if we got in that line, I headed up the escalator, luggage and Kim in tow. As soon as we got to security, our line merged with another, forming one very long line—and Kim began whining again. Fortunately, she is adept at moving quickly in lines. She stands so close behind people that she bumps them. It's uncomfortable for them, but they see she's disabled and often let us go ahead.

When we got to the scanners, Kim wouldn't put her speech computer on the conveyer belt. She started arguing with the security person, typing out, "It's my voice." I yanked her "voice" out of her hand and put it on the belt, and she restarted her whining. Of course, security was suspicious of my "seeJesus" box, so a particularly scrupulous guard scanned it meticulously.

Once through security, we had twenty minutes before our gate closed. I checked the screen. We were in the wrong terminal. We were in Terminal C, but our flight was in B. There was no way we'd make it. I threw myself in front of one of the carts that carry people around and begged for a ride. The driver agreed and whisked us away, but as we came down the long ramp of Terminal B, we got stuck behind a man on his cell phone. Our cart was emitting a loud, persistent beeping, but the man did not pick up his excruciatingly slow pace. As Kim saw me getting tense, she started to smile again.

We made it to the plane, and after settling into our seats, my shoulders relaxed as I hooked Kim up to her audiobook. Then the flight attendant came by and told Kim to turn off her electronic devices. Kim turned off her audiobook, but refused to turn off her speech computer. I reached over and shut off the device—and Kim resumed her whining. A few minutes later, the captain announced, "We have eleven planes ahead of us, so it will be fifteen minutes before departure." Even though she could not see the line of planes, just knowing we had to wait led Kim to a complete meltdown. I started to say, "Kim, if you don't stop, we aren't going to Disney," but that was one of my reasons for taking her on this trip, so I swallowed my threat. Helpless and embarrassed, I said to myself, "This was a mistake. I will never do this again."

The next day, Saturday, as I reflected on my reaction, I realized I'd forgotten the J-Curve, the idea, frequently articulated by the apostle Paul, that the normal Christian life repeatedly re-enacts the dying and rising of Jesus. I call it the J-Curve because, like the letter J, Jesus's life first went *down* into death, then *up* into resurrection.

Just like the earthly life of Jesus, the J ends higher than it starts. It's the pattern not only of Jesus's life, but of our lives—of our everyday moments. When Kim and I were sitting in the back of the plane, I thought everything had gone wrong. No, the apostle Paul says, the J-Curve is the shape of the normal Christian life. Our lives mirror Jesus's. In the diagram below you see Jesus's J-Curve and our present J-Curves.

Fig. 1A. Jesus's J-Curve and Our J-Curves

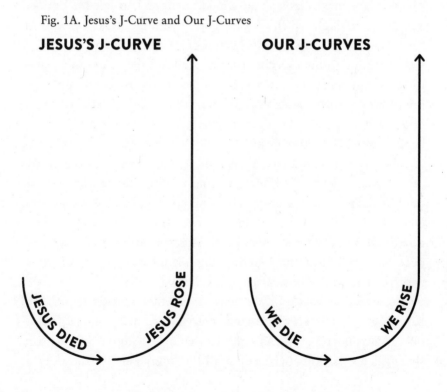

> The J-Curve is the shape of the normal
> Christian life. Our lives mirror Jesus's.

Keep in mind that Jesus's J-Curve atones for our sins; ours don't. His is once for all—we have multiple J-Curves that echo his. (For the sake of clarity, when I use the term J-Curve by itself I'm referring to our *present* J-Curves.) As we shall see, our J-Curves each have their own unique cadences, but they all

1. enter some kind of suffering in which evil is weakened or killed;
2. weaken the flesh and form us into the image of Jesus;
3. lead to a real-time, present resurrection.

Dying and Rising on the Way to Florida

As I reflected on how our travel disaster was the beginning of a J-Curve, our trip went from a lifeless gray to vibrant and multicolored. Like Jesus, I experienced a death followed by a resurrection. The two are inextricably intertwined. Friday's trip left me drained and weary (dying), which created a spirit of humility as I taught on Saturday (rising). On Saturday, I was in front of a group of people who were listening to my every word. I'm thankful they were such eager listeners, but being at the center of people's praise is potentially toxic. I'm prone to the leadership sins of overtalking and underlistening, so Friday's dying was God's gift to inoculate me against the pride lurking behind success and popularity.

The work of love that happens in a J-Curve exposes our hearts in unexpected ways. On Friday, in front of three different crowds (at the bus shelter, in the security line, and on the plane), I was far too concerned with how I looked. In fact, my desire to hide my "seeJesus" box at the bus shelter showed I was ashamed of him. The sign was dead-on—see Jesus in his humility; don't run from his path of weakness. In fact, that's the message of this book.

Resurrection has multiple faces. After that Florida trip, I told Kim I'd give her $50 for letting me interview her at a Young Life banquet in Washington, DC. As I interviewed her about our Florida trip, she giggled, smacking her head at all the funny parts of the story. It was a delight to watch her. After the interview, I stepped aside so she could take her speech computer off the podium and sit down, but she didn't budge. Instead with 250 people listening, she typed out on her speech computer, M-O-N-E-Y. In other words, "Dad, show me the money!" How's that for a resurrection?

The Right Time to Rediscover the J-Curve

The "collapse" Kim and I went through on our Florida trip is a microcosm of the cultural collapse Western civilization is going through. The rising tide of unbelief and the lure of secular liberalism touch almost every Christian home. Fifty years ago, we called the occasional child who walked away from the faith a black sheep. Now almost every Christian home has children walking away from the faith.

And that's just the tip of the iceberg. A young wife, "Sarah," from a healthy church confided to a friend of mine, "I think I've outgrown my marriage." That's something you might say about an immature boyfriend, but Sarah said she had "outgrown" her sacred vows to her husband. She used therapeutic language to mask her betrayal.

Sarah's feelings operated at the center of her decision making. Almost certainly, Sarah encountered some immaturity in her husband, instinctively discarded the biblical morality she grew up with ("Be faithful in marriage"), and reached for the central moral vision of our age, which I'll call *feelism*.[1] By making "How does it/you make me feel?" our moral grid, feelism makes faithfulness—the glue of life—almost impossible. Feelism drives emotions to the center, distorting and amplifying them in the process. As we'll discover, the J-Curve not only balances our emotions but helps them come alive.

Our world is increasingly filled with people like Sarah who have inhaled the spirit of this age. To quote William Butler Yeats's poem "The Second Coming," "the centre cannot hold." So how does the church survive and even thrive when the world is going crazy from

---

1. A leading moral philosopher, Alasdair MacIntyre, writes, "The unrecognized philosophical power of emotivism is one clue to its cultural power." *After Virtue: A Study in Moral Theory*, 3rd ed. (Notre Dame, IN: University of Notre Dame Press, 2007), 20. See pp. 6–22 for MacIntyre's description of the grip that emotivism (feelism) has on our culture. My son John and I coined the word *feelism*.

the care of the sacred self? As we shall see, there's no better time than now to rediscover what Jesus's dying and rising means. That's why I've written this book, to help prepare the bride, the wife of the Lamb, for suffering.

The J-Curve not only balances our
emotions but helps them come alive.

But this is not a book on coping with suffering. My goal is to draw you, the reader, into the dying and rising of Jesus—to reset your sense of the normal Christian life, freeing you from cynicism and despair. Inhabiting the J-Curve promises to transform your entire vision of how you engage life, freeing you from the world of resentment, touchiness, and just plain old grumpiness, and inviting you into Jesus's world, a world rich with joy, hope, and love.

We will pay attention to two cultural lenses that prevent us from living the J-Curve: the lenses of the manager and the therapist.[2] For example, the manager looks at my flight with Kim and says, "You should have left more time for traveling with Kim" (true), "It's not wise to combine too many things like speaking and caring for Kim" (possibly), and "You should have brought someone to help you" (yes, I did that the next time). The therapist tells me, "You need to do something for yourself" (true), then asks, "Do you have a problem with anger?" (yes, Kim brings out the best and the worst in me) or "Have you thought of putting Kim in a home?" (no, she's God's gift to us; plus she's one of my best friends). Both the manager and the therapist have pieces of wisdom, but they miss love. Because they play it safe, they miss life in all its richness. They miss that not only was God resurrecting my soul and saving me from pride during my trip with Kim, but also that my mini-death gave Jill a mini-resurrection. That's how love works.

When I felt ashamed and frustrated with Kim, I mirrored the state of the church. I'd forgotten the J-Curve. Just as Martin Luther redis-

---

2. I prize the skilled work of many managers and therapists. I do both in my work. I'm critiquing, as you'll see, a whole cultural mind-set or value system.

covered justification by faith in the early 1500s, we need to rediscover the J-Curve in today's rising storm of unbelief and evil.

Like a diamond, each facet of the J-Curve refracts the light in a slightly different way on the wonder of Jesus's death and resurrection. In the upcoming pages, we will journey with the apostle Paul as he lives and teaches the J-Curve in his writings and his life.

You might think I'm overstating the importance of the J-Curve. But the apostle actually writes more about the J-Curve than he does justification by faith, which is his focus in Romans and Galatians. But the J-Curve dominates Philippians, 1 and 2 Corinthians, Romans 6 and 8, Colossians 1 and 3, and Ephesians 1, and it is modeled in Philemon, 1 Thessalonians, and Acts. Beginning with Philippians, we'll focus on Paul's J-Curve writings.

When I explained the J-Curve to a group of pastors, they wondered why they'd never heard it before. One said, "I guess we are more focused on the theological than the practical." I said, "No, our theological vision is too narrow." My goal is to add to our Romans/Galatians lens a neglected Pauline lens: the J-Curve.

At each point, our understanding of the J-Curve and how it transforms our everyday life, even our emotions, will become clearer. Here's an overview of what we'll cover:

- Part 1, "Discovering the J-Curve," introduces the J-Curve and explores the relationship between the J-Curve and three great truths of the Reformation: (1) the flesh, (2) justification by faith, and (3) union with Christ. The lack of integration of the J-Curve with these truths has led to theological imbalance and thus weakness in how we do life.
- Part 2, "Dying with Jesus," is where we begin to follow the path of the J-Curve down into death and then up into resurrection. Part 2 gives an overview of three different types of J-Curves, then takes a deeper look at the *repentance* J-Curve, where we put to death our sins, and the *suffering* J-Curve, where outside suffering leads us into dying with Jesus.
- Part 3, "The Descent of Love," explores the *love* J-Curve, where love leads to suffering, by looking at Jesus's descent of love. We examine the DNA of love—humility and incarnation. By DNA, I mean a deep structure that permeates the whole. We

also look at the danger of getting stuck in dying and making an idol out of humility.

- Part 4, "Rising with Jesus," focuses on the resurrection side of the J-Curve. We watch Paul look at life through a resurrection lens. He creates a tapestry of love as he embodies Jesus's dying and rising in his and his coworkers' lives. We follow Paul in his travels to discover insights into the art of living life in the dying and rising of Jesus.
- Part 5, "Forming a J-Curve Community," shifts our focus from the individual to the community. Paul uses the J-Curve to re-shape an entire community into the image of Jesus. We descend into the nitty-gritty of life in the ancient world as Paul uses the J-Curve to relentlessly confront a culture that has kept the gospel from forming a true Jesus community.

Because this book is about the gospel in everyday life, I've inter-twined my own stories with those of others—Luther, Mother Teresa, and Joni Eareckson Tada. But our main focus is on the apostle Paul's journey for Jesus and into Jesus. Along the way, we'll encounter leak-ing Dixie cups, bench-warming hockey players, a sheep named Ed, and a host of everyday problems. These stories don't illustrate the J-Curve; they embody it, with the goal of helping you retell your stories in the light of the death and resurrection of Jesus. To "embody" simply means that you give a tangible or visible form to an idea.

Welcome to our pilgrimage into the wonder of the gospel!

"I Take Your Place"

The Substitutionary Nature of Love

The Sunday after Friday's plane trip to Florida, I took Kim to Disney World. We just missed the tram, which meant a brief wait. With Kim whining in the background, I called home to see how Jill was doing. Our daughter Ashley answered, "Every five minutes Mom says, 'I can't believe how quiet it is without Kim.'" I got death and Jill got resurrection. Substitution is the heart of love.

Every great love story has substitution in it. For instance, in *Les Misérables*, when Jean Valjean steals the bishop's silverware, the police return him to the bishop to confirm the theft. The bishop, in a breathtaking triumph of love, assures the police that the silverware was a gift, and he even scolds Valjean for forgetting to take the silver candlesticks. Much to the disgust of the police, who know the bishop is covering for Jean, the bishop gives Jean the last of his silver, the candlesticks. The bishop substitutes his silver for Valjean's freedom. That's the structure of love.

Filling Up What Is Lacking in Christ's Afflictions

My discovery of the J-Curve began in the late 1980s after I'd written a course on how the gospel applies to our lives. I noticed the apostle

Paul didn't just preach the gospel, he relived it. This passage from Colossians 1:24 and others like it caught my attention:

> Now I rejoice in my sufferings for your sake, and in my flesh I am filling up what is lacking in Christ's afflictions for the sake of his body, that is, the church.

Fig. 2A. My Dying and Jill's Rising

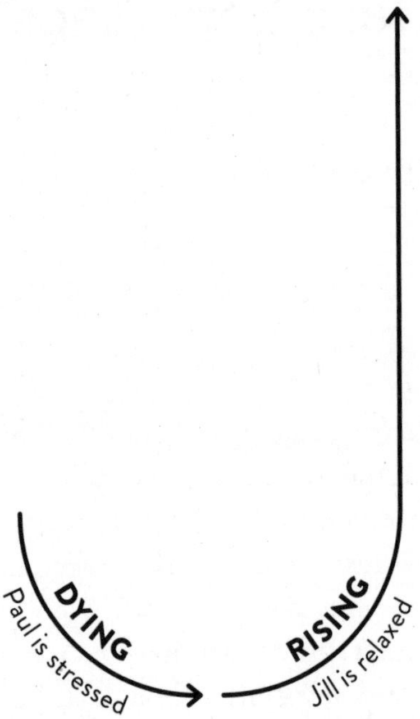

It seemed strange, almost uncomfortable, that Paul says he *rejoices in his sufferings.* Most of us endure or cope with suffering, but we don't rejoice in it. Then he says he is *suffering for their sake.* How can he suffer for the believers in Colossae? He isn't even close to them; he is in Rome, a month's travel from Colossae. Strangest of all, he says he is *filling up what is lacking in Christ's afflictions.* How can anything be lacking in Christ's afflictions? Jesus's death was "once for all." I'd never thought about this before. It seemed new and strange.[1] I'd seen

---

1. The influential scholar Albert Schweitzer called this pattern Paul's "mysticism." See *The Mysticism of Paul the Apostle,* trans. William Montgomery (Baltimore: Johns Hopkins University Press, 1998).

this verse applied to missionaries who suffered for the gospel, but not to me, not to everyday life.

How could anything be lacking in Christ's afflictions?

Paul's letter to Philemon, the companion letter to Colossians, especially riveted me. It's where I first discovered the J-Curve. Philemon, a wealthy leader in the church in Colossae, had a slave named Onesimus who ran away to Paul in Rome and was dramatically changed by his encounter with the apostle.[2] Paul sent Onesimus (his name means "useful") back to Philemon with this letter, which was read to the entire congregation. In the letter, Paul asks Philemon not only to accept Onesimus, but to welcome him as a brother. Paul hints that Philemon should give Onesimus his freedom.[3] The gospel permeates Paul's assumptions as he makes his case to Philemon. Look at Paul's seemingly innocuous comment to Philemon about Onesimus, the runaway slave:

> I would have been glad to keep him with me, in order that he might serve me on your behalf during my imprisonment for the gospel. (Philem. 13)

Paul suggests that Philemon "gift" Onesimus to Paul "that he might serve me on your behalf." Just as Jesus died for us, Paul assumes Philemon will want Onesimus to serve *on Philemon's* behalf. This is an expensive assumption—a male slave could be valued at as much as $150,000 in today's figures.[4] For Paul, the lived-out gospel trumps Philemon's property rights (according to Roman law, he owns Onesimus) and Roman justice (Onesimus ran away). Paul invites Philemon into a *fellowship of Christ's sufferings* (Phil. 3:10) in an offhand way, sure that Philemon has the same perspective. Paul presumes that

---

2. James D. G. Dunn, *The Epistles to the Colossians and to Philemon* (Grand Rapids, MI: Eerdmans), 304–5. We have at least one record of a slave running away from his master in Roman times to a potential mediator who appeals on the slave's behalf by letter.

3. See N. T. Wright, *Paul and the Faithfulness of God* (Minneapolis: Fortress, 2013) 12–15.

4. Mary Beard mentions two slave prices in Pompeii: 1,500 and 6,252 sesterces (one quarter of a denarius). *Pompeii: The Life of a Roman Town* (London: Profile Books, 2008), 179. A denarius would be worth about $100 (Matt. 20:2) in modern terms, showing that slaves could be very costly.

Philemon considers substitutionary love normal. "The DNA of Jesus has so shaped Paul that he can't imagine a Christian life that isn't radically shaped in this same way."[5]

Later in the letter, Paul offers to substitute himself for Onesimus:

> If he has wronged you at all, or owes you anything, charge that to my account. I, Paul, write this with my own hand: I will repay it. (Philem. 18–19b)

Paul assumes that both he and Philemon would gladly substitute themselves for each other; it's how they do life. For that reason, Paul's request doesn't seem odd to them.

Since Paul's letter to the Colossians is read to the church at the same time as his letter to Philemon, Paul's "off the cuff" remark about "filling up what is lacking in Christ's afflictions" also makes sense to them. That means that the J-Curve is their normal. The entire congregation sees life as defined by substitutionary love that participates in Christ's dying and rising. The gospel re-enacted functions at the DNA level for how the church does life.

Here's my paraphrase of what Paul says:

> I know that all of you at Colossae don't just believe the gospel; you act out the gospel in a life of dying love for one another. Just as Jesus substituted himself for you, so you live a life of substitutionary love. The gospel has radically reshaped your relationships. It's natural, then, for me to presume Philemon would willingly gift Onesimus to help me; that's how you do life. But I'm not asking for that. I simply want Philemon to receive Onesimus back not just as a slave, but as a brother.

Ed the Sheep

When I was discovering this in Philemon, our family, but especially Jill, was under enormous pressure. Our six kids, aged three to sixteen, were constantly fighting and whining. Caring for Kim, our fourth child, had depleted our savings; we were living from paycheck to paycheck. Jill did all her gift buying for the kids at thrift stores, putting

---

5. Jimmy Agan in personal correspondence.

the best face on it by packing their presents in boxes from brand-name stores. Our kids figured out what she was doing and started sniffing their stale-smelling presents when they opened the boxes! Then Kim was kicked out of a school because they didn't think she could learn.

Every area of our life had become extraordinarily difficult—and Jill felt the brunt of it. I didn't know what to do; I didn't know how to love her. She was hemmed in on every side. With Philemon in mind, I prayed God would allow me to experience what she was experiencing. I wrote this prayer in my journal in January 1991:

> *Father,*
> *How do I love her?*
> *How do I give myself up for her?*
> *How do I die for her?*

When I prayed this prayer, I wasn't sure what it looked like to "give myself up for her." Over the next few years, God began to show me what that looked like in everyday moments.

Here's one glimpse. We'd moved to the edge of Philadelphia's northern suburbs in 1993 to get better schooling for Kim. We had a place that allowed Jill to fulfill her childhood dream of having farm animals. Growing up on the streets of Philly with a concrete backyard, she had longed for some green acres. We had four pygmy goats and one big sheep named Ed.

In the winter of 1995, our local weather forecasters began predicting the storm of the century. A couple of days before the storm, Jill began worrying about her animals in their little wooden shelters. Since Ed had a six-inch-deep coat of wool, I wasn't concerned, but I called a local sheep farmer and asked if the animals would be OK. He said yes, as long as they had shelters. I shared this with Jill, and it seemed to calm her.

On Saturday evening, when we already had a foot of snow on the ground, Jill began to get nervous again. We knew the goats were savvy and would go into their sheds, but Ed wasn't the sharpest tack in the box. I went to bed about 10 p.m. and was drifting off to sleep when I heard Jill's voice from the next room: "Paul, would you check the sheep? I'm concerned about Ed." As I lay there, I plotted my response.

I'd remind her of what the farmer had said, then I'd explain the insulating value of snow, not to mention Ed's thick coat. But I knew Jill well enough to realize that none of this would convince her. She'd just go out into the blizzard by herself, which would just get me more irritated at her.

Then I remembered how Paul re-enacted the gospel. I thought, "This isn't complicated. I can substitute my warmth for her worry." The problem wasn't Ed, but Jill's anxiety. So I crawled out of bed, put on my boots and jacket, and checked Ed. He was fine, so Jill was too.

"This isn't complicated. I can substitute
my warmth for her worry."

In the morning, we trudged out together into a winter wonderland of snow to check on the animals, but especially Ed. As we called his name, we made a poem: "Where is Ed? Is Ed dead? Will he come out of his bed?" Finally, one of the lumps on the field began to move, and out popped Ed!

A New Vision of Normal

In this small act of dying, I loved my wife differently. I realized that in Philemon and elsewhere, Paul was re-enacting the gospel, Jesus's death *for* us. The word *for* means the weight of our sins comes on Jesus. Paul uses *for* when he defines the gospel:

> The Lord Jesus Christ . . . gave himself *for* our sins. (Gal. 1:3a–4b)

> Christ died *for* our sins. (1 Cor. 15:3b)

So just as Jesus substitutes himself for us, we substitute the pieces of our lives for others. Now I understood how Paul could *fill up what was lacking in Christ's afflictions.*[6] Jesus's death was once for all.

---

6. Richard B. Gaffin Jr. writes about Col. 1:24, "This union is such that not only can the sufferings of believers be viewed as Christ's and as being conformed to his death, but also the personal, past-historical sufferings of Christ and the present afflictions of the church are seen together as constituting one whole. Again, certainly not in the sense that the sufferings of the church have some additive atoning, reconciling value." "The Usefulness of the Cross," *Westminster Theological Journal* 41, no. 2 (Spring 1979): 242. See also John Murray, *The Epistle to the Romans* (Grand Rapids, MI: Eerdmans, 1959), 299.

His death for Jill was finished—mine was ongoing. I could substitute myself for the pieces of her life, like checking on Ed. So I had a mini-death, and Jill could live. Paul articulates this:

> For we who live are always being given over to death for Jesus' sake, so that the life of Jesus also may be manifested in our mortal flesh. *So death is at work in us, but life in you.* (2 Cor. 4:11–12)

Seeing this pattern of substitutionary love reoriented my vision of what it was to be a Christian. For example, in those years I enjoyed reading *Time* magazine. Instead of interrupting my reading of *Time* to love, I started interrupting love to read *Time*. It was the difference between a life of low-level irritation (when the kids interrupted my reading of *Time*) and a life devoted to people (when I interrupted my loving them by reading *Time*).

Here's the thing: when we understand that substitution is the heart of love, we see life through a different lens. We realize that all of life is love. Love is 24-7.

3

Marketing the Self

What We Do Instead of the J-Curve

What do we do instead of living the J-Curve? What's our default way of operating? Simple: we boast. The J-Curve goes down; we want to go up.

Paul describes his pre-Jesus self in Philippians 3 by recalling his boasting. He divides seven boasts into lists of-four and three. I've written them below as an ascending stair, to reflect Paul's boasting spirit.

If anyone else thinks he has reason for *confidence* in the flesh,
I have more: [Read from the bottom up.]

> as to righteousness under the law, blameless[!]
> (Phil. 3:4–6)[1]
> as to zeal, a persecutor of the church;
> as to the law, a Pharisee;
> a Hebrew of Hebrews[!]
> of the tribe of Benjamin,
> of the people of Israel,
> circumcised on the eighth day,

---

1. I have added exclamation marks in 3:5–6 to capture Paul's ending his lists with a closing "flourish."

Paul's first four boasts describe his blue-blood Jewish heritage. In a shame-honor culture (the entire ancient world), your identity came from your family, your birth order, and your tribe. Identity was given, not earned. Like all Jews, Paul was "circumcised on the eighth day." But he wasn't an ordinary Jew: he was "of the tribe of Benjamin," the only northern tribe that stayed with Judah when ancient Israel divided. Paul's parents proudly named him Saul after the first king of Israel, a Benjaminite. The tribe of Benjamin was the warrior tribe—the shock troops who led the Israelite army into battle.[2] Paul concludes his first list with a flourish, describing himself as "a Hebrew of Hebrews"!

Paul's next three boasts shift to his personal achievements. He had become an elite Pharisee, scrupulous in following the law, highly educated by a famous rabbi, Gamaliel (see Acts 22:3). But even among the Pharisees, Paul stood out because he zealously persecuted the church. *Zeal* was a code word for a devout Jew who fought the enemies of God, like Aaron's son Phineas, who speared an Israelite man committing adultery with a Midianite woman (Num. 25:6–13; Ps. 106:30–31).[3] Paul ends with another crescendo—"under the law, blameless!" As he writes elsewhere,

> I was advancing in Judaism beyond many of my own age among my people. (Gal. 1:14a)

He was the best of the best!

The Flesh—Our Ancient Allergy to God

Paul's boasts move him up from shame to honor, from failure to boasting. I've charted Paul's boasts on the Failure-Boasting Chart below.

Our English word *boast* is misleading because it has a narrow, negative meaning. The Greek word *boast* encompasses the ideas of "glory" or "rejoice," so it's often translated that way. For example, in February 2018, the Philadelphia Eagles won the Super Bowl for

---

2. Gen. 49:27; Judg. 5:14; 20–21; and Hos. 5:8 fit this picture of the Benjaminites as a warrior culture.

3. See Dane C. Ortlund, *Zeal without Knowledge: The Concept of Zeal in Romans 10, Galatians 1, and Philippians 3*, The Library of New Testament Studies (London: T&T Clark International, 2012), 150–65. Ortlund writes, Paul "was so deeply and passionately concerned about maintaining Jewish solidarity and adherence to Torah [law] that he would go to any length, even Phinehan-like violence, to snuff out perceived threats to such cherished loyalties" (154).

the first time. The day before the game, as my plane landed in Philadelphia, one of the Southwest Airlines flight attendants led the whole plane in the Eagles' fight song, "Fly, Eagles Fly"! For the next six months in my travels, I boasted—that is, I gloried and rejoiced—that we'd won. That is good boasting. It's what humans do. We are always glorying in something. The problem is the object of our glory.

Fig. 3A. The Failure-Boasting Chart

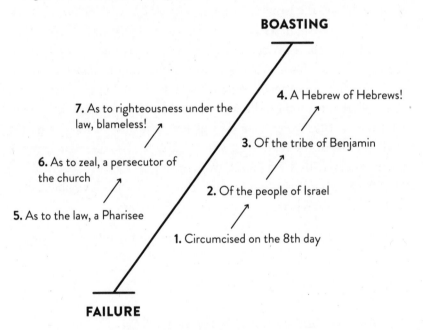

BOASTING

7. As to righteousness under the law, blameless!

6. As to zeal, a persecutor of the church

5. As to the law, a Pharisee

4. A Hebrew of Hebrews!

3. Of the tribe of Benjamin

2. Of the people of Israel

1. Circumcised on the 8th day

FAILURE

You can see the wider meaning of *boast* in our text above when Paul talks about his "confidence in the flesh." The problem isn't confidence—we are all confident in something—but the object of Paul's confidence—his flesh. Paul glories in his flesh.

Flesh is Paul's short-hand for our ancient allergy to God, our natural bent toward evil.[4] The flesh is us on our own, independent of God,

---

4. John Calvin writes about "confidence in the flesh": "For under the term *flesh* he includes everything of an external kind in which an individual is prepared to glory . . . he gives the name of *flesh* to everything that is apart from Christ. He thus reproves . . . the perverse zealots of the law, because, not satisfied with Christ, they have recourse to grounds of glorifying apart from him. He has employed the terms *glorying*, and *having confidence*, to denote the same thing. For confidence lifts up a man, so that he ventures even to glory, and thus the two things are connected." *Com-*

relentlessly promoting ourselves. Paul isn't dealing with the isolated sin of boasting, of openly praising ourselves; he's dealing with the *boasting self*, our secret quest for our own glory. We might never actually boast, but we might live our life dominated by the *boasting self*—critical, judgmental, and quietly superior. You see, in the *boasting self*, praise due to God turns in on ourselves.

Our flesh reverses the two great commandments: instead of loving others, we love ourselves (pride); and instead of loving God, we seek other gods (idolatry). Pride and idolatry work hand in glove. Paul's alternative god or idol was *obedience to the law*.[5] The law was life for Paul.[6] That, in turn, provided a path for Paul to exalt himself. We can feel that as he ends each of his two lists with a flourish. Our false gods not only promise life, but make us look good. Judaism was a platform for the display of Paul.[7]

Paul's boasting embodies the flesh just as Jesus's dying and rising, the J-Curve, embodies goodness. Good and evil don't float; they are always personified. So just before Paul's seven boasts, he warns the Philippians about the Judaizers who demand that Gentile believers be circumcised:[8]

> Look out for the dogs, look out for the evildoers, look out for those who mutilate the flesh. For we are the circumcision, who worship by the Spirit of God and glory [or "boast"] in Christ Jesus and put no *confidence* in the flesh—though I myself have reason for *confidence* in the flesh also. (Phil. 3:2–4)[9]

Notice Paul doesn't say, "Look out for the flesh" or "Look out for legalism." He says, "Look out for men who embody 'the law as life.'"

---

mentaries on the Epistle of Paul the Apostle to the Philippians, Colossians, and Thessalonians, trans. John Pringle (Grand Rapids, MI: Baker, 2003), 89 (emphasis added).

5. Rom. 1:16–3:18 is Paul's "brief history of the flesh." The flesh's most basic move is rejection of God and the worship of alternative gods or idols.

6. See also Douglas J. Moo, *Galatians*, Baker Exegetical Commentary on the New Testament (Grand Rapids, MI: Baker Academic, 2013), 100; Ortlund, *Zeal*, 138–39.

7. Geerhardus Vos makes this point: "In its extreme form it [the law-method] assumes the character of enmity against God. . . . The method formulated breaks down . . . [in] its inevitable lapse into the sin of 'boasting' before God. . . . [It is] a profoundly irreligious attitude towards God as the rightful possessor and sole legitimate recipient of religious glory." *The Pauline Eschatology* (Phillipsburg, NJ: P&R, 1994), 274.

8. The Judaizers were Jewish followers of Jesus who insisted that Gentile converts also follow the Jewish law.

9. Regarding "boast" as a synonym for "glory" in this passage, see Frank S. Thielman, *Philippians*, The NIV Application Commentary (Grand Rapids, MI: Zondervan, 1995), 168.

By demanding circumcision, these "cutters" "mutilate the flesh." In fact, Paul says, "We Christians are the *real* circumcision, the authentic Jews, because we've shifted our boast from ourselves to Christ." Paul never stops boasting; he just shifts from boasting about himself to boasting about Christ.

Boasting Was Like Breathing

Paul's pre-Jesus self wasn't satisfied with merely going up; he was compelled to announce it. I mean, what's the point of being awesome if no one notices?

That was my dilemma in 1991 at the end of an hourlong meeting with my boss (my dad) and our mission's communications director. I realized it wasn't clear that I was the one who had come up with the idea we were discussing. At least, no one had mentioned that it was my idea. I could have easily corrected this oversight with an aside, such as, "When I first came up with this idea . . ." As I began to think of a discreet way to say this, I sensed the dissonance between my desire to "provide clarity" and not wanting to appear boastful. I'm not sure why I felt that dissonance because boasting was like breathing in our family. But my desire to manipulate the conversation ever so slightly bothered me, so I remained silent.

As the door closed, I was overwhelmed
with a sense of despair and loneliness.

The meeting ended and my coworkers left. As the door closed, I was overwhelmed with a sense of despair and loneliness. I felt unbelievably empty, like I was disappearing. Life no longer had any point. Why bother putting so much energy into the mission? I turned off the lights and went over to the window, opened my Bible to John 6, and read Jesus's conversation with the crowd at Capernaum the morning after his feeding of the five thousand. In response to the crowd manipulating him to give them more food, Jesus said,

> I am the living bread that came down from heaven. If anyone eats of this bread, he will live forever. And the bread that I will give for

the life of the world is my flesh. . . . For my flesh is true food, and my blood is true drink. (John 6:51, 55)

As I read, I was overcome with an enormous hunger for Christ. My desire to boast seemed distant, out of place. Something new was drawing me. I felt strangely full.

Look how this story maps on the Failure-Boasting Chart below. I'd come up with a good idea that, to my mind, placed me high on the chart. My coworkers' silence suggested they viewed me lower, an oversight I could fix with an offhand comment, which would enlarge their vision of me and move me up the chart. Like the apostle Paul, I wanted my success in ministry to be seen. I was using God-work to elevate myself.

Fig. 3B. Our Flesh

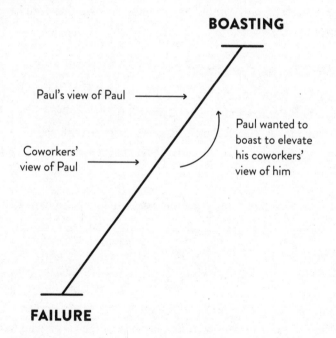

Why did I feel so empty when I didn't boast? Think of the flesh as a monster that must be fed. Addiction simply means you have regular feeding times for your flesh. Usually a steady diet of low-level boasting fed my flesh, but now my stomach was growling.

Like a drug addict, I needed a fix. My silence cut off an alternative source of life.

But what was the source of my overwhelming hunger for Christ that seemingly came out of the blue? Faith. Faith grew out of awareness of my emptiness. My faith shifted from my coworkers' approval to God's. Very simply, faith replaced the boast. If we constantly feed our addictions, we miss the real feast.

Notice how feeding on Christ reshaped and stabilized my feelings. When I wanted to boast, I felt neglected, overlooked, and unappreciated. If I'd made those feelings absolute (feelism), that would have fed a creeping resentment and nourished a victim narrative. *Feelism* doesn't understand that feelings emerge from the heart. If my heart is off, then my feelings will also be out of tune. So when I said no to my flesh, not only did those old feelings disappear, but new feelings emerged—sadness and emptiness, which opened the door to a new love for Christ.

Faith Replaces the Boast

After Paul's seven boasts, he turns in disgust from himself to faith in Jesus. Three times Paul goes back and forth between his old loves and his new love. Watch Paul's growing disgust with the flesh on the one hand and his growing love for Jesus on the other. First, he simply reflects,

> But whatever *gain* I had, I counted as *loss* for the sake of Christ. (Phil. 3:7)

He realized his confidence in his past achievements, his *gain*, is really a *loss* compared to *Christ*. Paul's intensity grows as he reflects a second time,

> Indeed, I count *everything as loss* because of the surpassing worth of knowing Christ Jesus my Lord. (v. 8a)

With growing passion, Paul realizes that *everything* outside of Jesus is a *loss*! Why? Because nothing compares to "the surpassing worth of knowing Christ Jesus my Lord." This is because Christ is "the only knowledge worth having, a knowledge so transcendent in value that it compensates for the loss of everything else!"[10]

As Paul reflects a third time, he becomes even more impassioned:

> For his sake I have suffered the loss of all things and *count them as rubbish*, in order that I may gain Christ and be found in him, not having a righteousness of my own that comes from the law, but that which comes through faith in Christ, the righteousness from God that depends on faith. (vv. 8b–9)

Paul ends with a flourish, asserting that anything other than Christ is not just a *loss*; it's *rubbish*—a polite translation for *manure*. He retches not only at the thought of his boasting, but also at the entire system of the flesh, his preoccupation with himself and how he's doing. It's all manure. His seven boasts told the story of Paul, of how amazing he was. That story now disgusts him; he's now completely enamored by the story of Jesus. Both our flesh and our faith *boast* or *glory*. In other words, Paul has just shifted from worship of himself to worship of Jesus.

Just as the old Paul embodied the flesh, so the new Paul embodies faith. Embodiment is a lost category of our faith. If you miss embodiment, you'll see Paul's trust but miss his wonder and love. I've asked multiple mature Christians to tell me how, in Philippians 3:7–9, Paul relates to Jesus. No one ever mentions love. Eventually I hint, under the influence of Kim, "Don't think in spiritual categories—think of Disney princess movies." Then someone says, "Paul's in love!"

Frankly, I don't expect anyone to say *love*, partly because we seldom hear about Paul's love for Jesus or people. Consequently, we lose a sense of Paul as a person. When we come to things like faith, we put on spiritual hats and forget the real world. This is a lingering effect on the church of Greek Stoicism, which deprecated the physical and muted categories such as "in love."[11] But here Paul overflows with love. He's enchanted with Jesus.

---

10. F. F. Bruce, *Philippians*, Good News Commentary (San Francisco: Harper & Row, 1983), 88. One commentary translates Phil. 3:8 "because of the *one supreme value*, namely, a *personal knowledge* of Christ Jesus my Lord." Gerald F. Hawthorne and Ralph P. Martin, *Philippians* (Nashville: Thomas Nelson, 2004), 190.

11. Greek Gnosticism said that the spiritual was more real, had more weight, than the physical. See Ronald K. Ritgers, *The Reformation of Suffering: Pastoral Theology and Lay Piety in Late*

Since the Reformation, the church (in general) has been better at seeing sin and idols than seeing and celebrating love. We have a clear vision of what we shouldn't be, but a dull vision of what we should be. Our wonderful Reformation emphasis on sin and grace needs to be enlarged to encompass a vision of beauty and love. Otherwise, we'll get stuck in the darkness. Our cynical age amplifies this tendency because cynicism is the craft of seeing evil in others' motives. If we are not captured by a larger vision of the beauty of Jesus, we will see evil everywhere—especially in the church. You see, one of the flesh's most toxic characteristics is its ability to rivet you on evil. We see this characteristic of the flesh in J. R. R. Tolkien's *The Lord of the Rings*, when the wizard Saruman, though initially good, becomes entrapped by evil by looking into the crystal ball at the evil Sauron.

In summary, seeing how our flesh works is oddly encouraging. A clear-eyed vision of how our idolatry and pride work together helps us see how critical faith is to shifting our boast from ourselves to Christ. As we shall see, what we do instead of the J-Curve (the flesh) helps us understand how the J-Curve repeatedly unmasks and emaciates the flesh's power by inverting the Failure-Boasting Chart. It is the ultimate flesh-killer.

> We have a clear vision of what we shouldn't be,
> but a dull vision of what we should be.

Medieval and Early Modern Germany, Oxford Studies in Historical Theology (New York: Oxford University Press, 2012), 259–63.

4

Liberating the Self

The Foundation of the J-Curve

Now that we understand the problem (the flesh), we are ready to understand the solution. We will begin by exploring the foundation of the J-Curve: justification by faith. At times, the church has separated the J-Curve from its faith foundation, and thus distorted its impact. So in this chapter, we will go down into the basement and look at the J-Curve's supporting structure.

Our passage in Philippians 3 reflects the foundational character of justification by faith. Right after Paul calls his flesh *rubbish*, he describes his new identity: justification by faith. Paul says,

> [I want to] be found in him, not having a righteousness of my own that comes from the law, but that which comes through faith in Christ, *the righteousness from God that depends on faith*. (Phil. 3:9)

My understanding of how justification by faith—"the righteousness from God that depends on faith"—applies to everyday life began in the spring of 1982. Just a few months after Kim was born, my dad invited me to a Bible study in the old Victorian garage behind his house. Just a handful of people showed up. That didn't bother my dad. He loved the work of creating disciples and knew it starts small.

At our first meeting, we read Martin Luther's introduction to his commentary on Galatians. I was transfixed.[1] I knew justification by faith, the unbelievably liberating truth that God declares us righteous because of our faith in Christ, but something about how justification had captured Luther's soul arrested me. I had grasped the importance of justification by faith for salvation, but I had not thought about its implications for sanctification (the process of becoming like Jesus). I remember coming home, putting Luther's introduction on the kitchen table, and telling Jill, "If the church really gets this, it will change things." I sensed this was a game changer. I suspected that justification by faith could transform my identity as a person, but I didn't know what that looked like—until the crisis of the Dixie cup.

The Dixie Cup Crisis

When our son Andrew was three, he often asked for a drink in the middle of the night. I'd stumble out of bed, get a Dixie cup from the bathroom dispenser, fill it with water, and take it to him. Often, several hours later, he'd ask for a second cup. So to save myself a second trip, I began to get two Dixie cups of water on the first trip. The only problem was that Dixie cups sweat; the second cup left a stain on the dresser. Jill asked me not to take the second Dixie cup, so I said OK and took just one Dixie cup. That's what good husbands do.

Several weeks later, about six o'clock in the morning, Jill called from Andrew's bedroom, "Paul, you left a Dixie cup on the dresser. Don't leave Dixie cups on the dresser." I stood in the closet where I was dressing, thinking, "I only took one Dixie cup." I bristled at Jill's presuming I had left the second Dixie cup. It implied that I was the kind of husband who leaves Dixie cups on dressers. I was about to correct Jill's declaration of me as a failure as a husband, as unrighteous, when I remembered Paul's words: "the righteousness from God that depends on faith."

Reflecting on the gospel helped me realize that my haste to correct Jill's opinion of me was a form of self-righteousness. While it is entirely appropriate to defend ourselves from false accusations—Jesus and

---

1. Many people, including John and Charles Wesley, the founders of Methodism, have been influenced by Martin Luther's introduction to his Galatians commentary.

Paul do it frequently—what struck me was my *rush* to defend myself. I didn't want a vague, detached righteousness from God; I wanted a "real" righteousness of my own, a righteousness with substance. Jill was declaring me unrighteous, and I wanted her to declare me righteous! I wanted Jill to justify me, not God.

For the first time in my life, I connected God's justification of me with how I related to another person. The result? I shut up. I didn't defend myself. I quietly rested in "the righteousness from God that depends on faith." My silence was a form of love. Love comes from faith.

For the first time in my life, I connected God's
justification of me with how I related to another person.

What about the Dixie cup? Who left it? It was likely me. Either I forgot or it was the original cup I got on the first trip. But, really, who cares? That's what faith does. You see, realizing I was justified by faith in that moment killed my desire to create my own identity. Not defending myself over a Dixie cup was a big step for me in putting feet on what it means to believe the gospel in everyday life.

God's Justification or Jill's?

With the help of Figure 4A below, let's reflect on how justification by faith works:

1. Jesus dies for me.
2. Then I look to Jesus's death for me. That's faith. Faith means resting in the fact that my identity is rooted in Christ and his work, not my own.
3. But even faith is a gift. My heart's bent toward myself, my flesh, is so powerful that I need Jesus in me (the Spirit) in order to look at Jesus outside of me.
4. Then the Father counts me righteous because I'm in Jesus by faith. Notice that I don't look to my own justification, but to Jesus's work for me on the cross. If we focus on our justification in the abstract, it can become a way of feeling good about ourselves. Justification is something we rejoice and rest in, but we look to Jesus and his death for us.

Fig. 4A. Justification by Faith

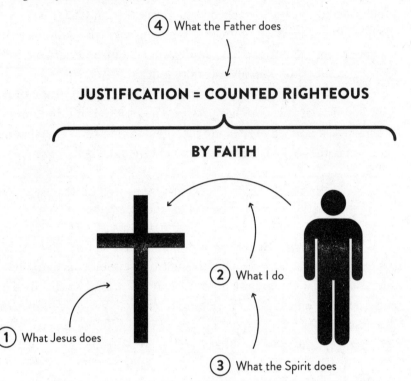

Now let's look at the justification I was seeking: justification by Jill. While the chart below, Justification by Jill (Fig. 4B), mirrors the chart just above, Justification by Faith (Fig. 4A), instead of looking to Jesus's righteousness:

1. I point to my own righteousness: "I didn't leave a Dixie cup on the dresser."
2. Instead of exercising faith, I defend myself: "I'm a good husband."
3. Because my flesh focuses on my own righteousness, I see no need for the Spirit.
4. I want Jill to declare me righteous.

Here's Philippians 3:9 rewritten to reflect what I initially wanted:

A righteousness that comes from being a good husband, the righteousness from Jill that depends on her declaring me righteous.

Fig. 4B. Justification by Jill

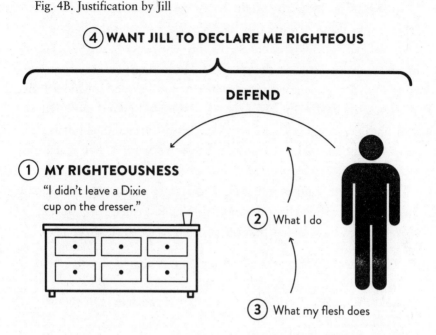

The Dixie cup incident was only a crisis because my identity as a *good husband* was threatened. My touchiness showed that being viewed as a good husband had become a source of life for me. Jill's offhand comment lowered me (in my mind) down the Failure-Boasting Chart from *good husband* to *bad husband*.

My fragility over a ring left by a Dixie cup struck me as odd. I am not alone. With the life of faith weakening in our culture, the modern self's fragility is increasingly on display. People's inability to laugh at themselves is just the self set on a hair trigger. Seeming slights ("You left the Dixie cup") take on a life of their own. Little communication problems become quarrels, making us touchy.

The same quest for righteousness occurred in my meeting with my coworkers that I recounted in the previous chapter (I wanted *a righteousness of my own* that came from being seen as creative. I wanted a "real" righteousness, one my coworkers saw. Of course, their opinion would have been no more real than a passing vapor. Soon my restless flesh would have been hungry again.

Justification by faith stabilizes our restless selves outside of ourselves in the cross of Christ. In *Les Misérables*, after the bishop gives Jean Valjean the silver candlesticks, he whispers, "Jean Valjean, my brother, you no longer belong to evil. With this silver, I have bought your soul. I've ransomed you from fear and hatred, and now I give you back to God."[2] The bishop's act of substitutionary love shattered Valjean. Likewise, the gift of righteousness shattered the apostle Paul. Jesus bought Paul. He was no longer his own man; he had an entirely new relationship to Jesus *and* to himself.

So faith undermines our need to boast, to constantly defend and display ourselves; it kills the boast. It kills, in principle, a touchy, defensive spirit. Paul makes that point in his letter to the Romans:[3]

> *Then what becomes of our boasting? It is excluded.* By what kind of law? By a law of works? No, but by the *law of faith.* For we hold that one is justified by faith apart from works of the law. (Rom. 3:27–28)

Notice also how the gospel reshaped my feelings. If you had asked me when I was about to defend myself, "What are you feeling?" I would have said, "Unappreciated, hurt, and criticized unfairly." That's the victim narrative of *feelism.* The gospel destroyed the victim narrative that fed those feelings and replaced it with peace.

Justification by Seinfeld

Justification isn't just a religious idea; we all long for it. Michael Richards, who played the quirky Cosmo Kramer on *Seinfeld*, craved justification after he flew into a racist rant at the Laugh Factory in Hollywood when he was taunted by a disgruntled patron in 2006. After yelling "Shut up!" to a heckler, Richards said, "Fifty years ago they'd have you hanging upside down with a _____ fork up your _____. Throw his _____ out!" He repeatedly labeled the man with a

---

2. *Les Misérables*, directed by Bille August (1998; Culver City, CA: Sony Pictures Home Entertainment, 1998), DVD, 9:21–9:36.

3. Paul tells the Ephesians the same thing: "For by grace *you have been saved through faith.* And this is not your own doing; it is the gift of God, not a result of works, *so that no one may boast*" (Eph. 2:8–9).

racial slur. On video of the incident, you could hear a woman gasping in the background, "Oh, my God!"[4]

After the video went viral, Richards went on *The Late Show with David Letterman* to "do atonement." He told the audience, "I said some pretty nasty things to some African Americans. . . . You know, I'm really busted up over this and I'm very, very sorry."[5] The confession didn't go well. Richards slipped into his comic routine while apologizing, sending a confusing signal to the audience. Jerry Seinfeld, who introduced Richards on the show, had to tell the audience to stop laughing. Afterward, Richards's shame was so profound he stopped doing standup comedy.

Years later, Seinfeld tried to redeem his friend by inviting him on his new Internet show *Comedians in Cars Getting Coffee*. Seinfeld picked up Richards in an old VW van, and they went for coffee. You could still feel Richards's shame as he told Seinfeld, "I busted up after that event seven years ago. It broke me down." Seinfeld encouraged Richards to let it go, saying, "That's up to you, to say, 'I've been carrying this bag long enough. I'm going to put it down.'" But Richards couldn't. He just said, "Yeah, yeah."[6]

Richards couldn't "put it down" because deep down he knew he couldn't justify himself. He instinctively realized that even Seinfeld, with all his good will and fame, couldn't declare him righteous. Justification by Seinfeld didn't work. Justification by confession didn't work either. Neither would "forgiving yourself."

Why not? We've sinned against a holy God. Only God can justify. Only God can forgive. Only the blood of Christ can satisfy the insatiable thirst of a guilty conscience.

When the video of Richards's rant went viral, nothing could remove his shame, not even YouTube taking the video down or Seinfeld repeatedly going to bat for him. You see, the real problem isn't that Richards *looked* bad (shame). It's that Richards *was* bad (guilt before

4. Paul Farhi, "'Seinfeld' Comic Richards Apologizes for Racial Rant," *The Washington Post*, Nov. 21, 2006. http://www.washingtonpost.com/wp-dyn/content/article/2006/11/21/AR2006112100242 .html.

5. Farhi, "'Seinfeld' Comic Richards Apologizes for Racial Rant."

6. David Haglund, "Seinfeld and Kramer, Together Again," *Slate*, Sept. 28, 2012. http://www .slate.com/blogs/browbeat/2012/09/28/michael_richards_with_jerry_seinfeld_on_comedians_in _cars_getting_coffee_watch_it_here_video_.html.

a holy God). When we understand the real problem, the gospel converts shame into guilt, and forgives guilt. If the Father counts the obedience of his Son to Richards, then Richards's shame becomes Jesus's shame, and Richards is free.

Failure Is Not Faith

Richards's angst reminds us of a subtle but stark difference between the bottom of the Failure-Boasting Chart and the bottom of the J-Curve. Beating ourselves up for failure is not the same as faith. In fact, it can easily become a form of penance, where we try to pay for our sins emotionally. True, failure is often God's door to faith, but it doesn't equal faith.

Real faith cries out for grace. God wants us *off* the Failure-Boasting Chart and in Jesus. We can be in despair, but still stubborn. Judas appeared broken, at the bottom of the Failure-Boasting Chart, but he didn't cry out for grace. He still wanted to be in charge of his life, in control of his despair. He turned inward and saw bottomless corruption. Then, in one final act of self-will, he ended his life. Right up to the end, he was in charge. Faith is helplessness *plus* crying out for grace.

Faith is helplessness *plus* crying out for grace.

The following excerpt from John of Landsberg's *A Letter from Jesus Christ* captures the feel of a heart despairing but not yet trusting:

I know those moods when you sit there utterly alone, pining, eaten up with unhappiness, in a pure state of grief. You don't move towards me but desperately imagine that everything you have ever done has been utterly lost and forgotten. This near-despair and self-pity are actually a form of pride. What you think was a state of absolute security from which you've fallen was really trusting too much in your own strength and ability . . . what really ails you is that things simply haven't happened as you expected and wanted.

In fact, I don't want you to rely on your own strength and abilities and plans, but to distrust them and to distrust yourself, and to trust me and no one and nothing else. As long as you rely entirely on yourself, you are bound to come to grief. You still have a most important lesson to learn: your own strength will no more help you to stand upright than propping yourself on a broken reed. You must not despair of me. You may hope and trust in me absolutely. My mercy is infinite.[7]

Connecting Justification by Faith with the J-Curve

We've learned that justification by faith sits at the heart of the gospel (the Richards story) and is a motivation for sanctification (the Dixie cup story). Now let's see how Paul connects faith (our identity in Christ) with the J-Curve.

Paul links faith and the J-Curve in an opening summary of Philippians:

> For it has been *granted* to you that for the sake of Christ you should not only *believe in him* but *also suffer for his sake.* (Phil. 1:29)

First, notice that faith ("believe in him") comes before the J-Curve ("suffer for his sake"). "Jesus lived the J-Curve for me, so that he can reproduce the J-Curve in me."[8] The foundation of *believing the gospel* frees us to *become like the gospel* (the J-Curve). *Believing* comes before *becoming.* For Paul nothing is more important than "*faith working through love*" (Gal. 5:6). Faith energizes love.

Second, the word *granted* is related to the Greek word *charis*, or "grace." God has not only *gifted* us with *believing* in Jesus, but also with *suffering for his sake* (the J-Curve). Paul mentions this specifically because we like *believing*, but we recoil from *becoming.* Both are gracious gifts.

I say that because we love the gift of justification by faith—*believing the gospel.* Nothing is more liberating than realizing that God welcomes sinners. In fact, only when we own up to our sin and stop creating "Good Husband Righteousness" or "Good Comedian Righteousness" do we receive grace. Christ's merit, not ours, is now

---

7. John of Landsberg (1542–1591), *A Letter from Jesus Christ*, ed. John Griffiths (New York: Crossroad, 1981), 58–59. Obviously, this parable is not the voice of Jesus.

8. Jimmy Agan in personal correspondence.

the foundation for our lives. Grace is amazing. But we recoil from the second gift—*becoming like the gospel*. It took me a while to see that the J-Curve is a gift.

Philippians 1:29 describes my journey. First, God gifted me with a new identity for everyday life when I rediscovered the wonder of justification by faith. Next, I found myself being drawn into the narrative of Jesus's dying and rising. After I discovered the J-Curve in Philemon, the following year, in the meeting with my two coworkers, I realized I lived on the Failure-Boasting Chart, the antithesis of the J-Curve. In time, I discovered the J-Curve also was a gift. As you journey with me, I hope you will as well!

5

In Harvard

Union with Christ Comes Alive

When I first stumbled onto the J-Curve, I wasn't sure how it connected with justification by faith. Over the next several chapters, we'll explore the relationship between the "basement" of justification by faith and the "first floor" of the J-Curve. When we step back and look at the house as a whole, we discover that the entire structure is *union with Christ*. Justification by faith and the J-Curve are both ways of being *in Christ*. Let me explain.

Paul's most frequent, cryptic description of his relationship with Jesus is "in Christ." Over 170 times, he uses some version of "in Christ," "in Christ Jesus," or "in him." One theologian describes union with Christ as the web that holds Paul's theology together.[1]

When Paul lifts the hood of "in Christ," we encounter a J-Curve. In Romans 6, Paul answers the charge, "If we are justified by faith and our sins are completely forgiven, why not just sin more to get more grace?" He anticipates a problem many have struggled with in the church—if we are declared righteous by faith, why bother trying to be righteous? That is, how do we balance *believing* (faith) with *becoming* (love)? Paul's answer:

---

1. Constantine R. Campbell, *Paul and Union with Christ* (Grand Rapids, MI: Zondervan, 2012), 441.

How can we who died to sin still live *in it*? Do you not know that
all of us who have been baptized *into Christ Jesus* were baptized
into his death? We were buried therefore *with him* by baptism *into
death*, in order that, just as Christ was raised from the dead by the
glory of the Father, we too might walk *in newness of life*. (Rom.
6:2b–4; I've italicized all the phrases where Paul speaks of us as
in something.)

Notice that Paul doesn't reply, "That's where the law comes in."
Neither does he point to grace. His points to our *union with Christ*.
This is not an abstract *union*: we are united with Jesus in his death
and resurrection. Baptism re-enacts the J-Curve as we go down into
death and then up into resurrection. Dying with Jesus kills sin; rising
with him creates new life and new obedience. Our entire identity is
imprinted with his story. I call this mysterious union with Christ's
dying and rising the *faith* J-Curve. Our *present* J-Curves are based
on the *faith* J-Curve. It shows how dominant the story of Jesus was
for Paul and the early church—everything came back to Jesus and
his story.

To recap, Paul's answer is, "No way; you can't continue *in sin*
because the old you died and rose with Jesus. Jesus's J-Curve becomes
your J-Curve. Now you live *in him*." Scholars have pointed out that
since the Reformation, the church has swung back and forth between
Jesus as Mediator (faith) and Jesus as example (love) because we've
neglected John Calvin's teaching of twofold grace, that both our justification (believing) and our sanctification (becoming) are ways of
being *in him*. Union with Christ encompasses both a finished state and
an ongoing process of becoming like him.[2]

---

2. Recent Reformed scholarship has unconvered John Calvin's emphasis that union with
Christ ("in Christ") encompasses both justification and sanctification. See Mark Garcia, *Life
in Christ: Union with Christ and Twofold Grace in Calvin's Theology* (Colorado Springs:
Paternoster, 2008), 89–147, 264. Richard Gaffin articulates how missing that sanctification
is part of our union with Christ has weakened the centrality of the person and work of Christ.
See Richard B. Gaffin Jr., "Justification and Union with Christ," in David W. Hall and Peter A.
Lillback, eds., *A Theological Guide to Calvin's Institutes: Essays and Analysis* (Phillipsburg,
NJ: P&R, 2008), 248–69. William Evans traces out how we lost Calvin's vision of union with
Christ: "We must note the persistent problem for Reformed thinkers of . . . the relationship
of the various elements of salvation to one another and to union with Christ. In Calvin . . .
justification and sanctification are both grounded in a third element, the deeper reality of our
union with Christ. Later, however, there was a shift to a bipolar soteriology in which justification and sanctification related more directly. In this context, it was all but inevitable that one
and then the other would dominate, leading to the oscillation of the tradition between legal-

The concept of being *in Christ* is mystical—that is, we can't reduce it to categories we can see and touch. But the same is true of beauty, love, and almost everything we value. Being *in something* is one of life's most basic realities, part of what it means to be human. Paul describes both his life before and after Jesus as being *in something*. He summarizes his boasting, pre-Jesus self as *in Judaism*:

> For you have heard of my former life *in Judaism*, how I persecuted the church of God violently and tried to destroy it. And I was advancing *in Judaism* beyond many of my own age among my people, so extremely zealous was I for the traditions of my fathers. (Gal. 1:13–14)

Fig. 5A. The Faith J-Curve

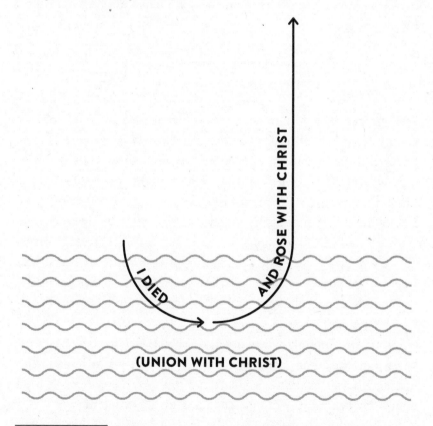

Just as the Failure-Boasting Chart sits at the center of *in Judaism*, so the J-Curve sits at the center of *in Christ*. But what does it look like in our lives to be *in something*? If you stop and reflect, you'll see we are all trying to be *in something*. I wanted to be *in Harvard*.

In Harvard

When I was in high school, my oldest sister, Roseann, was admitted to Wellesley College in Boston, and she introduced me to the world of Ivy League schools. She only needed to say once, "Paul, you could get into Harvard," and I began to plan my future. Getting into Harvard would identify me for life as one of the elite of our culture. That, in turn, would open all kinds of doors. I wanted to be *in Harvard*. Of course, I didn't get in. Neither did I get into Yale or Princeton. Instead, I went to Temple.

She only needed to say once, "Paul, you could get into Harvard," and I began to plan my future.

Several years ago, a humble friend who attended Harvard told me a story from his college days, saying, "When I was at college . . ." I perked up at his missed opportunity to name-drop. Why didn't he say "Harvard"? Since I went to Temple, I usually say "college." But I found a way to get in Harvard by the back door. A couple of times, I've found myself quoting my friend, saying, "My friend who went to Harvard said . . ." By linking myself to my friend, I create a virtual link to Harvard and elevate the value of my comment. My friend who went to Harvard doesn't mention Harvard because he's *in Jesus*. But I, who didn't go to Harvard, am still trying to get in forty years later! God be merciful to me, a sinner!

Notice the interplay of two ways of being *in Jesus* here. As a believer, I'm *already* in Jesus by faith, but I'm *not yet* in Jesus in this instance, but *in Harvard*. Scholars call this *already, not yet*. It is an immensely helpful way of understanding the Christian life.

Here's what my attempt to be *in Harvard* looks like on our Failure-Boasting Chart.

Fig. 5B. In Harvard

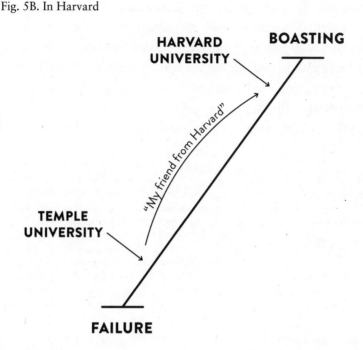

If I'm *in Harvard*, I ascend the Failure-Boasting Chart. All the benefits of Harvard flow into my life, just as being *in Jesus* allows the benefits of Jesus, his righteousness and his love, to flow into my life.[3] Justification by faith emerges out of our union with Christ. Recall that in Philippians 3, Paul wanted to *"be found in him*, not having a righteousness of my own" (v. 9). Our justification is *found in him*. Justification doesn't float; it is located in Jesus. Because we are in Jesus, we have his righteousness.[4] Calvin wrote,

> As long as Christ remains outside of us, and we are separated from him, all that he has done for the salvation of the human race remains useless and of no value to us.[5]

---

3. Paul embeds justification by faith in our union with Christ (1 Cor. 1:30; 2 Cor. 5:21). As Martin Luther says, "It is impossible for one to be a Christian unless he possesses Christ. If he possesses Christ, he possesses all the benefits of Christ." *Lectures on Galatians*, in *Luther's Works*, gen. ed. Jaroslav Pelikan, 55 vols. (St. Louis: Concordia, 1963), 26:168.

4. See Evans, *Imputation and Impartation*.

5. John Calvin, *Institutes of the Christian Religion*, ed. John T. McNeill, trans. Ford Lewis Battles, The Library of Christian Classics, vols. 20–21 (Philadelphia: Westminster, 1960), 3.1.1.

Whatever we are *in* justifies us. Justification always occurs in some kind of virtual community. It's not abstract; it's embedded in communities that give us identity. The question is, does that justification work? Michael Richards's community of friends, led by Jerry Seinfeld, tried to justify Richards, but it failed because the attempt wasn't grounded in the finished work of Christ.

Look at this comparison between *in Harvard* and *in Jesus*:

	IN HARVARD	IN JESUS
How do you get in?	By your own merit. You need either great test scores (predicted merit) and grades (past merit) or family connections (blood merit). It helps to have good connections.	By Jesus's merit. That connects you with the Trinity, the family of Jesus. Based on the blood of Jesus, his merit, the Father invites you into his family. It helps to have good connections.
Whose record is on the application?	Yours.	Jesus's.
What group lets you in?	The admissions committee.	The Trinity—the Father calls, the Son dies, the Spirit indwells.
Who gets in?	Only a few of the best and the brightest— or the well connected.	Anyone who calls on the name of the Lord.
Is there a formal ceremony for admissions?	A letter in the mail and a welcome ceremony.	An open confession of faith plus baptism, where you re-enact the dying and rising of Jesus.
How do you participate?	You faithfully attend classes and go to extracurricular activities. You are physically *in Harvard*.	The church is Jesus's body. Participating in the life of the church is a way of being *in Christ*.
Whom do you meet?	Other smart, good-looking, well-dressed, well-rounded, well-connected people.	All the richness of the body of Christ: rich and poor, disabled and healthy, adults and children.

	IN HARVARD	IN JESUS
What do you get when you leave?	A piece of paper with the hope of a better life, including an "in" to better jobs and relationships.	You never leave. The Spirit is always with you. You keep going deeper into Christ.
What if you destroy Harvard or Jesus physically?	It would be rebuilt. The endowment is intact.	They did.
What happens if you destroy society's esteem of Harvard or Jesus?	Harvard dies.	That's what happened. They crucified Jesus to shame him; but his resurrection converted the instrument of his shame into a sign of triumph.

Going Deeper in Him: The J-Curve

Paul's immersion *in Judaism* was transformed into an immersion *in Christ*. He embodied *in Christ* when he turned in disgust from his seven boasts and was captured by the wonder of Jesus (Phil. 3:7–9).

In his next breath, Paul goes even more deeply *in Christ*. He says he wants to gain Christ so that:

> I may know him and the power of his resurrection, and may share his sufferings, becoming like him in his death, that by any means possible I may attain the resurrection from the dead. (Phil. 3:10–11)

Notice the familiar contours of the J-Curve. Paul wants to share in Jesus's *sufferings* and then experience the power of his *resurrection*. This isn't mere theology for Paul; it's the climax of a love affair. His passionate love for Jesus spills over into an entire participation in Jesus's life. Paul gets to know the love of his life as he re-enacts his life.

This isn't mere theology for Paul;
it's the climax of a love affair.

To recap, in this chapter we've been exploring how our identity (justification by faith) and the shape of our life (the J-Curve) are embedded in union with Christ. Paul first experiences a *faith* union with

Christ. Then, in the J-Curve, he experiences a *present* union as he re-enacts the story of Jesus's dying and rising in his everyday life. The J-Curve makes union with Christ come alive: it's not just an idea we believe, but a present reality. For most Christians, union with Christ is a vague, even sterile idea, but when you begin to experience in the J-Curve the *doing* part of the union, the *being* part of the union comes alive. In the following chapter, we will see this illustrated in a story about my daughter Emily.

6

In Sports or In Christ?

How Location Changes Everything

I enjoyed watching my sisters and then my daughters play field hockey. Prior to some growth in sanctification, I used to combine cheering from the sidelines with free coaching tips, which led one coach to remind me she was the coach, not me.

When my youngest daughter, Emily, was in the eleventh grade, she and her friend were benched. The word on the team was that the coach was playing favorites. Neither Emily nor I enjoyed this. Her J-Curve was my J-Curve. I asked her if she wanted me to talk to the coach, but she said, "No, I'll do it, Dad." I was thankful for her maturity.

I ran into another parent at the gym during all this, and she said, "I can't believe what the coach is doing with Emily and her friend." I said, "I'm actually thankful Emily has this low-level suffering on my watch. Life is much more like sitting on the bench than starring in a game." I can still see the shock on this mom's face. It was like she had met a Martian.

In Sports or In Jesus?

Notice the role justification played in both our worlds. The mom saw Emily slipping down the Failure-Boasting Chart, losing "sports-righteousness."

On the other hand, Jill and I were concerned Emily was going up. She and her best friend were cute, athletic, and had boyfriends. Our daughter was developing *a righteousness of her own* that came from being in the "in group." It was enough of a concern for Jill and me that when faced with a choice between buying a new car or an old car, we bought the old one. We didn't want Emily using a new car to elevate herself with her friends.

Fig. 6A. Mom's World vs. Paul's World

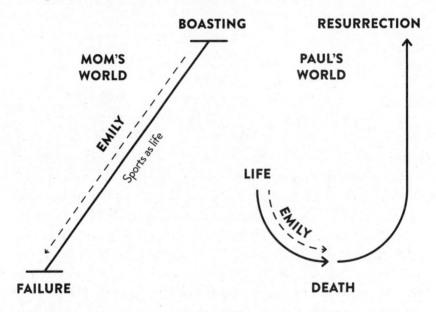

While our children played hockey at the same Christian school, in that moment, this mom and I were living in separate worlds. I'd spent the last fifteen years in a multilayered *fellowship of his sufferings*, so *in Jesus* had become a way of life for me. For that reason, when Emily encountered suffering, I was disappointed but not devastated, even thankful for an opportunity for her to be drawn into Jesus. My thankfulness startled this mom. It seemed strange to her.

We were both looking at the same scene: two girls sitting on a bench. But our *locations*, what we were *in*, shaped what we saw. The mom saw disaster; I saw an opportunity for Emily to be drawn into a *fellowship of his sufferings*.

Notice how similar Paul's *in Judaism* is to the mom's *in sports*. Both forms of life outside of Christ became centers of worship for them and distorted their views of the world. Sports, of course, is not the problem. The problem is sports as an idol. In fact, *in ministry* can be every bit as destructive as *in sports*. Remember, I was tempted to boast with my two coworkers because I'd made ministry into an idol.

The mom assumed we were both *in sports*. She was being kind, empathizing with me that my source of life (sports) was cut off. She was attempting to strengthen a community bond between the two of us. But I didn't live in her community; my community was Jesus, so my mind-set was shaped by the narrative of his dying and rising. Of course, this mom was a believer and thus *in Christ* by faith, but in this incident, when it came to her sanctification, how she did life, she was *in sports*.

I saw Emily slipping into a community shaped by this story: "Sports is everything. If your child is treated unfairly by a coach, go to war, demand justice—don't let people push you around." That false narrative was embedded in a larger narrative seducing her that looks, success, and money were all she needed. That toxic narrative would not deliver life to her. I had a larger vision for her, that the normal Christian life re-enacts the dying and rising of Jesus. I'd been praying that she would "not love the world or the things in the world" (1 John 2:15), so I saw her bench-warming as God's gift. What we are *in* shapes how we react to life. Notice that idolatry (in sports) and union with Christ have the same structure. Both are sources of life—one false and the other true.

Likewise, what we were *in* shaped how this mom and I viewed the coach. Because this mom was *in sports*, she saw the coach as "the enemy." He had sinned against her sports idol, and thus against the community. I wasn't happy with the coach, but because I was *in Christ*, I saw the coach as God's instrument to potentially draw Emily into Jesus. The mom was mildly upset. I was concerned, waiting, and praying. My location *in Jesus* shaped my response to Emily's bench-warming. It took the steam out of me. Union with Christ thrives under stress, because stress drives us more deeply into Christ. On the other hand, union with sports wilts when your daughter is sitting out the game on the bench.

Union with Christ thrives under stress, because
stress drives us more deeply into Christ.

Faith and the J-Curve

Most parents embrace our culture's mind-set: "If you don't stick up for yourself, no one will" or "Don't let people push you around." There's truth in these statements, but at heart they preserve the self. That's toxic. On the other hand, submitting to an unjust authority, in this instance, would draw Emily and me into the humility of Christ.

Faith isn't just critical to justification; it's also critical to accepting a *fellowship of his sufferings*. Faith allowed me to see the benchwarming through the narrative of Jesus's dying and rising. I wanted Emily *in Jesus*, off the Failure-Boasting Chart and in the J-Curve. She knew she was justified by faith, but that knowledge sat on the surface of her life. I knew Christ's dying and rising offered Emily the hope of making *in Christ* a present reality. She wouldn't just *believe in Jesus*; she would *become like him*. She would participate in his life.

Justice and the J-Curve

What about justice for Emily? Was I neglecting my duty as a parent?

To clarify, if my daughter had been nine years old, I would have talked to the coach, but as a seventeen-year-old, Emily was mature enough to talk to the coach herself. I even asked her a second time if she wanted me to talk with the coach, but she assured me she preferred doing it herself. Frequently, when parents pursue justice, especially in sports, it is just a mask for demanding their rights.

Field Hockey and Resurrection

Greek Stoicism, which dominated the elite culture of Paul's day, taught that suffering is good for us. It toughens you up. Paul knew that suffering matures you, but he wasn't interested in any old suffering, only in the *fellowship of Jesus's suffering*.[1] Likewise, I didn't want Emily on the bench because "it was good for her." I wanted resurrection.

I didn't know the shape or timing of resurrection, but I knew God would hear my prayers for my daughter. God had helped me so many times that hope had become a habit. So in the midst of a confusing situation, I had clarity: I knew the story Emily and I were in (Jesus's story); I knew where she was in that story (dying); and I knew the outcome (some kind of resurrection). Clarity calms the soul.

> God had helped me so many times
> that hope had become a habit.

The resurrection quietly emerged over the next few years. After Emily finished high school, Jill encouraged her to take a year off and work in an orphanage in Guatemala. We knew that loving a community of orphans, many struggling with their own self-absorption, might open a door in Emily's spirit to a *fellowship of his sufferings*. Sure enough, the work of love in a hidden place led to a new and deep work in Emily. She returned a different person.

The Emotional Life of the J-Curve

As we've seen, doing life through the lens of the dying and rising of Jesus reshapes our emotions. Emotions can go wrong in many ways—we can underfeel and suppress our emotions or overfeel and give full vent to them. Especially in situations like the one with Emily and her coach, it's easy to overfeel and become intense. Intensity then operates like a multiplier, escalating conflict.

Knowing that Emily was potentially embedded in the story of Jesus's death and resurrection enabled me to relax. A key component of relaxing, especially in relational conflict, is not talking about the pain repeatedly with the people involved. That's why I redirected the

---

1. Reflecting on 2 Cor. 1:7; 3:9–10; and Rom. 8:17–23, Richard Gaffin writes, "Until Christ returns, then all Christian existence continues to be suffering with Christ. . . . With Calvin, we must recognize that as Christ's whole life was nothing but a sort of perpetual cross, so the Christian life in its entirety, not just certain parts, is to be a continual cross (*Institutes*, 3:8:1, 2)." Richard B. Gaffin Jr., "The Usefulness of the Cross," *Westminster Theological Journal* 41, no. 2 (Spring 1979): 237, 239.

mom's comments into the larger story of how God uses suffering to shape and mature us. Good theology made for good emotions.

When we view life through the J-Curve, it gives our emotions a peculiar cadence. I was bummed when Emily was on the bench, but I wasn't consumed by my sadness. Knowing Emily was in a J-Curve let me feel the weight of the path, but not be overwrought by it. It gave my feelings a frame. In our *feelism* culture, "how I'm feeling" operates like a new kind of legalism, constantly shifting with the winds of emotion. The path of Jesus's dying and rising offers sanity and stability to our emotions.

We can see the same emotional pattern in the apostle Paul when he explains to the Corinthians the feel of the J-Curve:

> We are afflicted in every way, but not crushed; perplexed, but not driven to despair; persecuted, but not forsaken; struck down, but not destroyed; always carrying in the body the death of Jesus, so that the life of Jesus may also be manifested in our bodies. (2 Cor. 4:8–10)

The apostle Paul was "afflicted . . . but not crushed." He was down, but not out. Watching Emily from the bleachers, I was disappointed, but not devastated. That is, I didn't underfeel. I'm no Stoic trying to suppress or manage my emotions; I'm free to experience negative feelings. But neither did I overfeel. I could feel the effect of minor evil without it dislocating me. Why? Because the more familiar we are with the dying and rising of Jesus as a way of inhabiting life, the more capacity we have to absorb slights, discouragements, and weakness. We do life with a lighter touch.

This story of Emily on the bench gives us a feel for how potentially liberating the J-Curve is in the rough and tumble of life. Internally, it balanced Jill's and my emotions and reduced our anxiety. Externally, it calmed a quarrel and gave us clear directions for the future. It shaped both our goals for Emily and how we pursued those goals, not by pulling us out of the world of sports, but by helping us relax in that world. Location is everything.

7

It's All About Who You Know

Knowing Jesus in the J-Curve

Jill and I looked at Emily's bench-warming through the lens of the J-Curve because we wanted her to know Jesus, not just through saving faith, but through a living faith that participated in his life. In fact, a saving faith is a living faith that participates in his life. Paul articulates this dual vision in Philippians 3:8–11. He puts these two complementary ways of knowing Christ in parallel.[1] The first centers on justification by faith; we saw this in the Dixie cup story. The second centers on the J-Curve; we saw this in the field hockey story.

> Indeed, I count everything as loss because of the surpassing worth of *knowing* Christ Jesus my Lord. For his sake I have suffered the loss of all things and count them as rubbish, in order
>
> [1] that I may gain Christ and be found in him, not having a righteousness of my own that comes from the law, but that which comes through faith in Christ, the righteousness from God that depends on faith—

---

1. Moisés Silva writes, "This verse [3:10] is best understood as a second purpose clause introduced . . . by '*that I may know.*' This construction parallels the . . . clause that begins at the end of verse 8 and continues through verse 9. . . . Paul appears to define *knowing Christ* as the believer's experiencing of Christ's own death and resurrection." *Philippians*, Baker Exegetical Commentary on the New Testament (Grand Rapids, MI: Baker Academic, 2005), 163.

[2] that I may *know* him and the power of his resurrection, and may share his sufferings, becoming like him in his death, that by any means possible I may attain the resurrection from the dead.

The word *knowing* shapes this passage. The sense of the Greek (no. 2) is "I want to know him *in* the power of his resurrection, *in* sharing his sufferings" (Phil. 3:10).[2] By embracing Jesus in his dying and rising, Paul knows Jesus in ways he would not if he were simply meditating on or resting in justification by faith (no. 1). The word Paul uses for "share" is one of his favorites: *koinonia*. It means a binding partnership in which two are embedded in one another.[3] As Paul re-enacts the suffering and resurrection of Jesus (no. 2), it knits him to Jesus. If Emily embraces the fellowship of his sufferings in her benching, it will join her to Christ in ways she has not experienced before.

We still live by faith, but now we are active in love.

Once again we see that justification by faith is the foundation of the J-Curve. Faith comes first.[4] *Believing* comes before *becoming*. So in Figure 7A below, I've put justification by faith at the bottom. We are passive, receiving the gift of justification. The J-Curve is at the top. We still live by faith, but now we are active in love.

When Emily was playing field hockey, she had no. 1, the foundation—she *believed the gospel*. She could say, "Jesus died for me." But she experienced no. 2, *becoming like the gospel*, on the bench. Sitting out the game on the bench gave her an opportunity to enter into the life, death, and resurrection of Jesus. She could know Jesus better through the shame of the bench than through starring on the field.

---

2. Following Robert Tannehill, Gerald F. Hawthorne and Ralph P. Martin see the two halves of 3:10 as linked not only linguistically, but in the lives of believers, too. "The power of the resurrected Christ and the fellowship of his sufferings are to be thought of not as two totally separate experiences but as alternate aspects of the same experience." *Philippians* (Nashville: Thomas Nelson, 2004), 190.

3. Markus Bockmuehl, *The Epistle to the Philippians*, Black's New Testament Commentary (Grand Rapids, MI: Baker Academic, 1998), 34–38, 215; Kevin McFadden, in discussion with the author, April 23, 2016: Paul uses *koinonia* to describe his relationship with the Philippians (nouns in 1:5, 7; 2:1; verbs in 4:14, 15).

4. For example, Phil. 1:29 and Gal. 5:6.

Fig. 7A. Participating in Christ

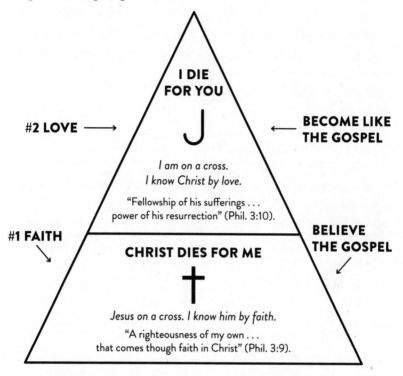

Two Complementary Ways of Seeing Jesus

Here's a brief summary of these two complementary ways of knowing Jesus. He comes alive when we see him with both eyes.

#1 Justification by Faith	#2 J-Curve
Symbol: Cross	Symbol: J-Curve
His suffering, not ours	Our suffering, in fellowship with his
Believe the gospel	Become like the gospel
Know him by faith, by resting	Know him by love, by doing
Saves us from sin's penalty	Helps us with sin's power
His story transforms my story	His story becomes my story
Christ died for me	I die for you
Gives us a new life	Gives us power to live out the new life
Deals with pride in principle	Deals with pride in practice

Paul can't imagine *believing* the gospel (no. 1) without *becoming* like the gospel (no. 2). For Paul, this is a single act of knowing. To believe the gospel necessarily leads to entering into Christ's dying and rising. Knowing Jesus in these two complementary ways makes our knowledge of him richer, more complete. We embrace the whole pattern of Jesus's life as the story of our own life.

To believe the gospel necessarily leads to
entering into Christ's dying and rising.

Here are some simple analogies to show how these two ways of knowing relate:

#1 Believing the Gospel	→	#2 Becoming Like the Gospel
Babysitting	→	Parenting
Business school	→	Starting a business
Boot camp	→	Combat
Falling in love	→	Marriage

In each case, we move from knowing *about* something to *entering* into a deep, personal knowledge. For example, what's the difference between babysitting and parenting? It's the level of ownership. Parenting is 24-7 love, while babysitting is just a few hours. Babysitters are hired hands, not shepherds who lay down their lives for the sheep (John 10:1–18). Babysitting doesn't change you. Parenting changes you. As soon as you have a child, you are a parent forever. Of course, the above analogies are imperfect, since both ways of knowing are located *in Christ*. Each is an aspect of union with Christ.

The problem with staying in the world of babysitting (no. 1) is that our will remains unchallenged. Our thin-skinned age, in which so many cultivate the memory of past hurts, desperately needs to learn this two-part way of knowing Christ. Look at the difference between the Touchy Person and the Jesus Person:

The Touchy Person. When Melissa encounters even low-level suffering, she demands (self-will) the suffering be removed. Consequently, small irritations are overwhelming. The work of collecting

and harboring slights leaves her with little capacity for love or dealing with evil. In short, suffering + *self-will* = bitterness, irritation.

The Jesus Person. When Tanya encounters low-level suffering, she
absorbs it. She presumes the world is unbalanced, so, by love, she
works to rebalance it. Consequently, she barely notices small irritations. She's in a constant state of forgiveness and forbearance,
resulting in an enormous capacity for love and dealing with evil.
In short, suffering + *surrender* (embracing Christ in the suffering) = J-Curve. The mundane becomes magnificent!

When we embrace the *fellowship of his sufferings*, it changes everything. Instead of nourishing slights and running from the suffering
inherent in life and love, we embrace Christ in the suffering. It's all
about who you know.

In the next two chapters, we will explore the danger of marginal-
izing either justification by faith or the J-Curve. Theological imbalance
leads to lives out of balance. A balanced emphasis gives us sanity in
an increasingly crazy world.

8

Missing Justification by Faith

The J-Curve without Justification

Mother Teresa is a poster child for the J-Curve. She embodied the dying love of Christ. Like him, she loved going low. She and her sisters converted a temple of Kali, the fearsome dark mother of Hinduism, into a home of compassion for the dying poor. When Malcolm Muggeridge, the British journalist, visited her in Kolkata, he was deeply moved by her love for "the least of these."

What motivated Mother Teresa? She repeatedly said when she cared for the dying, she cared for Christ. She experienced Christ as she loved the dying, knowing him in a *fellowship of his sufferings*. She said this about why she loved the poor on the streets of Kolkata:

> Suffering by itself is nothing. But suffering as a share in Christ's Passion is a great gift. Man's greatest gift is the possibility of sharing Christ's Passion. Yes, it is a gift and a sign of God's love. This is the way the Father showed his love for the world: giving us his Son to die for us. This is the way Christ showed that the greatest gift is love: he gave himself in suffering for us.[1]

---

1. *Stories of Mother Teresa*, ed. Jose Luis Gonzalez-Balado (Liguori, MO: Ligouri, 1983), 13.

Notice that Mother Teresa didn't embrace suffering for its own stake. She was no Stoic. She shared Christ's suffering. Her focus on Jesus's passion goes back to the early church. The disciples were riveted by *how* Jesus died. Forty percent of the Gospels is devoted to Passion Week. Just one example of many: The Gospel of Mark is a discipleship course that descends into Jesus's death. Mark equates discipleship with joining Jesus in his dying.[2] As a result, martyrdom, re-enacting the death of Jesus, became the coveted prize of the early church.

Loving dying beggars helped Mother Teresa know Christ more deeply. Her love deepened her faith. *Love creates faith.* But only as we enter into the dying of Christ does our faith grow. The field hockey bench potentially did the same thing for Emily that a beggar on the streets of Kolkata did for Mother Teresa. It joined Emily to Christ in ways she had not experienced previously.

One of my most enduring experiences of *love creating faith* occurred over a ten-year period when I experienced almost incessant humiliation. My pride and will were constantly exposed and stripped. During this time, I got to know God like I never had before. He took away everything I loved in ministry and gifted me with his enduring presence. In my repeated descents into death, prayer became like breathing. It is a knowledge you experience only down low. Enduring in love deepened my faith.[3]

Missing Justification by Faith

Mother Teresa and Martin Luther have a fascinating common heritage—the medieval mind, which was dominated by the J-Curve. She embraced it. He reacted against it.

Before Luther rediscovered that faith (resting) comes before love (doing), he thought he had to get right with God in his own strength.

---

2. See Richard V. Peace, *Conversion in the New Testament: Paul and the Twelve* (Grand Rapids, MI: Eerdmans, 1999), 105–279.

3. Martin Luther's rediscovery of justification by faith removed our love (our doing) from salvation. Roman Catholic Cardinal Joseph Ratzinger (who became Pope Benedict XVI) articulated the medieval Catholic position, which merged faith and love: "Love, which lies at the center of the Catholic faith, is dropped from [Luther's] concept of faith. . . . Luther's insistence on 'by faith alone' clearly and exactly excludes love from the question of salvation. [For Luther,] Love belongs to the realm of 'works' and, thus, becomes 'profane.'" "Luther and the Unity of the Churches: An Interview with Joseph Cardinal Ratzinger," *Communio* 11 (1984): 219.

That's because, when it came to salvation, the medieval church merged faith and love by combining our sufferings (the J-Curve) with Jesus's suffering. When we merge faith with love in salvation, we don't just muddy the waters—faith loses. Faith must be pure. If saving faith isn't pure, we re-create the works righteousness of the Judaizers. That was Luther's struggle.

If salvation depended on Luther's doing, then confessing all his sin was critical. Luther describes the angst he experienced:

> I often repeated my confession and zealously performed my required penance. And yet my conscience would never give me assurance, but I was always doubting and said, "You did not perform that correctly. You were not contrite enough. You left that out of your confession."[4]

When Luther looked inward at his own obedience, he kept finding more and more sin. His flesh—like ours—was bottomless. Overcome with self-preoccupation, he realized "we are bent in and curved in upon ourselves."[5] In effect, Luther tried to do the J-Curve without the foundation of justification by faith. That's why justification by faith was so liberating for him. Among other things, he realized he didn't need to confess every sin in order for it to be forgiven.

Not surprisingly, self-doubt also plagued Mother Teresa. From letters she wrote to her spiritual confidants, we know she had a lifelong struggle with spiritual depression. Here is an excerpt:

> I call, I cling, I want—there is no one to answer—no One on Whom I can cling—no, No One.—Alone. The darkness is so dark—and I am alone.—Unwanted, forsaken.—The loneliness of the heart that wants love is unbearable.—Where is my faith? . . . I am told God loves me—and yet the reality of darkness & coldness & emptiness is so great that nothing touches my soul.[6]

---

4. Martin Luther, *Lectures on Galatians*, in *Luther's Works*, gen. ed. Jaroslav Pelikan, 55 vols. (St. Louis: Concordia, 1963), 27:13.

5. Martin Luther, *Lectures on Romans*, ed. Wilhelm Pauck (Philadelphia: Westminster, 1961), 112.

6. Mother Teresa, *Mother Teresa: Come Be My Light: The Private Writings of the "Saint of Calcutta,"* ed. Brian Kolodiejchuk (New York: Doubleday, 2007), 187.

I say this cautiously, because depression has multiple causes and can be a dark cloud that can paralyze any of us. I had a bout with depression many years ago, so I have some sense of how debilitating it can be. But when you look closely at this picture of Mother Teresa's depression, she appears to be doubting God's love for her because she is looking at her feelings of that love. She looked for a sense of God, but felt nothing.[7] Mother Teresa was affected by what we've called *feelism*—her feelings were the measure of reality. She made the common error of looking at her faith and not at the finished work of Christ. When we look at our faith, we inevitably look at our feelings—and if you ground God's love for you in your feelings, neither your conscience nor heart will be satisfied. In effect, Mother Teresa embraced *justification by sensing God's love for her*. When we base God's love for us on how we feel about his love, it inevitably leads to self-entanglement, because we never have enough faith.

If you ground God's love for you in your feelings,
neither your conscience nor heart will be satisfied.

Mother Teresa's spiritual advisors, not surprisingly, used a medieval answer to a medieval problem. They told her she was in a *fellowship of his suffering*, that her melancholy resulted from the cost of her love.[8] Because they also lacked a grounding in justification by faith, they gave a good cure (the J-Curve) to the wrong disease (a sensitive conscience). "If her disease had been failure to live out the gospel in love for others, the J-Curve would have been the right cure. But for her condition, a conscience looking to its own ability to feel God's love, the real cure is justification by faith."[9] Figure 8A (p. 74) shows what Mother Teresa's situation looks like.

Looking at your faith will depress you, whereas exercising faith by looking to Jesus frees you. We are declared righteous because of Jesus's blood, not by the energy of our faith. Otherwise, we get

---

7. The dark night of the soul is a familiar theme in late medieval piety: God feels distant; we have no sense of his love.

8. Mother Teresa, *Mother Teresa: Come Be My Light*, 3–4.

9. Jimmy Agan in pesonal correspondence.

caught in endless mental traps. True faith frees the conscience like nothing else.

Fig. 8A. The J-Curve without Justification by Faith

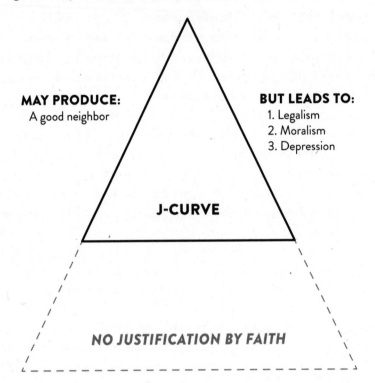

MAY PRODUCE:
A good neighbor

BUT LEADS TO:
1. Legalism
2. Moralism
3. Depression

J-CURVE

NO JUSTIFICATION BY FAITH

If Luther looked to his obedience and found it wanting, Mother Teresa looked to her faith and found it wanting. There is no greater cure for the sin-sick soul than realizing we are justified *by faith*. Justification grounds God's love for us in the finished work of Christ and not in our ability to sense God's love. Without the grounding of justification by faith, the *fellowship of his sufferings* is an unbearable weight.

There is no greater cure for the sin-sick soul
than realizing we are justified *by faith*.

9

Missing the J-Curve

Justification by Faith without the J-Curve

Martin Luther rediscovered that God accepts us not because we are good (by our love), but because Jesus is good (by our faith). Neither are we justified by a mixture of faith and love. We are justified by faith alone.

In thesis twenty-eight of his Heidelberg Disputation, Luther summarized the priority and purity of faith: "The love of God does not first discover, but creates, what is pleasing to it."[1] In other words, God doesn't find love in us; he creates love in us as we look in faith to Jesus. Faith is the energy for love. We can never begin with ourselves. Luther found that deeply liberating: "Here I felt that I was altogether born again and had entered paradise itself through open gates."[2]

Luther realized that faith not only had priority in salvation, but shaped the entire Christian life. His sermons—which were, in effect, his instructions for everyday life—focused on repentance ("I can't") and faith ("Jesus can"). He realized we never outgrow the cross; by faith we start our life as Christians, and by faith we repeatedly come to the end of ourselves. Faith is foundational for both salvation and sanctification.

---

1. Quoted in Gerard O. Forde, *On Being a Theologian of the Cross: Reflections on Luther's Heidelberg Disputation*, 1518 (Grand Rapids, MI: Eerdmans, 1997), 112.

2. Martin Luther, *Preface to the Complete Edition of Luther's Latin Writings*, in *Luther's Works*, gen. ed. Jaroslav Pelikan (St. Louis: Concordia, 1964), 34: 337.

In the early years of the Reformation, Luther was a *theologian of suffering*, in constant danger of his life. He had a rich theology of the cross, but in general, the J-Curve remained at the periphery of his main passion: preaching the law ("I can't") and gospel ("Jesus can"). That singular vision left little room for a theology of sanctification integrated with the Pauline theme of the J-Curve. As he matured, Luther increasingly saw the danger of lawlessness, but he never consistently grounded sanctification in the J-Curve with its dynamic of living in Christ.[3]

You can see the missing J-Curve in Luther's life. As he aged, he became increasingly bitter when others, especially the Jews, rejected the gospel. He wrote a diatribe, "The Jews and Their Lies," so awful I can't bear to quote it.[4] True, Luther's venom fit the spirit of his age, but he had defied the spirit of his age by rediscovering justification by faith. When the Jews failed to respond to the gospel, Luther didn't receive their rejection as a *fellowship of his sufferings*.

In contrast, Luther's mentor, the apostle Paul, did. Luther wanted to break the Jews, while Paul let his own heart break for them:

> I am speaking the truth in Christ—I am not lying; my conscience bears me witness in the Holy Spirit—that *I have great sorrow and unceasing anguish in my heart*. For I could wish that I myself were accursed and cut off from Christ for the sake of my brothers, my kinsmen according to the flesh. (Rom. 9:1–3)

In this passage, Paul doesn't push suffering away by making the Jews his enemies. Instead, he laments, letting his heart break because

---

3. Luther was a remarkably rich thinker, with one foot in the Middle Ages and one in the Reformation. He valued the medieval emphasis on a fellowship of his sufferings, calling himself a theologian of suffering. See Ronald K. Ritgers, *The Reformation of Sufferings: Pastoral Theology and Lay Piety in Late Medieval and Early Modern Germany*, Oxford Studies in Historical Theology (New York: Oxford University Press, 2012), 111–18. Later in life, Luther realized that the law gives us direction to live as Christians (the third use of the law), but cruciformity didn't take a significant role in his preaching. See Carl Trueman, *Luther on the Christian Life: Cross and Freedom* (Wheaton, IL: Crossway, 2015), 61–66, 95–97, 173–74. For additional reflections on Luther, see my essay "Luther: The Last Medieval Protestant" in the Virtual Appendix for this book, www.seeJesus.net/J-Curvebook.

4. I don't want to create a caricature of Luther that doesn't reflect his overall balance and love. For instance, two decades before his diatribe, he wrote a moving pamphlet on loving the Jews. Likewise, his pamphlet *Whether One May Flee from a Deadly Plague* (1527) called pastors and church leaders to stay and care for the sick and dying in Wittenberg, Germany, at great risk to themselves. Luther himself stayed behind. Nevertheless, he consistently struggled to love his enemies. His reaction to the 1525 Peasant Revolt was similar to his reaction to the Jews in 1543. For a balanced discussion on Luther and the Jews see Carl Trueman, "Luther and the Jews," audio recording on "The Reformation," Westminster Theological Seminary, available on iTunes.

they are his enemies; he receives the dying. His love for the other—even the hostile other—is so great that he, unbelievably, vows he is willing to give up his eternal salvation for them.

Paul inhabits the dying love of Christ for his enemies so thoroughly, so completely, he would die for them. For eternity, Paul is willing to enter hell for his fellow Jews, his enemies. Luther condemns the Jews to death. Paul wants to be condemned to eternal death for the Jews. Substitutionary love, one aspect of the J-Curve, is Paul's normal.

If we don't re-enact Jesus's dying and rising, then justification by faith can become a feel-good formula that gives us a positive self-image. The gospel turns in on itself and becomes one more thing to make us feel good about ourselves. Then individualism ("It's up to me"), materialism ("It's all about my money"), and narcissism ("It's all about me") shape the core of life, and suffering seems strange. Here's what that looks like:

Fig. 9A. Justification by Faith without the J-Curve

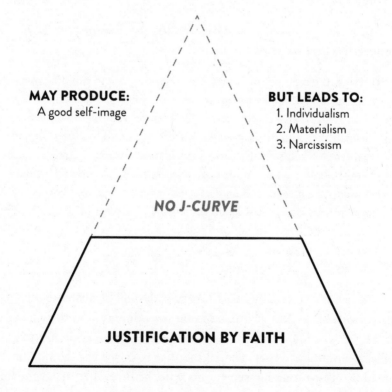

MAY PRODUCE:
A good self-image

BUT LEADS TO:
1. Individualism
2. Materialism
3. Narcissism

NO J-CURVE

JUSTIFICATION BY FAITH

Missing the J-Curve Illustrated

Pastor Tom's story (not his real name) shows us what happens when you separate justification by faith from the J-Curve. Tom, a best-selling author and megachurch pastor, made Luther's emphasis on the present value of justification by faith the center of his ministry. Tom wrote,

> The gospel alone liberates you to live a life of scandalous gener-osity, unrestrained sacrifice, uncommon valor, and unbounded courage.

When Tom had an affair, his church released the following state-ment about him:

> Several days ago, Pastor Tom admitted to moral failure, acknowl-edging his actions disqualify him from continuing to serve as se-nior pastor or preach from the pulpit, and resigned—effective immediately.

Tom then released this statement to *The Washington Post*. I've italicized where he spins the narrative:

> I resigned from my position at church today due to ongoing mari-tal issues. As many of you know, I returned from a trip a few months back and discovered that *my wife was having an affair.* Heartbroken and devastated, I informed our church leadership and requested a sabbatical to focus exclusively on my marriage and family. As her affair continued, we separated. Sadly and embar-rassingly, *I subsequently sought comfort in a friend* and developed an inappropriate relationship myself. . . . Both my wife and I are heartbroken over our actions and we ask you to pray for us and our family that God would give us the grace we need to weather this heart wrenching storm.

Tom told us (actually, all of America) that his affair was a response to his wife's. By publicly mentioning her adultery and the timing of it, he reduced his shame. By shaming her, he becomes the victim. His silence would have been a small sacrifice to cover her shame. But in-stead of substituting himself for his wife, he threw her under the bus.

He betrayed her in the adultery, then he betrayed her in the narrative. Twice Tom chased his feelings. First, he "sought comfort in a friend." Then he sought comfort by exposing his wife. In neither case did he embrace a *fellowship of his sufferings*.

The result? An even more broken relationship with his wife. Not surprisingly, after she read Tom's press release, she sent her own.

> The statement reflected my husband's opinions but not my own. Please respect the privacy of my family at this time, thank you.

Tom knew little of a love that takes someone else's place. He understood that Jesus died for him, but he didn't know how to die for his wife. He *believed* the gospel, but he didn't *become* like the gospel. Tom's grace-only lens harmonizes with the therapeutic vision of the fragile self—hunting for balance, security, and identity. Both the grace-only lens and the therapeutic lens reinforce people's self-absorption. Tom was self-absorbed.

Missing the J-Curve

Tom frequently used grace to denigrate the work of love. Here is a typical quote: "We spend more time asking what would Jesus do instead of what did Jesus do." Here, he makes a false dichotomy between love (what would Jesus do) and faith (what did Jesus do). We can see his limited vision here: "Contrary to popular belief, Christianity is not about good people getting better. If anything, it is about bad people coping with their failure to be good."

This vision was incomplete and unbalanced. Christianity has a dual vision: bad people realizing they can't be good (faith), and bad people becoming good (love).

Tom's vision of knowing was limited to Jesus's work for us in the atonement. This narrow vision eventually ended his ministry. While his story is extreme, I've seen multiple milder versions. I often hear grace-centered teaching that marginalizes obedience.

Some are unbalanced in the other direction, with little room for grace in how they relate to people. They have grace-centered doctrine, but they are weak in graciousness. My dad, Jack Miller, commenting about his own tradition, Reformed theology, said, "We have created this wonderful castle of grace, but someone forgot to put in a door to the castle—the welcoming heart of God."

The church tends to oscillate between abusing grace (forgetting the law) and forgetting grace (legalism). Some emphasize "believe more" and some emphasize "be good." As Richard Gaffin observes,

> Too much of church history . . . has gotten trapped in a false dilemma, the dilemma between Atonement (Christ as Mediator) and conformity (Christ as example). . . . [Christ's] footsteps lead, as Paul tells us, into "the fellowship of his sufferings" and "being conformed to his death" (Phil. 3:10).[5]

In general, since the Reformation, our vision of the J-Curve has been weak.[6] Most Christians are puzzled by the apostle Paul's references to participating in the dying and rising of Christ. I grew up memorizing the great catechisms of our faith. Their overall pattern is God-Creation-Fall-Redemption-Law. When it comes to the Christian life, the teaching focuses on the Ten Commandments. That's good, but we have something better. What's missing is not an emphasis on sanctification, but the spine of sanctification—dying and rising with Christ as the normal Christian life. The combination of some theologians' nervousness about imitating Jesus, combined with our nervousness about suffering, means we have a weak vision of the J-Curve.[7] Gaffin writes,

> Risking a generalization . . . the churches of the Reformation have shown a much better grasp of the "for us" of Christ's cross and the gospel than they have of the "with him" of that gospel, particularly *suffering* with him.[8]

---

5. Richard B. Gaffin Jr., "The Usefulness of the Cross," *Westminster Theological Journal* 41, no. 2 (Spring 1979), 244.

6. Reformed scholar Jason Hood, writing in the *Westminster Theological Journal*, reflects on this: "A number of factors contributed to the eclipse of imitation as a Christian practice. The controversial nature of the imitation of Christ and others in Socinism, by Abelard and his followers, as well as the Roman Catholic emphasis on merit in the sufferings of believers (sometimes taken to torturous lengths) all played a role, as did the eucharistic wars over the finality and significance of Jesus' death." Jason B. Hood, "The Cross in the New Testament: Two Theses in Conversation with Recent Literature (2000–2007)," *Westminster Theological Journal* 71 (2009): 289–90. Themes of the J-Curve linger on particularly in Pietism.

7. See Jimmy Agan, "Departing from—and Recovering—Tradition: John Calvin and the Imitation of Christ." *Journal of the Evangelical Theological Society* 56, no. 4 (2013): 801–14.

8. Gaffin, "The Usefulness of the Cross," 244 (emphasis original). Hood writes, "*The biblical teaching on the imitation of the crucified Christ is the most neglected aspect of recent work*

Linking Faith and Love

So how do we balance faith and love, justification and sanctification? Like the two natures of Christ, his divinity and his humanity, these two ways of participating in Christ (justification by faith and the J-Curve) must

1. *never be separated.* If we separate them, justification by faith can become an excuse for just feeling good about ourselves.
2. *never be merged.* If we merge them, we think our suffering pays for our sins.
3. *never be reversed.* If we reverse them, we put obedience before faith. Faith comes first.

If we don't keep faith and love together, we weaken our walk with Christ. Here are some of the dangers from isolating justification by faith or the J-Curve:

Justification by Faith *without* the J-Curve	The J-Curve *without* Justification by Faith
Jesus is distant—just need him for salvation	Jesus is distant—the dark night of the soul
Suffering feels strange—avoids suffering	Hunts for suffering to find Jesus
Wants to feel good, to protect the self	Wants to experience suffering to get rid of self
Avoids dying	Stuck at the bottom of the J-Curve
Pride unwittingly cultivated	Pride in humility
Doing what feels good	Legalism

To recap the last few chapters: Luther rediscovered that *faith creates love*, while Mother Teresa embodied that *love creates faith*. The activity of caring for dying beggars (love) helped Mother Teresa experience Jesus (faith). *Love creates faith* (the J-Curve) is a central principle for sanctification, but when love becomes the *means* for salvation, then Jesus's death isn't enough.

---

on the NT message of the cross. This neglect is particularly acute among works produced in Reformed and evangelical circles" (emphasis original). Hood, "The Cross in the New Testament," 286.

Here's a simple way to link these two patterns:

Fig. 9B. Luther and Mother Teresa

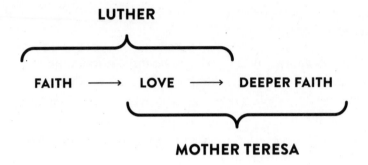

In other words, we must begin with faith and keep returning to faith (Luther), but only as we enter into a life of dying to self, of dying love (Mother Teresa), do we grow deeper in faith. As our world collapses around us, there is no better time to rediscover Gaffin's observation that "Until Christ returns, then, all Christian existence continues to be suffering with Christ."[9]

Like never before, the church needs *both* Luther and Mother Teresa's vision. Luther offers the foundational liberation of justification by faith. He helps us see *why* Jesus died and *how* that helps us live as liberated sons and daughters of God. Mother Teresa offers us a living example of the normal Christian life as dying with Jesus. She focuses on *how* Jesus died and *how* we re-enact that as slaves of Jesus. Luther provides the *foundation* for life. Mother Teresa models the *shape* of life.[10] Faith and love must be linked.

———

Now that we've located the J-Curve in Paul's ideas of union with Christ, the flesh, and justification by faith, we turn our attention in

9. Gaffin, "The Usefulness of the Cross," 237.
10. My affirming of one aspect of Mother Teresa's theology is not an endorsement of other parts of it. Neither am I suggesting we need a synthesis of Luther and Mother Teresa. When Roman Catholic theologians speak of justification by faith, they mean that righteousness is imparted instead of imputed.

Part 2 to understanding the dying side of the J-Curve, which, surprisingly, not only makes sense of our lives, but fills us with hope, because rising, not dying, is the last word.

Like never before, the church needs *both*
Luther and Mother Teresa's vision.

PART 2

DYING WITH JESUS

What Are the Different Kinds of J-Curves?

What Is the Connection between
Suffering and Love?

How Does the Presence of Evil Change
the Shape of Our J-Curves?

What Does It Feel Like to Live in This Strange
Time between Jesus's Resurrection and Ours?

10

Dying to Self

Understanding Different J-Curves

Now that we've explored the larger world that surrounds the J-Curve, let's take a closer look at the J-Curve itself. To continue our house analogy, we first explored the basement (justification by faith), then we went outside and saw the whole house (union with Christ). Now we explore the first floor (the J-Curve itself), which has three rooms, each with a distinctive focus. The location of the evil or problem gives each of the three kinds of our *present* J-Curve their unique character.

In the *love* J-Curve, you pursue a problem outside of yourself. Love leads you to go after evil, to absorb pain. For example, I entered a *love* J-Curve when I took Kim to Florida and when I checked on Ed the sheep. In both cases, I was proactive, initiating action, moving outside of my comfort zone. Similarly, Mother Teresa modeled this when she left the relative comfort of a school for Indian girls to care for dying beggars. As you move outside your world to engage with a problem, you embrace Jesus's suffering, the cost of love.

In the *suffering* J-Curve, evil comes at you from the outside, unwanted and unasked. You're not pursuing it. Pain finds you. This happened when Emily sat on the bench. Both of us wanted to be rid of this problem.

In the *repentance* J-Curve, evil is in you. You're the problem. You cause the pain. Here, you kill evil in yourself; you crucify it. When I didn't boast with my coworkers, I began a *repentance* J-Curve. When I was tempted to defend myself over the Dixie cup, I put to death my desire to create my own righteousness by not defending myself. If Christ is to be formed in you, the pieces of you need to be nailed to the cross. What makes this J-Curve unique, and more than a bit painful, is you're doing the nailing!

If Christ is to be formed in you, the pieces
of you need to be nailed to the cross.

Fig. 10A. 3 Present J-Curves

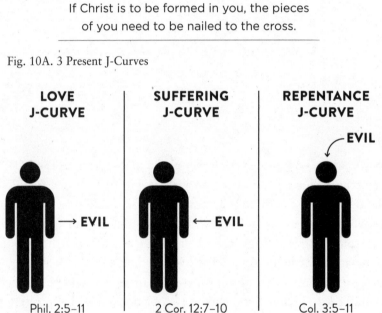

LOVE J-CURVE	SUFFERING J-CURVE	REPENTANCE J-CURVE
Phil. 2:5–11	2 Cor. 12:7–10	Col. 3:5–11

Each of these three J-Curves participates in Christ's dying *in the present*. Each embraces a form of his suffering as it envelops, absorbs, or pursues evil. As such, each is subsumed in a *dying to self*.[1] The source of the dying changes for each, but for all three, *dying to self* shapes the contours of the normal Christian life. Each embraces Jesus's command to *take up your cross and follow him* (Mark 8:34), and

---

1. Insight from personal communication with David Powlison, "This dying to self J-Curve is a positive J-Curve of comprehensive humility, the daily offering of oneself to God as a living sacrifice, turning away from self-trust and confidence in what I do, and turning to trust in our Savior and in what he did, does, and will do."

Paul's desire to enter a *fellowship of his sufferings* (Phil. 3:10). For Paul, *dying and rising in him* is the most basic structure of how we "do Jesus." From this dying, the beauty of an obedient, humble life that reflects Jesus rises. So just before a long passage on love, Paul writes,

> I appeal to you therefore, brothers, by the mercies of God, to present your bodies as a living sacrifice, holy and acceptable to God, which is your spiritual worship. (Rom. 12:1)

Figure 10A above shows the three different kinds of our *present* J-Curve (each with representative passages), each a different manifestation of *dying to self*.

To review, behind these *present* J-Curves are two *past* J-Curves. Lying behind all our J-Curves is Jesus's J-Curve: Jesus's life, death, and resurrection for our sins. We participate in his J-Curve by faith. I called our mysterious union with Christ in his *past* dying and rising the *faith* J-Curve (see chap. 5). All of our J-Curves *past* and *present* participate in Jesus's J-Curve. Here's what our past and present J-Curves look like:

Fig. 10B. Jesus's J-Curve and Our J-Curves

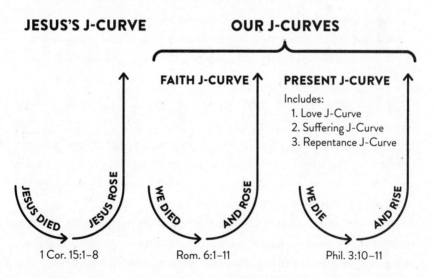

Martin Luther's rediscovery of justification by faith protected the church from merging the *original* J-Curve (Jesus's suffering) with our *present* J-Curves (our suffering). Our suffering doesn't pay for our sins, but it does imprint us with the image of Jesus. If we neglect the *present* J-Curves, suffering becomes strange, primarily to be avoided. If we miss the crucial role of our *present* union with Christ, we'll lose a vision for the beauty of Jesus imprinted on us.

Missing pieces of DNA can have an enormous impact. Kim's disability comes from a microscopic deletion of the *p* arm of her first chromosome, called 1p36. Because the first chromosome maps the other chromosomes, that microscopic damage spread to all her DNA. So with the church, the neglect of our *present* J-Curves has damaged the church's DNA. This book offers a chromosomal repair!

In this and the next several chapters, we examine in detail some of the multiple ways that *dying in Christ* shapes our lives, beginning with the *repentance* J-Curve.

The Feel of Death

In the *repentance* J-Curve, we put to death evil in us. In Colossians 3 (and Romans 8) Paul grounds our sanctification in the dying and rising of Christ. Dying with Christ imprints us with his image:

> *For you have died*, and your life is hidden with Christ in God. . . .
> *Put to death* therefore what is earthly in you: sexual immorality,
> impurity, passion, evil desire, and covetousness, which is idolatry.
> (Col. 3:3, 5)

In this passage, Paul refers to two deaths: one in the past ("you have died") and one in the present ("Put to death"). By faith, we mysteriously died with Christ in the past (the *faith* J-Curve), but in the present, we are not yet dead to our sin. Paul links our past death with the present by inviting the Colossians to re-enact Jesus's death by putting to death their sinful habits.

A *repentance* J-Curve, like the *love* or *suffering* J-Curve, encounters pain as it puts to death a hidden or stubborn piece of the flesh. When I didn't boast in the meeting with my two-coworkers, I was overcome with sadness. My silence killed a piece of my flesh, joining me to Jesus in his death. That hurt. Recognition of my work had been life for me, so when I didn't seek recognition, I felt an enormous loss. Given the modern obsession with living in a pain-free world, it is helpful to know that victory over my flesh will result in pain and even sadness. In other words, in that moment, I *should* have felt sadness. The J-Curve helps our emotional life come alive.

My silence killed a piece of my flesh,
joining me to Jesus in his death.

I frequently experience the sadness of repentance when it comes to sexual lust. I pray daily, "Father, help me to look at women with the eyes of Jesus, as sisters and daughters, but if I can't, help me to look away." Initially, I struggled to pray this because doing so required that I acknowledge this particular temptation. Now, when I look away, I feel a twinge of sadness. It's poignant for me. In fact, the more I've done it, the more I've become sensitized to my sadness.

Every other object of beauty in my life I can linger over—my wife, my daughter Kim, a sunset, our golden retrievers, the fall leaf colors— but God forbids me to lust over another woman's beauty. It's God's solitary no over my enjoyment of beauty. By regularly bowing to that no, I put to death my lust, and I follow Jesus into a light fellowship of his sufferings.

Bringing Death to Someone Else

When I wanted to boast with my two coworkers, the Spirit alerted me to my sin, likely because I'd been immersing myself in John 6. But often we don't see ourselves well, so we need an honest word to invite us into a mini-death. We need others to help us put our flesh to death.

Jill's honesty helped our daughter Ashley put to death her flesh. Fifteen-year-old Ashley had been consumed by sports, boys, and her appearance. Twenty-five years later, she reflected on what happened in this Facebook post on her mom's birthday:

> When I was in 9th grade, my mom abruptly pulled me out of 4th period choir and sat me in our Miller minivan in the school park- ing lot. She flipped down the passenger mirror & told me to look hard at my face & examine my insides, because that was where the heart flows. Faced with a cloud of aerosol, caked makeup, &

pops of gold jewelry, Mom listened to the Holy Spirit. She stopped errands, pushed 5 siblings aside to challenge my heart in a parking lot. My mom was not concerned about grades, clothing, sports, or trying to make sure I dressed for the in-crowd. Her number one priority was fighting hard to show me my audience of 1: Jesus. She is a lover of God & lover of the Bible & lover of talking to God non-stop. Over the course of my adult years, the amount of Bible verses she has sent me could wallpaper my whole house. So grateful for u mom—ur beautiful inside & out!!! . . . I love you!

Ashley, like her sister Emily, had created a righteousness of her own that elevated her in a community dominated by the false narrative of physical beauty. Jill invited Ashley to forsake that narrative and enter into the story of Jesus. She wanted Ashley to move from *in boys* to *in Christ.*

The resurrection side of a *repentance* J-Curve waits for our obedience. Ashley told me later that she was so jolted by Jill that morning that she seldom wears makeup even today. (Frankly, she doesn't need to—she glows with Jesus.) In my meeting with my two coworkers, my mini-death was overwhelmed by resurrection as I fed on Christ by reading John 6. Dying and rising always go together—but we never know how or when the rising will come until after we enter into and embrace the dying.

The Ultimate Beauty Treatment

We can see all three of our *present* J-Curves at work in the stories of Ashley and Emily. Ashley went through a *repentance* J-Curve as she put to death her love of appearance and popularity. Jill went through a *love* J-Curve as she pursued Ashley by speaking an honest word. Emily went through a *suffering* J-Curve as she sat on the bench. Each of these J-Curves, though distinct, leaves an imprint of the image of Jesus on the one who enters into *the fellowship of his sufferings.* When his journey becomes our journey, his image becomes our image. It's the ultimate beauty treatment!

11

A Cascade of Love

Weaving J-Curves Together

My friend Joni Eareckson Tada became a quadriplegic after a diving accident when she was seventeen. This vibrant, effervescent teenager, one of the most popular and athletic kids in her school, was locked motionless in a medical frame for months on end. Joni slipped into a deep depression, even begging her best friend to help her commit suicide. She refused the story that God had permitted in her life. She wanted her old life back—serving as captain of the lacrosse team and riding her horse, Tumbleweed, in shows.

The first two years after the accident were brutal. At first, Joni held on to the hope that by sheer willpower she'd regain the use of her arms and legs, and eventually get married to her boyfriend. But then reality set in. She would not get better.

> I retched at the thought of living life without a working body. I hated my paralysis so much I would drive my power wheelchair into walls, repeatedly banging them until they cracked. Early on, I found dark companions who helped me numb my depression with scotch-and-cola. I just wanted to disappear. I wanted to die.[1]

---

1. Joni Eareckson Tada, "Reflections on the 50th Anniversary of My Diving Accident," The Gospel Coalition, July 30, 2017. https://www.thegospelcoalition.org/article/reflections-on-50th-anniversary-of-my-diving-accident.

In her autobiography, *Joni*, she describes her escape into her imagination:

> Friends who had come to visit me had saddled horses and gone on a trail ride. I was feeling sorry for myself comparing my lot to theirs. . . . I closed my eyes and visualized a similar day a couple of years earlier. In my daydreams, I was again with Jason, riding horseback together toward the forest, across the fragrant meadows, stopping in a deserted place. I relished memories of unrestrained pleasure, excitement, and sensual satisfaction—
>
> I was angry at God. I'd retrieve every tiny physical pleasure from my mind and throw it up to Him in bitterness. I couldn't accept the fact—God's will, they said—that I'd never do or feel these things again.[2]

Breakthrough came when she learned the pattern of the J-Curve from her friend and mentor, Steve Estes. She didn't stoically accept her fate; she received the *fellowship of his sufferings*. Steve paraphrased Philippians 3:10 for her, saying, "Joni, what is happening to you will advance God's cause! Paul had his prison chains; you have your chair. You can rejoice in suffering because He is allowing you to suffer on His behalf." Then he explained the J-Curve, quoting Philippians 1:29: "You are given, in this battle, the privilege of not merely believing in Christ but also of suffering for his sake."[3]

Steve recast Joni's story by calling on her not only to *believe* the gospel, but also to *become* like the gospel. This gave her a brand-new perspective on her wheelchair. Now, instead of it being a terrible burden, she saw it as a tool for God's work in her life. The chair became a blessing and, unbelievably, "an instrument of joy."[4]

Joni's accident put her in a *suffering* J-Curve: the evil came to her from the outside, unasked. The *suffering* J-Curve exposed her flesh in new ways. Outside evil usually exposes our inside evil. When Joni saw her inside evil, she realized she needed to repent of demanding her old life back. Entering the *repentance* J-Curve meant embracing the

---

2. Joni Eareckson Tada, *Joni: An Unforgettable Story* (Grand Rapids, MI: Zondervan, 2012), 114–15.

3. Tada, *Story*, 132.

4. Tada, *Story*, 135.

suffering J-Curve. So Joni put to death her old life by giving away her cherished hockey and lacrosse sticks, and selling her beloved horse. She stopped clinging to her past. "Now," she wrote, "I was forced to trust God."[5]

Joni didn't realize the depth of the change God had done in her heart until her friends took her to Baltimore one evening.

> One night, a few Young Life friends who liked to sing picked me up for a late night drive into Baltimore City. We ended up downtown at the railway station—a massive structure with travertine floors, marble columns, and vaulted ceilings. We found a corner and started harmonizing, our voices echoing throughout the station. An officious-looking guard approached and ordered us out of the building. "See that 'no loitering' sign? It's 11 p.m. and you kids don't belong here," he barked. Then he pointed at me: "And you put that wheelchair back where you found it. Right now!"
>
> "But sir," I insisted, "it's mine." He told me not to give him any lip and to put it back right away. When our little group started laughing, he realized his error. That night, when my friends got me home, one kneeled beside my chair: "Joni, that's the first time I've ever heard you call it 'my wheelchair.' Thank you for doing that. You're helping me own my problems, too."[6]

Joni *received* the wheelchair. She didn't push away *the fellowship of his sufferings*. Likewise, God has given each of us a wheelchair. It might be a critical spouse, a wayward child, an always-tight budget, or the prospect of lifelong singleness. These chairs are doors to knowing Jesus in ways we never imagined. But they must be received. We can't push them away. We need to say with Joni, "It's my wheelchair."

The Surrendered Will

The following diagram illustrates what happened with Joni. The heart works in three steps. I call this the Chain of Love:

---

5. Tada, *Story*, 122.
6. Tada, "Reflections."

What we *love* (desire) → What we *want* (will) → What we *do* (action)

What I *love* shapes what I *want*, which controls what I *do*.[7] This can be either positive or negative. Here's a negative example from Joni's life:

Joni loves her old life (desire) → She refuses her new life (will) → She experiences anger and fantasies (action)

What we love (desire) drives this whole chain. So how do we get at bad desire? Surprisingly, Joni got at desire indirectly with an act of her will. She *put it to death* by selling Tumbleweed. Instinctively, we want to get at desire by educating it, by renovating it, or by improving our hearts. But you can't improve the flesh; you must kill it. The cross is a place for dying, not improving. So the first move in a *repentance* J-Curve is death. For Joni to taste Christ, Tumbleweed had to go. Repentance works backward through the chain, moving decisively against our feelings. Joni loved Tumbleweed. But Joni had a new love, a new calling, and a new master, so with an act of the will, she did the opposite of *what she felt* and sold Tumbleweed.

You can't improve the flesh; you must kill it. The cross is a place for dying, not improving.

Acting reshapes the will, which chokes off bad desire. This creates a new chain of love that works like this:

Joni loves Jesus (desire) → She receives her wheelchair (will) → She experiences joy and love (action)

Some Christians, saturated with a grace-only lens, struggle with the simplicity of doing. They fear legalism, presuming that obedience should flow naturally from meditating and resting on the gospel. But the flesh is far too crafty to be cured by mere meditation on the gospel. You must kill it regularly.

---

7. Both Jonathan Edwards (in his *Religious Affections*) and Augustine of Hippo (in his *Confessions*) trace how what we love shapes our will. Alfred Edersheim traces how the master theme in Jesus's life is the surrender of his will to his Father. Jesus's dependence on his Father is one of the master themes of the Gospel of John, especially chaps. 5–12. *The Life and Times of Jesus the Messiah* (Iowa Falls, IA: World Bible Publishers, 1990).

The Love J-Curve

The *repentance* J-Curve freed Joni to embark on a *love* J-Curve. When her friends surrounded her, she realized God had given her a far larger calling: to draw the church into friendship with people affected by disability. When her friends embraced Joni in her suffering, they freed her to embrace the suffering of others. She entered the *love* J-Curve informally with friends and then by creating Joni and Friends, a worldwide organization that every year ministers to thousands of people affected by disability. (In the interest of full disclosure, when I say "my friend Joni," I should clarify that Joni has so many friends, she started a mission to keep tabs on them all!)

The resurrection that started in Joni's will when she received the suffering enabled her to lose sight of herself and draw others into an ever-widening circle of friends. She began inviting others to enter the world of the disabled, whom the church has so often kept at arm's length. Jill, Kim, and I participate in Joni's resurrection every year, not only in going to Joni Camp, but in the friendships we've made from that camp.

In Joni's life, as is often the case, the three different J-Curves blended together to form one interlocking story: a *suffering* J-Curve led to a *repentance* J-Curve that led to a *love* J-Curve. It was a cascade of love.

A Cascade of Love

The apostle Paul describes a similar cascade in the opening to 2 Corinthians. He begins with God's love comforting us in our suffering:

> Blessed be the God and Father of our Lord Jesus Christ, the Father of mercies and God of all comfort, who comforts us in all our affliction . . . (1:3–4a)

The cascade then spills over as a ministry of comfort to others:

> . . . so that we may be able to comfort those who are in any affliction, with the comfort with which we ourselves are comforted by God. For as we *share abundantly in Christ's sufferings*, so through Christ we share abundantly in comfort too. (vv. 4b–5)

Paul sees his suffering as *sharing in Christ's sufferings*. Dying is followed by rising, suffering by comfort. The work of love repeats both the dying and the rising of Jesus. Like Jesus, Paul suffers so that others can be comforted. Likewise, Joni's suffering flows over into comfort for thousands and thousands of people affected by disability.

Paul goes on:

> If we are afflicted, it is for your comfort and salvation; and if we are comforted, it is for your comfort, which you experience when you patiently endure the same sufferings that we suffer. Our hope for you is unshaken, for we know that as you share in our sufferings, you will also share in our comfort. (vv. 6–7)

In a *love* J-Curve, my dying is for your rising. Every act of love potentially re-enacts the gospel. I've pictured this in Figure 11A below. Christ's suffering flows into our lives as comfort, so as we are suffering, our suffering flows into others' lives as comfort.

Fig. 11A. A Cascade of Comfort

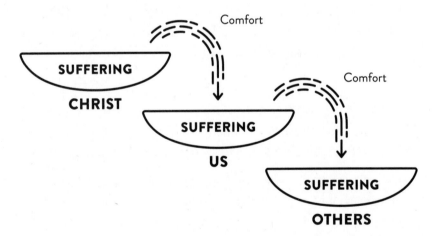

To give a feel for what Paul is saying, I've rewritten 2 Corinthians 1:3–7 with Joni's name inserted:

> Blessed be the God and Father of our Lord Jesus Christ, the Father of mercies and God of all comfort, who comforts Joni in all her

affliction, so that she may be able to comfort her friends who are in any affliction, with the comfort with which she herself is comforted by God. For as Joni shares abundantly in Christ's sufferings, so through Christ Joni shares abundantly in comfort too. If Joni is afflicted, it is for her friends' comfort and salvation; and if Joni is comforted, it is for their comfort, which they experience when they patiently endure the same sufferings that Joni suffers. Our hope for her friends is unshaken, for we know that as they share in Joni's sufferings, they will also share in Joni's comfort.

Suffering isn't strange for Paul. He isn't merely enduring suffering, coping with it, or even learning from it—he's celebrating a life that re-enacts the cross and the empty tomb. Paul is describing the *normal Christian life*. Because we've neglected Paul's emphasis on the J-Curve, suffering feels strange. We've lost sight of this vibrant way of doing life. Embracing the J-Curve as a way of life frees our inner self from a life of waiting for the other shoe to drop. In the same way that justification by faith frees our conscience, entering the dying and rising of Jesus liberates our spirit.

In the same way that justification by faith
frees our conscience, entering the dying
and rising of Jesus liberates our spirit.

Of course, it's one thing to put to death our fantasies, as Joni did by selling her horse, *but* it's another to live in a wheelchair with a broken body for fifty years. In the next chapter, we'll look at how the apostle Paul handles suffering that doesn't go away.

12

Life at the Bottom
of the J-Curve

Making Sense of Persistent Evil

Paul is no stranger to the *suffering* J-Curve. When his old nemesis, the Judaizers, slipped into Corinth and won people's hearts by boasting about their credentials, they attacked Paul for his lack of credentials. He responds in 2 Corinthians by revealing his resume. But because Paul inhabits the dying and rising of Jesus, he flips the Failure-Boasting Chart and boasts in his weakness. That's what living in the shadow of the cross does.

Paul's Flesh

One of Paul's weaknesses is his unknown thorn in the flesh.

> So to keep me from *becoming conceited* because of the surpassing greatness of the revelations, a thorn was given me in the flesh, a messenger of Satan to harass me, to keep me from *becoming conceited*. (2 Cor. 12:7)

You might be wondering why the great apostle Paul was tempted by conceit. The answer is the nature of the flesh. Like cancer, our flesh mutates, creating new forms of itself. For example, let's say I notice I have a tendency to boast. I repent of boasting and even stop boasting as much. Then I notice how much others boast. I mention to a friend how shocked

I am over how much other people talk about themselves. My good effort to stop a sin has created more sin. I've become a critic and a gossip. So I double down (in a good way) and fight my tendency to judge by cultivating humility. I grow in humility; then my flesh mutates yet again, and I discover I'm proud about my humility, turning into a boast.

The flesh is like email. You answer ten messages, but an hour later, twenty more appear. It helps to know, this side of heaven, that I will always be at war with a part of me. Nevertheless, evil's relentlessness can wear us down. Thinking about the flesh, Paul wrote, "Wretched man that I am! Who will deliver me from this body of death?" (Rom. 7:24).

As we mature as Christians, the flesh potentially becomes deadlier because we know more; we are wiser. Consequently, we can judge others more quickly and easily. So the more we grow in grace, the more grace we need. Paul feels that dynamic. With all his revelations, including an actual visit to heaven, he is tempted to think too highly of himself.

Paul's thorn draws him into a temporary death, the downward curve of the *suffering* J-Curve.

The Gift of the Thorn

Scholars speculate about Paul's thorn. It's possible it was bad eyesight (Gal. 4:15; 6:11), but his silence helps us because it makes *thorn in the flesh* generic, applying to almost any kind of suffering. His silence likely comes from prudence. Given our flesh's tendency to judge, sometimes less information is better.

Paul wants to get rid of the *thorn*. He never embraces suffering because "it's good for you." He's no Stoic; he's a resurrection guy. So he asks Jesus to remove it:

> Three times I pleaded with the Lord about this, that it should leave me. (2 Cor. 12:8)

Paul's desire for resurrection is a helpful insight into the J-Curve. Dying doesn't make a J-Curve—every pagan knew life descends into death. Resurrection makes a J-Curve. A resurrection is nothing less than "God hears my cry." If God answers prayer, then God will act against evil in my life.[1] So Paul prays, in effect, "deliver me from evil."

---

1. N. T. Wright, *The Resurrection of the Son of God* (London: SPCK, 2017), is immensely helpful, but he misses the simplicity that resurrection is embedded in answered prayer.

Here's Jesus's answer:

> But he said to me, "My grace is sufficient for you, for my power is made perfect in weakness." (v. 9a)

Jesus is saying, "I'm going to deliver you from evil by *not* delivering you from the thorn. I'm going to use outside evil (the thorn) to deliver you from inside evil (conceit)."

Here's how God's "power is made perfect in weakness." First, the thorn weakens Paul. When we get hit by a thorn, we feel drained, helpless, as if someone has pulled the plug out of our life. We feel weary beyond belief as we inhabit a peculiar poverty of spirit.

Jesus's answer connected Paul's thorn-derived weakness with Jesus's power: "My power is made perfect in weakness." Jesus permits this recurring weakness because the Spirit's power is perfected in humility. Down low, at the bottom of the J-Curve, pride is stripped from Paul. As he cries out for grace, he becomes like Jesus, who can't do life on his own (John 5:19). Paul's poverty of spirit, then, becomes the launching pad for the power of Jesus in his life, and he experiences a real-time resurrection.

Paul likely sees his experience with the thorn through the lens of Jesus's Passion. Like Jesus, Paul prays three times that the suffering will be removed (Matt. 26:39–44). Jesus has nails; Paul has a thorn. Both the cross and the thorn are instruments of weakness through which God pours his power.

Then, as Paul experiences resurrection power, his old nemesis, pride, returns, but just in time, the thorn reasserts itself, bringing him down again into death—and the cycle begins again.

When Jesus gives him the map of the J-Curve, Paul's world inverts—weakness becomes his boast:

> Therefore I will boast all the more gladly of my weaknesses, so that the power of Christ may rest upon me. For the sake of Christ, then, I am content with weaknesses, insults, hardships, persecutions, and calamities. For when I am weak, then I am strong. (2 Cor. 12:9b–10)

Paul now delights in his weakness, because weakness makes Christ fresh. Weakness is the location where he *knows* Jesus. Paul's resurrection is embedded in his death. He doesn't just know about Jesus; he inhabits Jesus's poverty of spirit. That's where the power is.

Here are the four steps that Paul articulates:

1. Paul faces the danger of conceit (2 Cor. 12:7a).
2. Jesus gives Paul a thorn that draws him into a mini-death (v. 7b).
3. Pride is stripped from Paul down at the bottom of the J-Curve. He becomes weak (v. 9a).
4. Paul experiences resurrection power in his life and ministry (v. 9b).

Here's what it looks like:

Fig. 12A. Boasting in Weakness

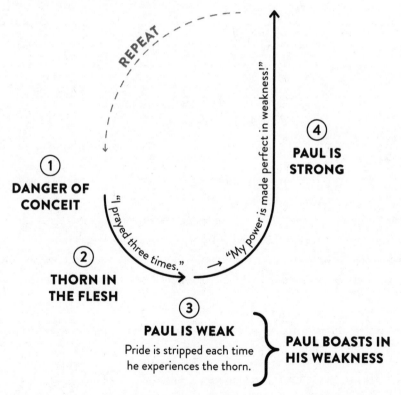

Repeat is the hardest word on this journey, but it defines a *suffering* J-Curve. We want our thorns to be over and done with. We recoil from repeated suffering. We much prefer one-time miracles, not the need for an ongoing miracle of a humble heart, but our ever-present flesh requires an ever-present solution: dying and rising with Jesus.

That's similar to my family's experience with Kim. During her pregnancy with Kim, Jill prayed, using Psalm 121, that God would "keep this baby from harm." But God gave us a harmed baby. That gap was agony, especially for Jill. Then we saw we were looking for the evil in the wrong place. The danger wasn't Kim's disability, but two proud, independent parents. Likewise, the danger for the apostle Paul wasn't the thorn, but his own conceit.

To be clear: God doesn't resurrect Paul's thorn. That stays. The resurrection is in Paul's spirit. An external dying from the thorn leads to an internal resurrection of humility, which spills out in an external resurrection of love and witness (power). In the *suffering* J-Curve, *external* dying leads to *internal* resurrection. With the map of the J-Curve, Paul doesn't get lost in the suffering. The narrative of the cross captures evil and puts it to work in resurrection.

The narrative of the cross captures evil
and puts it to work in resurrection.

Our Thorns

Paul includes a rich variety of suffering under *thorn:* "weaknesses, insults, hardships, persecutions, and calamities" (2 Cor. 12:10). Joni's thorn is her broken body. In 2017, she celebrated her fiftieth year in a wheelchair, which makes her one of the longest-living people in a wheelchair. The last few years have been particularly painful for her as she has lived with a misplaced hip and scoliosis. In 2010, when she got cancer, she reflected,

> It is very hard to go on. I mean privately I've wondered, gee, Lord, is this cancer my ticket to heaven? Because I sure am tired of sitting in a wheelchair, and my body is aching, and I'm so weary.[2]

But no, the rest of us needed to see the beauty of Jesus in her a bit longer. Joni wrote this at her fiftieth anniversary:

---

2. Joni Eareckson Tada, interview with WTTW, September 24, 2010. https://www.pbs.org/wnet/religionandethics/2010/09/24/september-24-2010-joni-eareckson-tada/7074/.

Suffering keeps knocking me off my pedestal of pride. . . . My displaced hip and scoliosis are sheep dogs that constantly snap at my heels, driving me down the road to Calvary, where I die to the sins Jesus died for. Sure, I have a long way to go before I am whom God destined me to be in glory, but thankfully my paralysis keeps pushing me to "strive to reach for that heavenly prize" (Phil. 3:14).[3]

A wheelchair is an extraordinarily challenging thorn, but it does have one upside: it looks like a thorn. Most Christians do not identify thorns very well. So a domineering mother, a lazy husband, or a sullen teenager are not seen as gifts that draw you into a real-time union with Christ. We focus on the thorn, and not on what God is doing through the thorn. Instead of receiving from God that dead-end job, we push it away.

God has permitted a relatively mild thorn in my life. Many years ago, at the start of seeJesus, we had a booth at a major conference. Marketing was tough—hardly anyone knew of our existence. I listened to the main speaker talk on how the gospel applies to our life. The gospel felt dull to me, so I asked God to make it come alive during his talk. Minutes later, I turned the page in the notes, and there was a chart I'd created that described how the gospel works on the heart. The chart illustrates how the more we grow in Christ, the more we see our sin. My imagination began to take flight. Would the speaker mention me? He was in my home city, so he might wonder if I was in the audience. Nothing fancy, just a quick mention.

> My imagination began to take flight.
> Would the speaker mention me?

The speaker explained how life-changing the chart had been for him. I edged forward on my seat. Then he said he wasn't sure who had created the chart; he thought it was (I held my breath) a person who on occasion had taken credit for my work. I sighed. I was back in familiar territory, dying with Jesus. Then I remembered my prayer. I wanted to be justified by the speaker, but my heavenly Father wanted me justified by faith.

3. Joni Eareckson Tada, "Reflections on the 50th Anniversary of My Diving Accident," The Gospel Coalition, July 30, 2017. https://www.thegospelcoalition.org/article/reflections-on-50th-anniversary-of-my-diving-accident.

I wanted to use this gospel chart to move up the Failure-Boasting Chart; instead, my Father offered me the path of the gospel, the J-Curve.

Fig. 12B. What I Want and What Jesus Wants

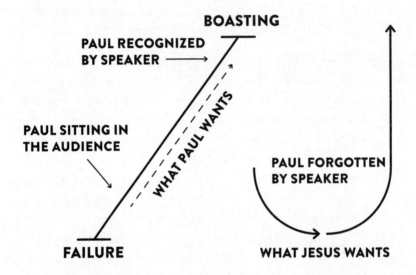

After the talk, I turned to my coworker, Julie, and told her about my prayer and how God had answered it. We laughed together. The more we grow in Christ, the more we see our sin! Each time something like this happens, I feel the sting of death. Then I remember Jesus's pattern of dying and rising, and I smile. You see, ten years had passed since I'd been hungry for my coworkers to give me credit (chap. 3). During that time, God had graciously taken me through multiple, deep J-Curves where he'd repeatedly exposed and stripped my pride.

The point is this: you can't cure pride simply by an act of repentance and faith. As important as faith is, unless we are actively reenacting Jesus's life, pride will regrow. Boasting is removed in principle at the cross; in practice, it is removed as we re-enact the cross. To see Jesus, we must do Jesus. The dying came from outside of me, but the rising was in me: a humbled spirit.

Boasting is removed in principle at the cross; in practice it is removed as we re-enact the cross.

The therapeutic vision has cast a heaviness over our culture, nourishing resentment and touchiness, and weakening our ability to laugh at ourselves. Again, look how the J-Curve revitalizes our emotions. When I realized I was in a gospel story, I became lighthearted; potential resentment was replaced by laughter. The situation was deescalated and I was emotionally transformed.

Linking Dying and Rising

Dying and rising often orbit around the same problem. For example, Joni's disability led to a ministry with people affected by disability. Jill's teaching our daughter Kim led to her creating the Bethesda Bible studies for people affected by disability.

But sometimes the hard thing (the dying) and the good thing (the rising) aren't connected in time and space. For Paul, the dying of the thorn exists in a different world from the danger of conceit. Kim losing her cool on the plane when I took her to Florida had nothing to do with my seminar the next day. And yet, knowing this deep structure of the J-Curve, I saw the connection. The Spirit connected the humility of dying on the plane with the blessing of the seminar. An eye alert to the pattern of the J-Curve links disconnected events.

This helps us not get thrown by the seemingly random difficult thing. You will often find dying in one area of your life matched by rising in another part. I've seen this so often in my own life that when I'm in a resurrection, I expect a dying as an antidote to my heart's pride. Likewise, when I'm in a death, I watch for a resurrection. Knowing the Spirit links dying and rising calms my heart. I don't get as disoriented by mini-intrusions of evil.

Our flesh tempts us to overread the flesh and to let evil have the last word. So at an otherwise wonderful Christmas dinner, when one family member is caustic or belligerent, we instinctively think, "He ruined the dinner." But everything hasn't gone wrong! Our Father's at work in the *suffering* J-Curve, protecting our hearts, humbling us. Seeing this pattern keeps us from crankiness. It helps us absorb the downs of life as we watch for how God will connect them with the ups.

13

Living in the Borderland

How to Thrive in a Broken World

Paul's analysis of his thorn in the flesh uncovers a uniquely Christian perspective: he separates his ego (pride) from his self (the whole person). Everyone else in the ancient world merged self and ego (as does everyone in the modern world), but Paul's Jewish roots prevented him from doing that.[1] Let's look again at Paul's thorn in the flesh, focusing on the relationship between the self and the ego.

In Figure 13A below, self and ego are merged (Step 1: I'm proud). As they go down into the acid bath of suffering, they separate (Step 2: I'm humbled). Self then soars in resurrection (Step 3: I'm blessed), only to be rejoined to ego when self thinks too highly of itself (Step 4: I'm boasting). Paul describes this pattern through the lens of the J-Curve:

> [We are] always carrying in the body the death of Jesus, so that the life of Jesus may also be manifested in our bodies. (2 Cor. 4:10)

---

1. If justification by faith lies at the core of the gospel, our ego or self-love resides at the core of the flesh. Paul's concept of flesh is larger than ego, just as the gospel is larger than its core, justification by faith. For Paul, the flesh encompasses both an entire rule or kingdom and an era or time period.

Paul "dies" as his ego is weakened and he "rises" as the life of Jesus is revealed in him. The dying isn't once and for all; it is a continuous dying joined to a continuous rising.

Fig. 13A. Continuous Dying and Rising

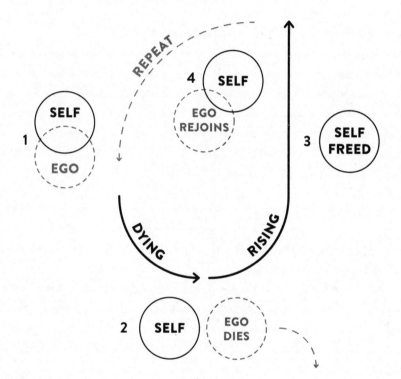

The Problem of Self and Ego

The Greek and Buddhist minds both recognized the problem of the intertwining of self and ego, but they had no vision of Eden, of a world before ego, so they had to destroy the self to destroy the ego. Ego was intrinsic to self.

For the Greeks, that meant life was inherently tragic, because *hubris* or pride eventually took even great men down. No answering resurrection rescued the downward pull of death. The Greek solution was the disembodied life of the mind that allowed the wealthy few to rise above the body. A higher knowledge or *gnosis* let a person rise above the riffraff.

For Buddhists, the desiring self is the root problem. To get rid of desire, Buddhists immerse the self in the All. We reach nirvana when our existence, like a drop of water in a vast sea, dissolves in the All. The self disappears. So both Greeks and Buddhists jettisoned the human body. Getting rid of their bodies freed them from their sin natures.

The Jewish Vision of Self Liberated from Ego

The Jews had a better solution. They didn't merge self and ego because the self, the person, was originally created good. God repeatedly calls his creation good (Genesis 1). Later, the fall corrupted creation (Genesis 3). This understanding let the Jews distinguish between the self and ego, between the person and pride, making it logically possible to separate sin from self. So repentance, the forsaking of ego, was a real possibility. For the Jews, ego was a cancer-like intrusion to be identified and fought at every step.

That gave rise to the Hebrew prophetic tradition—bold, fiery men and women who spoke truth to power. So the prophet Nathan confronts King David over his adultery, and David repents. (Other kings killed the prophets.)

The Jewish vision of a good original creation combined with God's promise to restore our world explains the fierceness of the laments in the Psalms. The Jews didn't want to be lifted above the mess or dissolved into the impersonal All; they looked to an infinite-personal God to invade and transform their world.

But the Hebrews had a problem. While it is logically possible to separate self from ego, it seldom happened. Human history is one long declaration of independence from God, riddled with Towers of Babel, monuments to our pride. Paul indicts humanity in Romans 1–3: evil is so pervasive, so powerful, that no human can separate self from ego: "None is righteous, no, not one" (Rom. 3:10).

The only solution was a new kind of person, an egoless self. We needed new DNA. To do that God gave us the gift of his incarnate Son, Jesus of Nazareth, righteous to the core with a self wholly devoted to his Father. When we are born into him, into his family, we join a new race of men and women who participate in his journey by continually re-enacting his dying and rising.

The World of Adam and the World of Jesus

Our new Jesus DNA presents a problem though; now we live simultaneously in two worlds—the world of Adam, where ego dominates, and the world of Jesus, where ego is destroyed.

Each world has a distinctive story. Understanding those stories and the interplay between them sorts out the complexity of what it feels like to be a Christian. In Romans 5, Paul tells the story of Adam and his followers, and the story of Jesus and his followers. Each man is a founder of a way of doing life. Adam's story begins with an act of rebellion—eating the forbidden fruit; Jesus's earthly life was one long submission to his heavenly Father, climaxing with his death on the cross. The final result of Adam's story is condemnation leading to death; the final result of Jesus's story is justification leading to life. For Paul, these two stories control two different kingdoms, even epochs.

Like parents, our founders shape our lives. Muslims follow the Sunna or path of Muhammad. They do everything as Muhammad did, from taking out the garbage to using the toilet to personal grooming. Buddhists re-enact Siddhartha's life by seeking nirvana. As descendants of Adam, left to ourselves, all of us re-enact Adam's story by living a life of self-seeking. I've captured that in Figure 13B below with the little thrones in the world of Adam.

Fig. 13B. The World of Adam

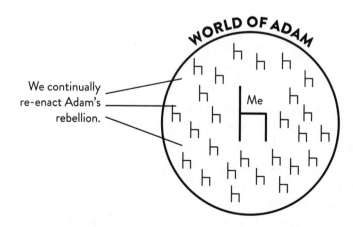

We continually re-enact Adam's rebellion.

WORLD OF ADAM

Me

The exit strategy from the world of Adam is Jesus's death and resurrection. Jesus went on this path alone for us. By living a life of Father-seeking obedience, Jesus shattered the world of Adam. The original J-Curve, Jesus's death and resurrection, created a new world, the world of Jesus. His path not only redeems us, but determines the shape of our own paths. As his followers, we now live in the world of Jesus, the world of Father-seeking obedience. We have his DNA. Every time we submit to what the Father has given us, every time we love, every time we enter into the mess of someone else's life, we re-enact Jesus's dying love. These are the little Js in the world of Jesus.

Fig. 13C. The World of Jesus

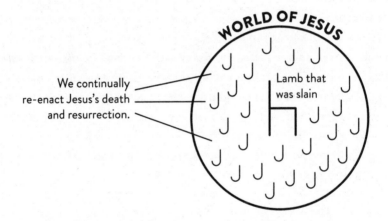

I've drawn these worlds as separate circles, but in our everyday experience, they are enmeshed. Our flesh constantly pulls us back to the old world of Adam, the world of self-love, while the Spirit draws us back into the world of Jesus.

It makes sense, then, that the principal means of leaving the world of Adam is re-enacting Jesus's death and resurrection. Every time we re-enact Jesus's path, we again leave the world of Adam and enter the world of Jesus. That's Paul's experience with his thorn. When he's tempted to sit on his throne, boasting of his trip to heaven, his thorn takes him on a Jesus journey, and once again he enters into the world of Jesus.

Already, Not Yet, and Right Now!

As Christ's followers, we inhabit a strange borderland where we are *already* in the world of Jesus, but *not yet* completely freed from the world of Adam. That explains how Paul talks about pride. To the Romans, Paul emphasizes that pride *already* is broken. After explaining justification by faith, he writes, "Then what becomes of our boasting? It is excluded" (Rom. 3:27a). But his thorn in the flesh shows that pride is *not yet* conquered.

Already, not yet applies to every aspect of the J-Curve.[2] We've *already* died with Jesus in the *past*, but because of the ever-present flesh, we've *not yet* died completely to the power of sin. We look forward to the *future*, when our flesh will be completely dead. In Christ, we are *already* resurrected, but until Jesus returns, we are *not yet* fully resurrected. We are *already* saints by virtue of our justification, but we are *not yet* saints, that is, people whose sanctification is complete. So we live in a peculiar borderland, with one foot in the past work of Christ and one foot in the future.[3]

But *already, not yet* can miss the present. Paul repeatedly emphasizes our present participation in the dying and rising of Jesus. Christ lives with us now in the borderland as we re-enact his life. Each of the three J-Curves—love, suffering, and repentance—re-enact Jesus's life in the *present*. A richer summary of Paul's thinking is *already, not yet, and right now!*

In 2 Corinthians 1, Paul gives an example of real-time dying and rising immediately after his "cascade of love." (I've italicized his dying and underlined his rising in the passage below.)

> *For we do not want you to be unaware, brothers, of the affliction we experienced in Asia. For we were so utterly burdened beyond our strength that we despaired of life itself. Indeed, we felt that we had received the sentence of death.* <u>But that was to make us rely not on ourselves but on God who raises the dead. He delivered us</u>

---

2. "Already, not yet" isn't just about our hearts, but refers to a rule and an epoch. The "already" is actually the future invading the past and the present. For the classic summary of the "already, not yet" position of Geerhardus Vos, see his *The Pauline Eschatology* (Phillipsburg, NJ: Presbyterian and Reformed, 1986), 36–41. "Already, not yet" was popularized by George Eldon Ladd, particularly in his *A Theology of the New Testament* (Grand Rapids, MI: Eerdmans, 1993).

3. I borrowed the term *borderland* from John Mark McMillan's song "Borderland."

<u>from such a deadly peril, and he will deliver us. On him we have</u>
<u>set our hope that he will deliver us again.</u> (2 Cor. 1:8–10)

Paul looks at his present hardship through the lens of Jesus's dying and rising. In the dying, ego dies and self is liberated. He experiences a present resurrection from a "God who raises the dead." God comes alive in the J-Curve.

Linking Past and Present

So we are torn between two sets of DNA: Adam's and Jesus's. Wherever we go, we see Adam's kids. We look just like him. The imprint of Adam—selfishness and self-preoccupation—is universal. Likewise, Jesus's children bear his imprint. We were mysteriously in Adam back in the garden of Eden, even as we were mysteriously in Christ in the garden of Gethsemane and the garden tomb.

In order for love to be formed in me in the present, I must *put to death what is earthly in me* (Col. 3:5). So I conquer impatience not merely by repenting, but by committing to love people who are slow, tiresome, or inefficient. I learn patience down low. Love always pulls me down into other people's lives. So the activity of reliving the dying of Jesus gives me humility in fact, not just in principle. I live it. Without the J-Curve, without a present participation in Jesus's journey, I'll merely dabble in the world of Jesus; but his world resists dabbling. In fact, I'll coast, growing less like him as I age.

So an act of repentance or love re-enacts the dying of Jesus in the present. Our J-Curves complete what Jesus started. In this strange borderland where beauty and brokenness live side by side, the beauty of Jesus shines through us and we lose sight of ego. His self becomes our self.

Finding Hope in the Borderland

In closing, let's reflect on the multiple blessings of living thoughtfully in this borderland:

1. It keeps us from being overwhelmed or disoriented with the persistence of our flesh by redefining normal as living in a borderland where we repeatedly move back and forth between the flesh and the Spirit, between dying and rising.

2. If moving back and forth between dying and rising is God's normal, that gives a certain feel to the Christian life, a mixing of joy and sadness, even an enmeshing of the two. Otherwise, we chase joy and recoil from sadness, which always yields a fragile, jittery self. Instead, with the borderland in view, we can revel in even fleeting joy, knowing this is a down payment on future joy, and embrace sadness, knowing that dying with Christ is the launching pad for joy. Knowing we live in a borderland anchors our emotions.

3. If dying and rising with Christ is the new normal, then when we encounter dying, we don't have to collapse or withdraw into ourselves. We can be weak, even depressed. This frees us from our tendency to be depressed about our depression. Because depression avoidance is such a high value in our culture, when people are depressed, they think something is wrong. It's a relief to realize that if we're dealing with hard things, we should be depressed. Jesus models depression for us in his Passion as he is overcome by the weight of his coming death. Our modern obsession with creating a pain-free self lays a great burden on us. When we see that our life is shaped by Jesus's commonsense narrative, dying no longer controls us.

4. Living in Jesus's path keeps us from becoming cynical about rising. Many of us are fearful of good news because bad news awaits. We protect ourselves emotionally from being whipsawed back and forth between rising and dying by shutting down on rising. We would rather stay in death than be disappointed by hope, so we shut down our hearts from the enjoyment of even small resurrections. Fear of hope disappointing us leads us to denigrate hope, which feeds a culture of cynicism—always doubting the good. But the story of Jesus has a distinct path—rising, not dying, has the last word. Easter follows Good Friday. That allows us to enjoy joy! We don't have to try to freeze the story in rising either; we can trust the Spirit to weave as he wills.

5. It gives us an expectation of continual hope, encompassing evil. The J-Curve shreds and crushes evil *now*. Evil no longer has the last word.

6. Our struggle is part of a larger cosmic struggle. It's not just little old me, battling it out by myself. My victories are part

of a larger victory over evil. Even if I find myself drifting back
to the old kingdom, the old era, I now live in Jesus's kingdom,
his epoch.

———

Now that we have a sense of the three different kinds of J-Curves
and how they give us hope in the borderland, we turn our attention
in Part 3 to the fascinating dynamics of the *love* J-Curve. We'll also
unpack multiple new concepts—such as embodiment, incarnation,
and *the good*—and see how rediscovering them holds out the promise
of shaping us all into the image of Jesus.

> Our modern obsession with creating a pain-
> free self lays a great burden on us.

PART 3

THE DESCENT OF LOVE

How Does the J-Curve Map Our Lives?

How Is It Helpful to See That
the J-Curve Is a Path?

Do We Incarnate Like Jesus Did?

Why Is It Important to Embody
Love? How Do We Do That?

What Key Role Does Our Will Play in the J-Curve?

How Does the J-Curve Promote Reconciliation?

14

Love Loses Control

Discovering the Shape of Love

Every summer, Jill and I go with Kim to Joni Camp. It's the highlight of Jill's year. She loves being with people who understand her world.

A number of years ago, on a Monday, the first day of camp, Jill made friends with Kayla, a volunteer "missionary" who had spent $500 and devoted a week of her vacation in order to serve families like ours. It is challenging but rewarding work to be part of a team embodying the love of Jesus with "the least of these." Jill helped Kayla give free manicures, which is odd, since Jill's nails look like she's been cleaning goat barns for twenty years.

Trouble started on Tuesday, when Kayla was in the food line; another mom said she had overheard Kayla belittle her parenting. In the world of camp, this is a serious offense. The mother complained to the camp directors, who questioned Kayla. But Kayla had no recollection of saying anything about this mom's parenting, so there was no resolution—just a murky impasse. It wasn't long before most of the camp staff knew about this mom's concerns. It had become a big drama. Like it or not, Kayla was the center of the problem. The camp leadership could not declare Kayla innocent or guilty. A cloud hung over her.

On Wednesday morning, Kayla came to us, distraught. For her, it felt as if her ministry was over. We didn't think the charges against her were true, but there was no way of proving it. Because of my immersion in *a fellowship of his sufferings*, I told her, "On Monday, you were in a transaction. It was a good transaction. You were giving your time and money, and receiving back thanks and the joy of knowing you were helping others. But now, instead of honor, you are getting dishonor. Instead of thanks, you are getting misunderstanding. You are entering the sufferings of Christ; the pattern of his life is now the pattern of your life. Now you are beginning to love and get to know Jesus in new and deeper ways. This is your glory!"

Monday and Wednesday looked like this for Kayla:

Fig. 14A. Kayla's Monday and Wednesday

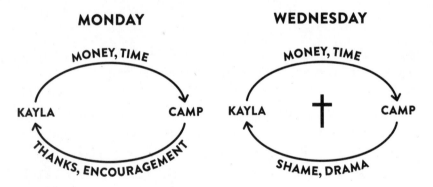

The Gold Standard of Love

My template for Kayla came from Philippians 2, the gold standard for what we've called the *love* J-Curve. Paul's imagination was so captivated by Jesus's descent into love that he created a work of art, a poem. His poem tells the story of Jesus, the original J-Curve, and then applies it to our lives.[1]

---

1. Phil. 3:7–11 is a summary of 2:6–8. In addition to similar meanings, multiple verbal patterns link the two passages: "the form of God" (2:6) and "the form of a slave" (2:7 AT) parallel being conformed to his death (3:10); "did not count" (2:6) parallels "counted as loss" (3:7) and "count . . . as loss" (3:8); "being found in human form" (2:8) parallels "found in him" (3:9). See Michael J. Gorman, *Apostle of the Crucified Lord: A Theological Introduc-*

Have this mind among yourselves, which is yours in Christ
   Jesus,

who, though he was in the *form of God*,
did not count equality with God a thing to be grasped,
but emptied himself,
by taking the *form of a slave*,

being born in the likeness of men.
And being found in human form,
he humbled himself
by becoming obedient to the point of death, even death on a
   cross. (Phil. 2:5–8 AT)[2]

Notice how the first and last lines of the first stanza match—"form
of God" is echoed by "form of a slave"—as well as the first and last
lines of the second stanza. The third lines of the two stanzas also
match: "emptied himself" matches "humbled himself."

Fig. 14B. The Descent of Love

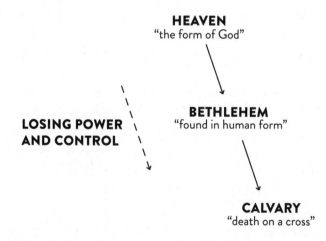

---

tion to Paul and His Letters (Grand Rapids, MI: Eerdmans, 2004), 442–43; L. Gregory
Blomquist, *The Function of Suffering in Philippians* (Sheffield, UK: Sheffield Academic Press,
1993), 102–3.

2. Following most recent commentators, I've changed *servant* to *slave* throughout this book.
See Murray J. Harris, *Slave of Christ: A New Testament Metaphor for Total Devotion to Christ*
(Downers Grove, IL: InterVarsity Press, 1999); and John MacArthur, *Slave: The Hidden Truth
about Your Identity in Christ* (Nashville: Thomas Nelson, 2010).

The first stanza is a *love* J-Curve, in which Jesus pursues evil outside of himself by entering our world. The second stanza is the *suffering* J-Curve, in which evil comes at Jesus unwanted because he is loving. In the *love* J-Curve, suffering shadows love. I've diagrammed the two steps of Jesus's downward movement above (p. 121).

The Shape of a *Love* J-Curve

Kayla's suffering was relatively mild. It would be over in a couple of days, and everyone would go their separate ways. However, it's in small incidents like this, when we've tried to do our best and then everything goes south, that we struggle to live out our faith. Often, the accumulated slights of low-level suffering operate like a hidden cancer, souring our relationships and suffocating our soul. Knowing the patterns of the *love* J-Curve is helpful, even liberating.

Kayla voluntarily took on a burden (camp) that became an involuntary burden (the mom). *Love* opened the door to *suffering*. This is what happens in almost every marriage I know. The commitment to love opens us up to suffering that we never would experience if we remained above the fray, distant and aloof. Typically, we define *love* as the love we choose, not realizing that the love *we choose* almost always draws us into love *we don't choose*.

Instinctively, we recoil from the suffering and rethink our commitment to love. That is, we work backward through the trajectory of *love* → *suffering* and say, "I never should have started this. This was wrong from the beginning." I said that when Kim was having a meltdown in the airplane. I regretted my love. Jesus feels this very human reaction when, facing the full weight of the cost of love at Gethsemane, he asks, "My Father, if it be possible, let this cup pass from me" (Matt. 26:39b).

Even small acts of love, like taking Kim to Florida or Kayla volunteering at camp, increase the possibility of suffering. The early slippage down the J-Curve is relatively easy. In my trip to Florida, adding Kim to the ticket, making arrangements, and traveling with her were inconvenient, but not costly. Her impatience and meltdowns were costly. The "easy" part of the J-Curve sets up the harder part.

As we slip deeper into a J-Curve, our control decreases. Initially, we choose to love; then, suffering chooses us. We usually don't mind the "easy" J-Curve, but we recoil as we descend the J-Curve and feel the weight of love. All *love* J-Curves have this distinct *love → suffering* pattern.

Here is a diagram of Kayla's camp week J-Curve:

Fig. 14C. Kayla's Love J-Curve

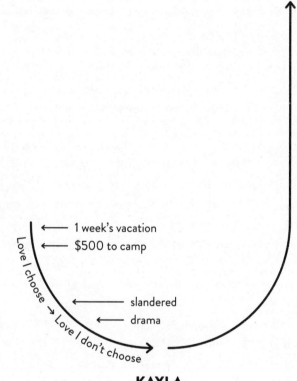

As we slip deeper into a J-Curve, our control decreases.

KAYLA

Victim or Sinner?

Unlike the *repentance* and *suffering* J-Curves, you initiate the *love* J-Curve by deciding to love someone. Frequently, when you pursue love, you are accused of not loving. That was Kayla's situation. It was also Jesus's. He who honored his Father more than any other person was accused of blasphemy. He who kept the Sabbath by healing the sick was accused of breaking Sabbath law. The only man who never yielded to Satan was accused of being controlled by Satan. One of Scripture's most basic rules is what happens to Jesus, happens to us.

The dissonance between a genuine desire to love and the false accusation of not loving is enormously unsettling. The more sensitive your conscience, the harder it is. In some ways, it would have been easier if Kayla had actually said something thoughtless about this mom. Then Kayla would have been a sinner. She could have done something with sin. She could have confessed, apologized, and lived with the consequences. Because she is justified by faith, she could have faced the worst about herself.

One of Scripture's most basic rules is what
happens to Jesus, happens to us.

But here Kayla was a victim. She was accused of something she (likely) didn't do. The power of a victim narrative comes from its truth—she had been sinned against. When you're a victim, it's easy to get lost in a sea of confusion and anger. For your own sanity, you want to retell your story just to set the record straight. Kayla could tell from the furtive glances and the awkward silences that people were talking, but she didn't know who was talking or what they were saying, so she couldn't defend herself. Shame lurked around every corner.

When you are a victim, you want to stand up and protest, like Mr. Wilson in the movie *Dennis the Menace*: "I'm not the bad guy here. I'm the victim." Left to itself, the victim narrative becomes the seed for bitterness. It can be a great burden to be sinned against. It's easier to sin and repent than to be sinned against.

We instinctively recoil from undeserved shame, but quietly receiving the shame as from the Father initiates a small act of dying. Kayla may have felt trapped, as if she didn't have any choice, but she actually had two choices: she could either take a victim exit (bitterness, withdrawal, anger, or gossip) or she could receive the shame as a *fellowship of his suffering*.

Here's what that looks like in a diagram:

Fig. 14D. Kayla's Choices

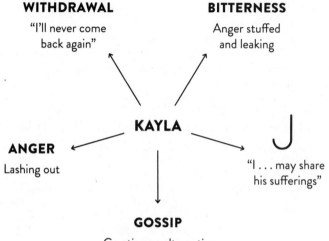

WITHDRAWAL
"I'll never come
back again"

BITTERNESS
Anger stuffed
and leaking

KAYLA

ANGER
Lashing out

"I . . . may share
his sufferings"

GOSSIP
Creating an alternative
community of empathizers

The J-Curve provided Kayla with an alternative narrative that put her in the right story. Instead of seeing herself as a victim, she was drawn into the story of Jesus's dying and rising. Knowing she was in a *fellowship of his sufferings* liberated her from the tyranny of the victim narrative and allowed her to endure and forgive.

Endurance, hanging in there in the work of love, is by far the most important quality of love. Without it, love collapses into either hot air or bitterness. When you see yourself embedded in Jesus's larger story, forgiveness comes more easily because your life no longer depends on removing the shame. By embracing the shame like Jesus, you rob it of its power.

To summarize, justification by faith frees us when we are wrong. The *love* J-Curve frees us when we are right.

Justification by faith frees us when we are wrong.
The *love* J-Curve frees us when we are right.

Answering Life's Questions

The *love* J-Curve offered Kayla a comprehensive vision of life that is true to both the beauty and brokenness. Using her story as an example, let's see how the J-Curve answers life's most basic questions.

1. Where Am I?

When Kayla came to us on Wednesday morning, she was not just upset but confused. Evil dislocates us, leaving us unsure of where we are. The *love* J-Curve is particularly disorienting because in the midst of doing good, we are accused of doing evil. But if Kayla knows she's in a J-Curve, that locates her. She knows where she is in the story—at the beginning, taking the descent of humility. If she knows that *love* opens the door to *suffering*, she's not thrown. She knows she didn't make a mistake with love, because suffering follows love. She's back in familiar territory, in a real-time union with Christ. She's *in him*. So instead of treating the suffering as strange, she can expect it in the work of love. With a "gospel map," she knows where the story is going—resurrection.

Since then, we've watched Kayla return to camp and become a well-loved and respected leader. Her trial that week was *light and momentary.*

2. Who Am I?

The J-Curve clarifies Kayla's identity. True, she's both a sinner and a victim, but neither is her primary identity. Like Jesus, she has *taken the form of a slave* (Phil. 2:7). Remarkably, this frees her spirit: she doesn't have to grovel by confessing something she didn't do, and neither does she cultivate bitterness.

3. What Should I Do?

If Kayla is a slave, she knows what to do—serve cheerfully for the next three days. There's no point in putting energy into redeeming her name. In this situation, that's a lost cause. Her path is clear. She throws herself into her work, knowing Jesus took *the form of a slave.* Her cheerfulness might be disorienting to some, but that's not her problem.

Joy in the midst of judgment shifts the confusion from Kayla's heart to theirs!

4. What Do I Feel?

As we've seen, the "map" of the J-Curve can shape Kayla's expectations and thus guide her emotions. On Wednesday, she knows what's coming: more shame. So serving cheerfully for the rest of the week feels, at times, as if she is *becoming like him in his death* (Phil. 3:10). When negative feelings surface, she doesn't need to suppress or be captured by them. She is free to be sad, to feel the shame, because she is in a mini-death.

Anticipating her feelings allows her to receive the dying as opposed to opening the door to hidden bitterness or open venting. You see, Kayla needs to love even "the camp." But openly venting her feelings not only fails to love "the camp," it also intensifies the problem by adding to the drama. By leaving space for feelings without being mastered by them, she can strike a remarkable balance seldom seen in our world, which worships feelings.

If Kayla isn't captured by her feelings, she is free to see the mom as a door to fellowship with Jesus. She can be kind to this mom, although she needs to be prudent. Figure 14E below captures this movement from seeing someone as an enemy to seeing that person as a Christ channel.

Fig. 14E. Kayla vs. Mom

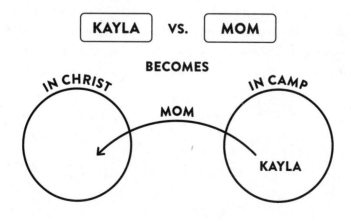

5. Why? What's the Point?

As we've seen, the three present J-Curves not only master evil, but form Christ in us. They are God's chisels to shape us into the likeness of his Son. Living in the story of Jesus stamps his image on us.

Here's a recap of how that works: the lower we go down the J-Curve, the more our motivations are unmasked. It's as if God says to Kayla, "I'm testing the depth of your love by stripping you of easy motivation and taking you deeper into my world, the world of love." Repeated dying strips our ego and breaks our will. What happened to Jesus in the original J-Curve happens to Kayla in the *love* J-Curve. Serving cheerfully when her ministry feels pointless draws her into fellowship with Jesus. Then her focus shifts from what others have done to her to how Christ is being revealed through her.

A Vision of Glory

When I told Kayla, "This is your glory!" strange as it might have sounded, I was excited for her. You see, Jesus and his path had captured my imagination. I didn't want suffering for her, but I'd been down the same path so often I knew the feel of glory. Embracing this fellowship of suffering would potentially reframe the worst part of her week. Then her story would become Jesus's story, transforming her shame into glory. That's what Peter had in mind when he said, "But rejoice insofar as you share Christ's sufferings, that you may also rejoice and be glad when his glory is revealed" (1 Pet. 4:13). Kayla was caught up into something far bigger than herself as she re-enacted the most magnificent story ever told, the story at the heart of the universe. To endure with joy, to not give in to bitterness, but to cheerfully serve as she was dying on the inside, was her glory. That's why martyrdom was so prized by the early church; re-enacting Jesus's Passion was their glory!

15

The Art of Disappearing
for Love

How the Incarnation Defines Love

We saw in the last chapter that the *love* J-Curve follows the path of Jesus's incarnation. But how do we incarnate? (To incarnate means to "step in another person's shoes," literally to become "enfleshed.")[1] What does it look like?

To answer that question, let's revisit Paul's portrayal of his flesh, where he takes seven steps up.[2] (Read from the bottom up.)

<blockquote>

as to righteousness under the law, blame-

less! (Phil. 3:5–6)

as to zeal, a persecutor of the church;

as to the law, a Pharisee;

a Hebrew of Hebrews!

of the tribe of Benjamin,

of the people of Israel,

[I was] circumcised on the eighth day,

</blockquote>

---

1. The verb *incarnate* is used in the world of biblical counseling.
2. There are multiple theories as to the form of Phil. 2:5–11. See Ralph P. Martin, *A Hymn of Christ: Philippians 2:5-11 in Recent Interpretation & in the Setting of Early Christian Worship* (Downers Grove, IL: InterVarsity Press, 1997).

Jesus's path could not be more different. Using seven verbs, Paul describes the *love* J-Curve with seven steps down. We are looking at a strand of Jesus's DNA.

> Have this mind among yourselves, which is yours in Christ Jesus, who, though he was in the form of God, *did not count* equality with God a thing to be grasped,

but *emptied* himself,
>> by *taking* the form of a slave,
>>> *being born* in the likeness of men.
>>>> And *being found* in human form,
>>>>> he *humbled* himself
>>>>>> by *becoming obedient* to the point of death,
>>>>>>> even death on a cross. (Phil. 2:5–8 AT)

Comparing the Two Paths

These two stories could not be more different. Jesus's story is humble, hidden, filled with love. He reaches out to people. Paul the Pharisee's story is proud, boastful, filled with hate. He pushes people away. Jesus slowly disappears to the point of death. Paul's path steadily expands with the wonder of Paul. Paul uses God's law to put Paul on display. Jesus's dying love displays God.

Roy Hession summarizes these two paths: "If Saul was the man going up, Jesus was the Man coming down. And when the man going up met that other one coming down, it broke him."[3] Paul realizes he's been living in the wrong story. He moves from the story of Paul to the story of Jesus. Paul still loves the limelight; he just has a different person under the lights: Jesus Christ. Paul displays Jesus by descending, following his path of humility. Union with Christ isn't just an idea for Paul; it's something he participates in every day.

Incarnating Goes Down and In

Notice the intimate connection between going *down* (humility) and *in* (incarnation). The only way to go *in* is to go *down*. So Jesus takes

---

3. Roy Hession, *When I Saw Him: Where Revival Begins* (Fort Washington, PA: Christian Literature Crusade, 1975), 40.

"the form of a slave"; he's born "in human form." Each step decreases Jesus's power and increases his humiliation. You can't incarnate without humbling yourself. They are inseparable.

Incarnation is the central move of love. It's radically different from how a Greek "god" temporarily took on human flesh. The god briefly descended, caused havoc while never losing his divine powers, then returned to Mount Olympus unruffled. This "incarnation" was more like bungee jumping than love. In sharp contrast, Jesus takes on our flesh. He becomes us. In every sense of the word, he enters our world.

The incarnation, the landing of Jesus, narrows his life. Here's a guess as to what "being found in human form" looked like: Jesus, weighing five pounds and seven ounces, with curly brown hair and olive skin, was born October 13 at 11:14 p.m. in the year 5 BC in a shepherd's cave in the city of Bethlehem. Love always constricts.

As Jesus went lower, he lost human power and control, resulting in an increase of suffering.[4] The same happens to us as we go lower, which is why we are so allergic to love. Maintaining control protects us from the suffering inherent in love. Paul emphasizes the brutality and shame of Jesus's death by adding one last twist: "even death on a cross" (Phil. 2:8).

We instinctively sense that love will narrow our life. It is one reason so many young men are fearful of marriage. They want to float above life. Of course, some men stay single like the apostle Paul for the sake of love, but many stay single to avoid love. Any chance I get, I tell young men, "Unless you narrow your life down to one woman, you will not mature. You've got to land in a specific life, to commit to love one person forever. Until you do that, your soul will remain shallow and light. You will have no weight as a person."

Let's see what going *down* and *in* looks like in our lives.

I tell young men, "Unless you narrow your life
down to one woman, you will not mature."

---

4. Of course, as the eternal God, Jesus always has infinite power, but he is clearly, "standing down," willing to not exercise his power. He does that in his temptations all the way to the cross. He doesn't avoid the consequences of his humanity. So the fully human, incarnate Son of God is constricted to the point where he can't move his hands or feet because he's nailed to the cross.

The Path of Incarnating

After praying and searching her heart, Lydia asks her husband, Richard, "Do you think you were harsh yesterday when you said . . . ?" Richard snaps back, "Well you had it coming, and anyway, you are harsh too." Lydia replies testily, "I'm not the problem here. You always throw things back on me. You never listen!" Richard doesn't miss a beat: "Well, that's because you don't see yourself very well. You are all high and mighty." Presto! We have a quarrel! Lydia thinks, "He's an idiot. He never listens. There's no point in talking to him."

Look at what Richard does. He shifts the focus off himself to Lydia. He pushes back in her face her attempt to do him good. He protects himself by reaching for power and shaming his wife. He pushes her down so he can go up. He's in the wrong story, the story of Richard and his greatness.

For the sake of simplicity, let's focus on Lydia and how she can respond with the mind of Jesus. When Richard pushes her down, she can recognize she is on the downward path of Jesus. Because she has located herself on the map of the gospel, when Richard says, "You are harsh too," she can ask without any barb, "How am I harsh?" She can respond to his lowering of her by receiving it as the path of Jesus. Nothing could be simpler. Nothing harder.

It feels crazy for Lydia to take the path of Jesus in this situation, like she's losing her mind. She might feel her identity as a person is being swallowed up by Richard's self-righteousness. But listening doesn't mean she agrees with Richard or his assessment of her. She is not a codependent; she is on the path of Jesus. She's gained the mind of Christ.

For Lydia to go *in*, to incarnate with her husband with a question, she has to go *down*. Going *down* and *in* does not mean she agrees with him. Here's Lydia's downward path:

Lydia already lives with Richard's harshness, which is a *suffering* J-Curve.
  Contemplating talking with him is painful for Lydia.
    Lydia searches her heart with a *repentance* J-Curve.
      She talks to Richard about his harshness, thus entering a *love* J-Curve.

He responds by blaming her.

Lydia doesn't quarrel, but asks him how she is harsh.

Given the modern mind, the downward path feels not only galling, but wrong. But Jesus lives in each one of these downward steps.

The only way Lydia can take the path of Jesus is if the Spirit of Jesus is in her. Later, we will see that the Spirit gives us the gift of Jesus's heart, which wants to go lower for love. Like Jesus, Lydia has to pray her way through the conversation, asking for grace to listen, to ask good questions, to check her anger, and to forgive.[5] Like Jesus, she realizes, "I can't do anything by myself" (see John 5:30). Richard's harshness drives her into *the mind of Christ*. She hears Jesus better because Richard doesn't listen.

Given the modern mind, the downward path feels not only galling, but wrong. But Jesus lives in each one of these downward steps.

To summarize, Lydia's husband responds harshly to her gift of honesty. She receives his harshness as a mini-fellowship of Christ's suffering, which allows her to incarnate. By incarnating, she prevents a quarrel and helps her husband with a good, honest word to penetrate his heart. The cost? The pain of humility—she loses her voice with Richard, but gains Christ's voice as she displays honesty, gentleness, and humility. Far from being a codependent, she boldly goes into dangerous territory (harsh people respond harshly to honesty) and plants a seed. She doesn't try to win, and she receives the death that comes with love. Just because someone refuses your honesty does not mean it wasn't a good gift. Jesus never measured his honesty by how people received it.

To be clear: I'd encourage Lydia to continue being honest with Richard. I'd encourage her to ask him to go to counseling with her. I'd encourage her to say at some point, "Richard, when I come to you

---

5. For a fuller discussion on how Jesus's prayer life as recorded in the Gospels connects with his dependence on his Father, see Paul E. Miller, *A Praying Life: Connecting with God in a Distracting World* (Colorado Springs: NavPress, 2017), 17–56.

about something, you usually say it's my problem. You seldom own you might be harsh." The therapeutic mind-set presumes that Lydia should not have to endure Richard's harshness. I don't wish suffering on Lydia, but frankly, there is no nonsuffering exit from the pain of Richard's harshness. If so, why not embrace Christ in the suffering?

The Narrative Shape of Life

Notice that when Paul says, "Have this mind among yourselves, which is yours in Christ Jesus" (Phil. 2:5), he doesn't give us a list of duties; he tells us to re-enact a story, Jesus's story. The writer Flannery O'Connor nails it: "A story is a way to say something that can't be said any other way, and it takes every word in the story to say what the meaning is."[6]

That we live in narratives or stories is one of life's deepest structures.[7] In the Old Testament, both good and evil are paths. Psalm 1 describes this: "For the LORD knows the *way of the righteous*, but the *way of the wicked* will perish" (v. 6). The Good Shepherd "leads me in *paths of righteousness*" (Ps. 23:3b). The good or bad path, or way, is a major theme in Proverbs. The wise person "will walk in the *way* of the good and keep to the *paths* of the righteous" (Prov. 2:20). In the New Testament, Jesus calls himself "the way" (John 14:6). He invites his disciples to "Follow me" (Mark 1:17). Not surprisingly, the church in Acts first calls itself "the Way" (Acts 9:2). Paul describes our Christian life as *walking with the Spirit* (Gal. 5:16).

The path for the early and medieval church was Jesus's path. His dying and rising defined goodness. Then, when the J-Curve lost its central role (as we discuss in chap. 17), we lost a narrative frame for goodness. I've asked multiple audiences to define holiness for me, and no one has mentioned the idea of a journey or of Jesus's path. If you miss the story character of our call to follow Jesus, you'll drift into depersonalized moralism and legalism, which obeys the law, but focuses on the self and its sanctification. You'll miss people.[8]

---

6. Flannery O'Connor, *Mystery and Manners: Occasional Prose* (New York: Farrar, Straus, and Giroux, 1969), 96.

7. Alasdair MacIntyre, *After Virtue: A Study in Moral Theory*, 3rd ed. (Notre Dame, IN: University of Notre Dame Press, 2007), 215–17. MacIntyre shows how life is lived in narrative structures. Morality is only comprehensible if we see our lives as stories.

8. Enlightenment thinkers (David Hume, Immanuel Kant), along with Søren Kierkegaard, inherited the narrativeless morality of the Reformation, so when they rejected "religion" as a

It's immensely helpful to think of evil and good as paths. Recall Las Vegas' marketing slogan: "What happens in Vegas, stays in Vegas." In other words, "Come to Vegas for a business convention, have sex with a coworker, and return to your spouse as if nothing happened. Vegas has no consequences; there is no path." The message of Vegas (a pleasure-seeking life is free of consequences or suffering) is, of course, utter foolishness. It assumes that a man who goes to Vegas isn't the same one who comes back. When you kiss your spouse as if nothing happened, you lie. You split yourself, creating an image of yourself as a faithful spouse when, in reality, you betrayed a sacred covenant. What you did in Vegas changed you. You've started on a new, deadly path that will create untold suffering in your life. Your soul has begun to die.

Life is a trajectory; our every step is connected to the previous step and the one that follows. This is how we slip easily into sexual sin. No one commits adultery out of the blue. You go down a path of linked steps, where every step prepares you for the next.

Below are seven downward steps that lead a person to adultery. Notice how self-preoccupied this person is. It's the very opposite of incarnating. He (or she) runs from a life of suffering love and embraces a life of pleasure-seeking:

1. Your heart is cold to God. The Word is dull. Church is boring. Your spouse is just irritating. Small things irritate you. Life doesn't have any point. Christians seem flat and cynical about the church. Christians are all hypocrites.

2. You are bored with life and increasingly restless. You begin hunting for excitement. You start looking at inappropriate TV shows or reading romance novels. Maybe you take up a new hobby or take a class. There's nothing wrong with that—but your heart goes on a hunt.

3. You lower your guard with someone of the opposite sex, beginning with low-level emotional intimacy. You share with this person some of your heart hassles. You put out subtle invitations.

---

basis of morality, all missed the story character of goodness, and their project to ground morality outside of God collapsed. See MacIntyre, *After Virtue*, 54–56.

4. You lower your guard even more, putting yourself in a position where low-level sexual sin is possible. You lie to yourself as to what is really going on. Seemingly "nothing has happened yet."
5. You cross a line, a very subtle one, where you open yourself up to the possibility of touching or being touched.
6. Excitement builds. You think about nothing else but this person. For the first time in years, you feel alive.
7. You touch. He (or she) answers with a touch. The thrill is unbelievable. Sex.

Of course, the final step is death (Prov. 7:27). Their families die. Their souls die. Their children are wounded. The seeking of pleasure leads to death, while Jesus's path of dying love leads to resurrection.

To summarize, each of us lives on a path or trajectory. This helps us in four ways. First, what I do today shapes who I become tomorrow. I'm becoming something new and different every day. The path I'm on shapes me.

Second, knowing I'm on a path can keep me from becoming overwhelmed. I can take one step today.

Third, a drumbeat of modern culture is "choose your own path." But there are really only two paths in life—the path of self (the Failure-Boasting Chart) and Jesus's path (the J-Curve). I don't "choose my own path in life"—I select one path or the other.

Finally, if I follow Jesus's path, I'm freed from trying to control the path, or take an early exit, because it's not my path; it's his. The Father sent his Son on it. I can trust my Good Shepherd to lead me—even if I, like Lydia, go through the *valley of the shadow of Richard*. The Father will set a table before me in the presence of my enemies; and yes, it ends well: I will dwell in the house of the Lord forever (Ps. 23:5–6).

There are really only two paths in life—
the path of self and Jesus's path.

16

Recovering a Vision
of *the Good*

The Wonder of the J-Curve

Several years ago, Jill asked me to videotape Kim walking from the close of a church service to her Sunday school room downstairs. Jill was creating a seminar to help the church relate to disabled people, and she knew from experience what the video would show. I walked behind Kim for twelve minutes with a video camera. It is a moving, almost silent video. In a very caring church we attended for many years, only two out of fifty people greeted Kim. *Why?*

Joni emailed me with the same question troubling her.

> Greetings Paul . . .   12/12/2014
>
> I hope you and the family are enjoying a blessed Christmas! At Joni and Friends, we've been deliberating why the church and its seminaries have a systemic problem when it comes to embracing special-needs families. Is something lacking theologically? Is it sociological? What has kept us from following through on Christ's commands to remember the poor, forgive seventy times seven, give our shirt when our cloak is required, and go out and find the disabled and bring them in?

Our discussion made me think of you. I recall an essay you wrote about living the Gospel daily; dying to self daily. I would certainly welcome anything you've written that might contribute to our discussion. After all, you're a theologian, but mainly, you're a special-needs dad. Love to Jill. . . . I'll be looking forward to hearing from you . . . and have a safe and blessed Christmas season!

Joni

In my reply, I agreed this was a church-wide problem:

You put your finger on the problem. In other words, "With all Jesus's attention to disabilities, why is the church, the body of Jesus, inattentive?" To deepen the puzzle, the "world" has often been ahead of the church. The problem of the church not enjoying and welcoming people affected by disabilities but actually distancing itself is strikingly pervasive.

In a very caring church we attended for many years, only two out of fifty people greeted Kim. *Why*?

I told Joni that the church is missing a significant piece of Jesus's DNA. That means the problem is far wider than just the church's inability to welcome the disabled. That's one of many tips of the iceberg encompassing all aspects of church life: spousal relationships, the celebrity culture of leaders, and even how parents handle their daughter being benched in field hockey.

I believe the problem is primarily theological. Of course, the heart is involved, but good theology provides a frame for the Spirit to shape our hearts. Weak theology leaves our hearts adrift. I believe the problem is not bad theology but missing theology. We know little about entering the dying and resurrection life of Jesus. *We lack a vision of the good*—of what it's like to embody the person of Jesus. The lack of a vision of *the good* distorts our vision of the gospel, of community, and effectively dumbs down holiness.

We all have a vision of *the good*—it's a vision of beauty, of perfection, that we are moving toward. Our phrase "the good life" retains the idea of *the good.* The Olympic athlete will endure endless hours of practice, manipulative coaches, and the shame of defeat because she envisions herself on a pedestal with a gold medal. Parents will push their kids to excel in school so they can get into a good college, which in turn will get them a good job and wealth. Almost all of our modern American visions of *the good* tend to move us up the Failure-Boasting Chart (wealth) or help us avoid slipping down (health).

The apostle Paul's vision of *the good* saturates his writing. Here's an example.

The Apostle Paul's Vision of *the Good*

Paul introduces the *love* J-Curve in Philippians 2 with a passionate call for unity:

> So if there is *any* encouragement in Christ, *any* comfort from love, *any* participation in the Spirit, *any* affection and sympathy, complete my joy by being of the *same* mind, having the *same* love, being *in full accord and of one mind.* Do *nothing* from selfish ambition or conceit, but in humility count others more significant than yourselves. Let each of you look not only to his own interests, but also to the interests of others. Have this mind among yourselves, which is yours in Christ Jesus. (vv. 1–5)

This stunning description of a loving, unified Jesus community begins with a multilayered, heartfelt plea, based on all that Christ has done for us, to create an astonishing, multifaceted unity, which can happen only if ego (pride) disappears. Then Paul shows us how to kill the ego by following the path of Jesus down to death. It's simple: for love to work, the ego must die. The result? A pristine picture of love purified of ego.

You can catch the purity of Paul's vision in the words I've italicized. He pleads for a radical decentering—the complete, ongoing death of self. He wants the Philippians to love all the time, to become 24-7 lovers. He's not dabbling at the edges of love; he's moved to the very center. There's no "Give it a try" or "do your best," no qualifying asides or caveats, but a cascade of pleas to allure the Philippians into a symphony of love. Paul paints for us something almost entirely missing from preaching today—an alluring picture of *the good*. He actually intertwines two distinct visions: the beauty of love and the beauty of what love creates (a Jesus community).

We usually miss what Paul is doing here, either by skipping over the surface of the text or by digging so deeply we miss the feel of the text. It's like looking at a beautiful painting through a telescope or a microscope. But the primary reason we miss Paul's vision is because we have no paradigm for it. We don't have a category for love in the same way we have a category for justification by faith. Love is "mere application," not a way of *knowing* Christ. Our faith-only paradigm has intruded into the world of love, emaciating it.

Paul's vision of *the good* permeates the book of Philippians, beginning with his opening prayer:

And it is my prayer that your love may abound more and more, with knowledge and all discernment, so that *you may approve what is excellent, and so be pure and blameless for the day of Christ.* (Phil. 1:9–11)

Paul's pagan audiences would have picked up on his vision of *the good* because they too were animated by a vision of *the good*. Purity for them meant floating above the despised underclasses instead of descending into them. Like the early church, the Greeks saw goodness as a path—but it was one that led away from the mess of life. Marcus Aurelius (121–180), the great Stoic philosopher-emperor, begins his *Meditations* by asking, in essence, "How do I cope with all the idiots I will meet today?" His answer? "Focus on your lofty vision of the good and the beautiful. Rise above the trash. Don't be swept into their stupidity."[1] Paul would answer, "We are all idiots in need of grace! My servant is as important as I am." Paul's answer lets us listen and value others who might be slower and less wise than we are. His vision ultimately triumphed over the Roman vision. The gospel transformed "idiots" into Christ bearers who lived lives of dying love.

---

1. Marcus Aurelius, *Meditations* (Mineola, NY: Dover Publications, 1997), 8.

> We don't have a category for love in the same way
> we have a category for justification by faith.

The Therapeutic Vision

Paul's call to love runs counter to the therapeutic spirit of our age. Here's my summary of the Christian therapeutic call to love: "God wants us to love one another, but I know life has been hard and people have wounded you, so be careful. Love is putting the other person first, but that doesn't mean you should endure in an abusive relationship. God won't give you more than you can handle. One way to do that is to make sure that you have clear boundaries."

Each thought, taken individually, has genuine biblical wisdom, but taken as a whole, this summary dilutes the entire feel of Paul's vision. Here's the contrast:

Therapeutic Call to Love	Paul's Call to Love
Pretend love	Real love
Protected, balanced self	Dying, unbalanced self
Dabbling at the edges of love	Full immersion in love
Calculated, qualified	Free, overflowing
Muddy, confusing	Effervescent, beautiful

The enshrined self of modern culture transforms Paul's call to love into a syrupy narcissism. It appears loving, but it is just a sugary glaze over the pursuit of a comfortable, protected, and often indulgent life. *Feelism*, with its commitment to feeling good about oneself, lurks behind this therapeutic vision of love.

Cultivating Wonder

Paul doesn't just describe love here. He captures our imagination; he stuns us with the beauty of Jesus's self-emptying.

In a sermon on Philippians 2, B. B. Warfield touches on the wonder of the incarnation. He first paints a picture of Jesus's self-emptying and then invites us into it:

He [Jesus] did not cultivate self, even His divine self; He took no account of self. He was not led . . . to brood morbidly over His own needs. . . . He was led by His love for others into the world, to forget Himself in the needs of others, to sacrifice self once for all upon the altar of sympathy.

Self-sacrifice brought Christ into the world, and self-sacrifice will lead us, His followers, not away from but into the midst of men. Whenever men suffer, there will we be to comfort. Wherever men strive, there will we be to help. Wherever men fail, there will we be to uplift. Wherever men succeed, there will we be to rejoice.

Self-sacrifice means not indifference to our times and our fellows: it means absorption in them. It means forgetfulness of self in others. It means entering every man's hopes and fears, longings and despairs: it means richness of development. It means not that we should live one life, but a thousand lives—binding ourselves to a thousand souls by the filaments of so loving a sympathy that their lives become ours.[2]

To summarize, Paul first enthralls us with the vision of a life completely devoted to the other (Phil. 2:1–4). Then he tells a story of the person of Jesus as he traces the letter J with his life of love (vv. 5–8). Unless we are animated by a vision of beauty (*the good*) that we are moving toward, love will remain either an occasional or a wearisome task. So cultivating a sense of the beauty of love and the oneness it creates is essential to the work of love.

---

2. B. B. Warfield, "Imitating the Incarnation," in *The Person and Work of Christ* (Phillipsburg, NJ: P&R, 1950), 574.

17

Celebrating Christ Bearers

Rediscovering Hidden Saints

If we had Protestant saints, Joni would be one. My wife, Jill, saw Joni participate in a momentary fellowship of Christ's suffering when Jill was in line to have Joni sign a book. The woman ahead of Jill saw Joni laboriously autographing her book by holding a pen in her mouth and said, "You poor thing."

Joni reacted instantly. She dropped her pen, lifted her head, and begin singing. She reacted to someone treating her as an object of pity by worshiping. Joni saw she was in a *fellowship of his sufferings*, received her suffering, and, like Paul in the Philippian jail, focused on the resurrection by worshiping. She was not overcome by this women's insensitivity, but enveloped her low-level evil with good (Rom. 12:21). She didn't just receive the dying, she re-enacted the resurrection, which lifted her spirits out of this woman's insensitivity.

If we had Protestant saints, Joni would be one.

I was struck by the quickness of Joni's response. You can react that way only if you've traveled repeatedly on Jesus's path. The process of habitually dying creates Jesus-like ruts in our life so that his ways become reflexes. Fifty years earlier, Joni had *received* from God her broken body. That gave her a map to *receive* this woman's thoughtlessness without a hint of irritation. Repeated living in a *suffering* J-Curve has tuned Joni's reactions to instantly love a thoughtless person. Joni's vision of *the good* allowed her to not only endure low-level evil, but to overcome it by embodying *the good* itself. She's a Christ bearer, that is, a person who uniquely embodies Jesus.

A Brief History of Christ Bearers

I was only half-joking when I said, "If we had Protestants saints, Joni would be one." Joni combines the best of Luther and Mother Teresa. Like Luther, she has a justification by faith foundation. Like Mother Teresa, she embodies the J-Curve.

We only have to look at Jesus, especially during his Passion, to see that some people embody love more than others. During the final twenty-four hours of his life, he washed feet, rebuked betrayers, sweated blood, forgave enemies, cared for his mother, and received his death. What Jesus was like under incredible pressure transfixed his disciples. That's why martyrs of the early church re-enacted his Passion. Stephen re-enacted Jesus's death when he rebuked and forgave his enemies as his face shone with glory (Acts 7). Taking the path of the J-Curve creates living saints.

This vision of *the good* permeated the medieval church and captured the vision of a former soldier, Francis of Assisi (1181–1226). You might have heard his famous quote: "Preach the gospel, and when necessary, use words." Except he never said that. The earliest written reference to that quote is in the 1990s! Francis was so in love with Jesus that when he was working as a chaplain on the Fifth Crusade, he badgered his bishop until he let him cross the Muslim lines to seek peace and share the gospel with the sultan of Egypt. Remarkably, he got an audience with the sultan and wagered that if he didn't convert the sultan, he would let the sultan martyr him. Equally amazing, when the sultan didn't convert, Francis made it home safely.

The passion of Francis's life was modeling Jesus's humility. Humility for Francis didn't exist as an abstract state, but was embedded in the narrative of Jesus's self-surrender, beginning with his birth in a lowly stable. Francis was so captivated by the lowliness of Jesus's birth that he wanted to visualize it, so he created the first-ever manger scene.

Yet in his desire to follow Jesus's downward path, Francis idolized it. For example, when his Franciscan missionary order became large, he appointed a successor so he could go lower, down the J-Curve. At their annual gathering, Francis sat up on stage at the feet of his successor, and when Francis wanted to say something to the gathered monks, he whispered in his successor's ear, and the monk told the assembly what Francis had said. In other words, Francis had the appearance of humility, but he still wielded power. In this instance, he pursued humility for its own sake.[1]

We've seen how easily we can treat good things, such as ministry or sports, as ultimate things. We can do the same with humility, making it an end in itself. If you separate humility from love and a foundation of justification by faith, you create an idol.

Francis's modern disciple, Mother Teresa, could also be caught up in seeking humility for its own sake. For instance, when she arrived in Rome to meet the pope, she refused the waiting limousine and instead took public transportation to the Vatican. Her desire was good—to reflect the poverty of Jesus's downward journey—but her focus was on humility, not love. By turning humility into a show, she actually made life more difficult for her hosts. Humility, not Jesus, had become central.

The downward path of humility for the apostle Paul is not an end in itself—it is in the service of love. We can easily turn humility into a boast. The truly humble person, according to C. S. Lewis, "will not be thinking about humility: he will not be thinking about himself at all."[2] Humility is the art of disappearing for the sake of love.

If you idolize the J-Curve, you create humility celebrities—that's what happened in the Middle Ages with the cult of saints who supposedly helped people get into heaven with their *merit*. The cult of saints even became an excuse to live a selfish life "because I'm not a saint."

---

1. Augustine Thompson, *Francis of Assisi: A New Biography* (Ithaca, NY: Cornell University Press), 89.
2. C. S. Lewis, *Mere Christianity* (New York: HarperOne, 2015), 129.

When Luther rediscovered justification by faith, he realized that all believers were saints in Christ. His merit is all we need. That's why Paul repeatedly addressed the churches as communities of saints. He never singled out one person as a saint, as if there is a higher category of Christians.

Humility is the art of disappearing for the sake of love.

Our Weakened Vision of Christ Bearers

The Reformation vision of *the good*—only faith, only Scripture, only Christ—corrected the medieval abuse, but over time, the J-Curve faded from view. Some feared the J-Curve would return us to works righteousness and to moralism—trying to be good in our own strength. The result? We lost a vision of Christ bearers.

If you isolate Luther's faith vision of *the good* from the historic J-Curve, you become good at detecting idols, but weak at drawing people into the perfection and beauty of a Jesus-shaped life.[3] You become good at seeing bad, but bad at seeing good. To be clear: our current vision of *the good* is wonderful, but incomplete.

I regularly hear this one-sided vision of *the good*. It's not uncommon for a preacher to say, "You don't know what a terrible sinner I am." The pastor genuinely wants people to see that he also needs grace, but he usually doesn't talk about how he's being transformed into a lover. Sometimes he'll quote Paul, who, at the end of his life, calls himself the chief of sinners (1 Tim. 1:15), but Paul is clearly referring to his pre-Christian persecution of the church.

I wonder about the pastor's confession. Is he overstating this for effect, or does he really mean he's a terrible sinner? I wonder, what has he done? Has he confessed it? Is someone holding him accountable? Is this is a besetting sin? Should he be preaching?

The pastor's lack of clarity suggests that he has confused the lifelong pull of our flesh with its power. The apostle Paul's vision of *the good* assumes that we will become more like Jesus as we regularly put the flesh

---

3. I don't mean Wesleyan sinless perfectionism. I mean God calling us to a perfection of beauty that reflects the beauty of his Son. Of course, the closer we get to the light, the more we see our sin, but even then, that should lead to a life of love.

to death. The pastor has taken Luther's emphasis on faith (coming to the end of ourselves) and made it the goal. He has confused the means (faith) with the goal (love). He has defined *the good* narrowly, as only brokenness or weakness. That's the foundation of *the good*, but it is not *the good* itself. It's like "Ready, Set . . ." with the "Go" missing. The "Go," *the good* itself, is a life overflowing with an other-centered love.

The medieval church did the exact opposite—it made love the means or the basis of our acceptance with God. So the medieval good—what I do—merged with the faith foundation. It confused the goal (love) with the means (faith). We've done the opposite with our grace-only preaching, thinking that faith is the end goal, and love is mere application.[4]

Modern Christ Bearers

Nevertheless, we've lost the sense that, while we are all saints in Christ, some reflect the beauty of Jesus in special ways. They are usually people who have suffered significantly and endured in a J-Curve or who live a life abandoned to the work of love.

Because we lack a paradigm or category for living saints, these Christ bearers are often hidden and not celebrated. Our neighbor, John Skilton, was one. When John retired from teaching Greek at Westminster Theological Seminary, he opened up his inner-city home to needy people, filling his life with "the least of these." One day, Jill and I stumbled into him at our local grocery store. At first, we didn't see his face because he had his hood up; he looked homeless. When he turned toward us, we were startled by his Jesus-like glow.[5] Outside, we said to one another, "It's like we saw the face of an angel."

Many in our church community remarked on John's life of love and his gentle, glowing appearance. And he was lighthearted. Once I asked him how old he was, and he said, "Seventeen. Since I turned eighty, I've started counting backward from one hundred."

We need to talk about people like John, to emulate them, to celebrate them. I'm struck by how often Joni celebrates hidden Christ

---

4. Of course, we are saved only by grace. By "grace-only," I mean teaching that focuses only on God's grace and not on God's call, inherent in our grace-only foundation, to live a life that reflects Jesus's dying and rising.

5. I'm not suggesting you can always see the presence of Jesus on someone's face, and neither do I equate a warm, glowing face with the presence of Jesus. Nevertheless, I've often seen faces like this on "Christ bearers."

bearers in her writing. It takes one to know one. We should add to our Reformation vision of *the good* (repentance and grace) a vision that sees and celebrates the beauty of Jesus in others. Unseen Christ bearers embody Paul's repeated calls for us to be 24-7 lovers who image Jesus.

In place of Christ bearers, we've elevated a culture of Christian celebrities. Nothing sums up that dissonance more than the question Edith Schaeffer was asked in an interview: "Who is the greatest Christian woman alive today?" Edith replied, "We don't know her name. She's dying in some cancer ward in India." Edith nailed it. The question, which came out of our evangelical celebrity culture, assumed a Christ bearer would be famous.

Secular Liberalism's Vision of Beauty

Secular liberalism's vision of *the good* is simply the person of Jesus secularized, Jesus's humanity stripped of his divinity. His virtues—inclusion, compassion, and love of the weak—become absolute. Secular-liberalism is trumping Christianity with its vision of *the good* summed up in a question like this: "How can you judge someone for being gay?" In other words, compassion for the gay person must trump God's law. This is compassion without a moral frame.

All the values of secular liberalism are historically rooted in Jesus of Nazareth. One of the first modern liberals, Thomas Jefferson, created his Jefferson Bible by removing the miracles of Jesus. He liked the person of Jesus, his compassion, but he didn't like Jesus's divinity, which ruined the modern quest for autonomy, for freedom.

Secular liberalism's vision of *the good* is simply the person of Jesus secularized.

Liberalism created a new vision of *the good* that, like Jesus, focused on the disabled, the weak, the outsider. Consequently, Jill and I found public schools more open to Kim and her disabilities than the church. In other words, Jesus-secularized was better at helping Kim than Jesus-depersonalized, stripped of his J-Curve.

Our daughter Courtney, as a gift for Jill, took a New Testament and cut out all the references to disabled people in the Gospels. When you leaf through the Gospels, almost every page has a hole in it. Like the Jefferson Bible, this Bible reflects our missing vision of *the good*.

In our modern world, three visions of *the good* vie for ascendancy: (1) Francis of Assisi's vision, which Mother Teresa embodied; (2) Luther's vision—faith—which he rediscovered as he reacted to the abuses of Francis's vision; and (3) secular liberalism's vision, which secularized Francis's vision. So we have the person of Jesus (Francis), the work of Jesus (Luther), and the love of Jesus (secular liberalism). This shows how powerful the beauty of love is, even when separated from its biblical moorings.

Francis's vision and secular liberalism's vision are, in some ways, more closely aligned because they both sit on the person of Jesus. As she lived out Francis's vision, Mother Teresa captured the imagination of our secular elites by embodying Jesus's descent of love. When she spoke at Harvard, her audience was so captivated by her love for the dying poor, they gave her a five-minute standing ovation. But instead of being seduced by their applause, this Albanian peasant entered into a *fellowship of his sufferings* by challenging one of the sacred tenets of our culture of narcissism, saying, "If a mother can murder her own child in her womb, what is left for you and for me to kill each other?"[6] I'm entranced by her simplicity of faith, which let her call our secular elites to repentance.

All of these concepts are intertwined. If you miss the J-Curve, you won't value Christ bearers or be drawn by the beauty of love, a vision of *the good*. There is no better time to rediscover the beauty of Jesus embodied in Christ bearers than now.

For the first time since the start of Christianity, our children by the millions are being seduced by a better vision of *the good*, a better vision of what is it to be human. In the public square, secular liberalism feels inclusive, compassionate, accepting, and nonjudgmental, while Christianity is portrayed as narrow, backward, uptight, and judgmental. The church is one generation away from its functional death and marginalization in America. We must recover a vision of the beauty of Jesus and the beauty of those who emulate his life. The original is far better than the secularized imitation.

---

6. "Mother Teresa—Acceptance Speech," Dec. 10, 1979, https://www.nobelprize.org/nobel_prizes/peace/laureates/1979/teresa-acceptance_en.html.

18

The Hinge of the J-Curve

Understanding the Will

I asked my seatmate on an airplane if she'd be a one-person focus group for a book I was writing, *Love Walked among Us*, about love and the person of Jesus.[1] With our culture's religious phobia, I thought she'd be interested in love but allergic to Jesus, but she said, "I'm actually interested in learning about what Jesus is like as a person, but I'm not sure I want to learn to love." It's true, we instinctively fear the work of love. As we've seen, we sense that love involves commitment, a narrowing of life, so we pull back, avoiding eye contact with love.

Paul helps us by embedding in his hymn to the incarnation (Phil. 2:5–8) a four-step pattern that promises to unfreeze us. Here are the four steps:

1. My Right: *He was in the form of God.*
2. My Choice: *He did not count equality with God a thing to be grasped.*
3. My Love: *He emptied himself by taking the form of a slave.*
4. My Cost: *He became obedient to the point of death, even death on a cross.*

---

1. Paul E. Miller, *Love Walked among Us: Learning to Love Like Jesus* (Colorado Springs: NavPress, 2014).

These four steps constitute one continuous whole; each step prepares for the next.[2] At first glance, these steps seem trite. The first two, in which Jesus recognizes and then disowns his status, especially seem unnecessary. Why state the obvious? The answer is simple: you can't disown what you can't identify. Nothing clings to me more than my status, my busy schedule—in short, my life. It defines me.

So Step 2 is the critical turning point. When Jesus *did not grasp at equality with God*, he gave up his demand for emotional safety and stability, and descended into the unknown. I say *demand* because Jesus wills his descent. In this chapter, we will focus on Step 2 and the critical role our will plays in the descent of love.

The Missing Will

Jesus's refusal to grasp his divinity is the critical hinge of the J-Curve. As we saw earlier, when he said no to the privileges of divinity, he set in motion a downward cascade of love, leading to his death. Likewise, when Joni stopped grasping at her memories, it set in motion a whole pattern of her life in which she received the suffering God had given her.

The *will* gets short billing in Christianity. Self-will and its opposite, a spirit of childlike obedience, are lightly taught in contemporary Christianity. We rarely hear about the joy or blessing of obedience. The church has focused on pride as the master sin; as we've seen, it lies at the core of our flesh, yet the first sin that emerges in a child is not pride but self-will, and the last sin we see in an older person with a fading life is generally self-will—thus, the prevalence of anger at the front and back ends of life.

Self-will, not pride, dominates Israel's forty years of wandering. Pride is mentioned only in Deuteronomy 8:17–9:4, and even then, Moses anticipates a future sin. They loved the food they had in Egypt, so they demand (self-will) to return. As we saw in chapter 11, what they loved shaped their will.

The Gospel of John, in particular, highlights Jesus's active dependence on his heavenly Father. The most outstanding feature of Jesus's

---

2. See Michael J. Gorman, *Apostle of the Crucified Lord: A Theological Introduction to Paul and His Letters* (Grand Rapids, MI: Eerdmans, 2004), 436. I am indebted to Gorman for the insights behind the four steps of love.

life is his obedience to his Father expressed in childlike dependence. Eve (and Adam) grasped at divinity when Satan promised, "You will be like God" (Gen. 3:5). Jesus did not grasp at divinity. Adam and Eve exercised their will to exalt themselves; Jesus surrendered his will to lower himself.[3] He is the good Son.

Satan entices Jesus in the wilderness to act on his own: "If you are the Son of God, command these stones to become loaves of bread" (Matt. 4:3). In other words, "*Since* you are God, use your divine power to protect yourself from the consequences of your humanity. Be like the Greek gods, who don't get dirty."[4] Satan invites Jesus to use divine power for self. But Jesus relinquishes that right so he can be fully human; he doesn't grasp at equality with God. He will do miracles out of love, but he won't do miracles for himself. He never separates power from love.

> He will do miracles out of love, but he won't do miracles
> for himself. He never separates power from love.

Jesus's will to obey his Father drives his descent down the J-Curve "to the point of death, even death on a cross." His determination to be fully human, to not use his divinity to protect himself from the consequences of his humanity, climaxes at the cross, when people taunt him, "He saved others; he cannot save himself" (Matt. 27:42). Scholar Alfred Edersheim nails Jesus's mind-set:

> His three great temptations resolved themselves into the question of absolute submission to the Will of God, which is the sum and substance of all obedience. If he submitted to it, it must be suffering, and only suffering—helpless, hopeless suffering to the bitter end; to the extinction of life, in the agonies of the Cross, as

---

3. Paul is likely making a subtle contrast between Adam and Jesus. See Morna D. Hooker, *From Adam to Christ: Essays on Paul* (Eugene, OR: Wipf and Stock, 2008), 88–100, for a study of the Adam-Christ contrast in Philippians 2. See also Moisés Silva, *Philippians*, Baker Exegetical Commentary on the New Testament (Grand Rapids, MI: Baker Academic, 2005), 102, 107.

4. "*If* you are the Son of God . . ." could mean "since," or Satan could be trying to introduce doubt, as in, "Are you sure you are the Son of God?" The latter is a common interpretation likely stemming from our evangelical obsession with identity and liberalism's desire to see Jesus in doubt about his Sonship, but Jesus never expresses the slightest hesitation about who he is. See Alfred Edersheim, *The Life and Times of Jesus the Messiah* (Iowa Falls, IA: World Bible Publishers, 1990), 291–307. See also my book *Love Walked among Us*, 137–46.

a criminal; denounced, betrayed, rejected by his people; alone in very God-forsakenness.[5]

By not grasping at the privilege of divinity, Jesus reveals his Father's heart. That's the sense of the Greek in the translation below:[6]

Precisely because he was in the form of God, he did not regard this divine equality as something to be used for his own advantage. (Phil. 2:6)

Precisely because Jesus was God, he didn't grasp at being God. When faced with evil, God doesn't isolate himself. He descends in the maelstrom we call humanity, to the point of death, even a shameful death on a cross. That's what God is like. That's why God is so present in a *fellowship of his sufferings*; he's at home in a life of suffering love. The downward movement of the J-Curve reveals God's mind, the mind of Christ.

How Do You Engage Your Will?

So how do we connect Jesus's obedience to ours when we are confronted with a J-Curve? Of course, the primary way we get the mind of Christ is from the Spirit of Christ. The Spirit makes Christ present. But the Spirit needs channels to run on, so I encourage people with this threefold pattern:

First, *see* that you are in a J-Curve. Recognize that you are reliving a gospel narrative. Jesus does this at Gethsemane when he asks his Father to remove the cup of suffering. He faces unbelievable grief as he contemplates separation from his Father, but he knows where he is located. He's not adrift.

Second, *receive* the suffering. Take the cup. Decide to own it as a gift from your Father (Phil. 1:29). This might seem odd, because suffering comes to us against our will. Jesus helps us here. He told his disciples,

---

5. Edersheim, *Life and Times*, 302.
6. Translation from Peter T. O'Brien, *The Epistle to the Philippians*, The New International Greek Testament Commentary (Grand Rapids, MI: Eerdmans, 1991), 202–3. See Ralph P. Martin, *A Hymn of Christ: Philippians 2:5-11 in Recent Interpretation & in the Setting of Early Christian Worship* (Downers Grove, IL: InterVarsity Press, 1997), 97–196, for a detailed analysis of this text.

I lay down my life that I may take it up again. No one takes it from me, but I lay it down of my own accord. (John 10:17b–18a)

As the soldiers are coming to take him away, Jesus takes the cup, saying, "Not my will, but yours, be done" (Luke 22:42b). So even though others willfully bring suffering into his life, Jesus surrenders his will. If all of life is orchestrated by our Father, then we can receive what the Father brings.

Now immersed in the mind of Jesus, we counter our heart's demand for safety and surrender to the work of love. Like Jesus, we *set our face for Jerusalem* (Luke 9:51, 53) and say, "Not my will, but your will, be done." We obey.

Third, *boast* in your weaknesses. I offer this as a dream to cultivate. When we are transformed by a vision of inhabiting the gospel, eventually our weaknesses become our boast. They become our glory, because in our weaknesses, Jesus shines through.

We've been focusing on the second step and the role of the will, but in the next chapter, we'll see how all four steps of love serve as a path to help a young father become a Christ bearer.

If all of life is orchestrated by our Father, then
we can receive what the Father brings.

19

The Four Steps of Love

Re-enacting Jesus's Descent

As he descends into the world of love, Jason, a young husband and father, moves through the four steps of love. Let's walk with him.

Step 1, My Right: He Was in the Form of God

At church, Jason notices a young man sitting with his mom. Jason thinks he might have Down syndrome. The young man can barely talk and makes odd noises during the service. Jason doesn't see a dad. The mom looks weary. He feels for her, but he doesn't know anything about disabled people, and frankly, during worship, the young man's noises annoy him. If he approaches the mom, he's not even sure what he'd say.

Jason greets her when he passes her in church, but feels relief when she moves on. The whole situation makes him uncomfortable. It's all so overwhelming. He thinks, "My life is unbelievably busy. Even if I had time, I have no idea what I'm doing, and I'd likely offend the mom. I don't even know if he can talk or if I'll be able to understand him. I'm more of a manager than a people person. This takes a specialist. Someone should start a ministry."

Notice how the managerial and therapeutic mind-sets freeze Jason. The manager looks at balance, time allocation, and specialization.

When Jason looks through a managerial lens, helping makes no sense. He kills projects like this all the time at work. It's an inefficient allocation of resources.

The therapeutic lens also keeps Jason distant. He instinctively wants to involve a professional, a specialist in the world of disabilities. Neither the therapist or the manager is driven by a vision of the beauty of love, so the appearance of wisdom suffocates love.

Remember my friend who actually went to Harvard? While doing an internship at a mental hospital, even though he wasn't yet a believer, my friend was struck that the two people who helped the patients the most were not the white-coated doctors, but a housekeeper and an aide. They related to the patients not as objects or problems to be diagnosed, but as people. The therapeutic mind-set mimics love, but tightens everyone up, creating categories (bipolar, schizophrenic) instead of friends. The managerial and therapeutic mind-sets provide Jason with a guilt-free, comfortable distance from this mom and her son. It's all "wisdom" and no love.

I described a scenario like Jason's in my email reply to Joni (referenced in the previous chapter):

> So the man in church who sees the Down boy instinctively realizes that to make friends with him will be work. It will disrupt his Stoic calm. It will be messy. He will make mistakes. But he has no paradigm for realizing that love is not just occasional, but 24-7. Love feels overwhelming, unusual, in fact, impossible. He'd rather hear about grace, about how much God loves him. With no theological frame to enter into God's life of grace, the J-Curve, he quietly recoils from any real relationship with the boy. The result? The Down boy and his mom remain alone, isolated and overwhelmed by life.

I'm belaboring this point because the pseudowisdom of the manager and the therapist neuter Jason. It is extraordinarily hard for him to say, "I am busy and I don't know what I'm doing, but I can at least take a first step toward this young man."

The therapeutic mind-set mimics love, but tightens everyone up, creating categories instead of friends.

The only way to break the grip of the manager and the therapist is to capture Jason's imagination with the wonder of love. Only the Spirit of Jesus can animate in him a vision of the path of Jesus, prompting him to recoil from his life of controlled and balanced self-seeking.

A new vision of love can free Jason to not grasp at a safe life. Step 1 potentially unfreezes Jason, because it allows him to identify the safety of his current position not as an absolute given, but as the first in a series of steps downward into love.

Step 2, My Choice: He Did Not Count Equality with God a Thing to Be Grasped

Now that he has identified his rights, Jason is free to disown them. He says to himself (and his wife), "I'm going to try to love this young man." He doesn't need a plan at this point—just a commitment. This crucial act of the will turns the story toward love and away from self. It clears Jason's emotional deck. He doesn't *count his suburban comfort as a thing to be grasped.*

But still, how does he begin? It's all so overwhelming. He can't unself himself, but he can ask for the Spirit of Jesus to help. So he prays, "I don't know how to love this boy. Give me the grace to walk over and introduce myself and listen. I don't know what I'm doing."

We can't go down and in unless the Spirit of Jesus helps us. After all, it's his path; he knows its shape.

The first move in a J-Curve is always prayer. It won't require a massive time commitment for Jason to pray for the mom and her son. He might pray for just ten seconds a day for several months. Jesus usually began his love by looking. Praying helps us look. We can't go down and in unless the Spirit of Jesus helps us. After all, it's his path; he knows its shape. Without realizing it, Jason has begun the actual descent in Step 3.

Step 3, My Love: He Took the Form of a Slave

Then one Sunday after church, out of the corner of his eye, Jason sees the mom and her son disappearing out a side door. His heart has begun to go out to her as he has prayed for her. Jason excuses himself from a conversation with a good friend and introduces himself to the mom while walking with her to her car. He no longer cares if he messes up, because he's stopped thinking about himself; he's entered the world of love.

Jason has *taken the form of a slave* by praying for this mom and her son, and by starting a friendship with them, but until love begins digging into his schedule or his wallet, he hasn't yet felt the cost of love. In order for love to come alive, Jason needs to incarnate, to experience the weight of her life. On the cross, Jesus felt the weight of our sin, so the weight of her life needs to come into his. Only then is he at the fourth step.

Step 4, My Cost: He Humbled Himself Even to Death on a Cross

Jason arrives back at his car, excited that he's taken this first step, only to encounter another J-Curve. The kids are whining, and his wife, Sharon, greets him with an irritated, "Where have you been?" As he starts to explain his conversation, she interrupts: "Next time would you at least tell me you are going to be late?" Jason apologizes and quietly absorbs the lack of affirmation. Sharon's not interested in what he has to say, so he goes silent. Now Jason's at Step 4, feeling the cost of love. He's in a mini-fellowship of Christ's sufferings. So without a hint of irritation, he cheerfully inquires how everyone is doing. He's in familiar territory; the pattern of Jesus's dying shapes not only how he relates to the mom, but also to Sharon. It's a double J-Curve. That's OK; all of life is dying and rising.

Most Sundays, Jason seeks out the mom and begins to get to know her son. He finds out a little of how Daniel (yes, he has a name!) communicates and begins to say hi. He asks Daniel's mom the Jesus question: "What can I do for you?" (see Mark 10:51). He's not thrown by her "Oh, nothing" response. He knows she's likely had so few people ask her that question that she doesn't know where to begin.

Jason's family shows little interest, and Sharon questions whether he's overcommitted. He doesn't dismiss her concerns. He listens to her, incarnating with her, the way he is with Daniel. Love, after all, must be pure, devoid of self-will. Jason can't surrender his will with this mom and her son, and then hold on to his will with Sharon. We're used to multitasking, but multilevel loving is rare. Death is ever present in the good work of love. And, as we shall see, so is life. But death comes first.

Seeing Jesus

Here's a summary of how Jason reenacts the four steps of love.

> Though Jason is a busy husband and father, uncertain how to begin, and fearful that he will make a mistake (Step 1), he doesn't grasp at comfort or a balanced life (Step 2), but enters a disabled boy's world by initiating a conversation with the mom and her son (Step 3). When he gets back to his car, his family, instead of thanking him, criticizes him for being late (Step 4). That stings, but he realizes he is on the path of Jesus, so he receives it as from his Father as part of the cost of love.

Jason encounters his most difficult "death" with his critical and self-absorbed family. He expected a J-Curve with the mom and her son, but not with his family. He's in a double J-Curve. It's the second one that blindsides us, because it is so unexpected. As we saw with Kayla, Jason initially has a measure of control over his suffering. He chooses to love. But it's one thing to voluntarily descend down the slope of the J-Curve; it's another thing to be pushed! When Sharon denigrates him, it stings. That's why the Spirit of Jesus is so critical to love. You can't take the path of Jesus unless you have the Spirit of Jesus. He knows the way down.

In Jason, we see three elements working together: a vision of love (Jason's imagination) + a story of love (the J-Curve) + a person embodying love (Jason obeying) = a life of love. Without realizing it, Jason embodies Jesus to his family. By becoming a Christ bearer, he inoculates his children against the siren call of secular liberalism by showing them a better vision of *the good* as he reenacts the dying of Christ for love. His children are watching. They will not forget. They see Jesus.

Death is ever present in the good work of love. And, as we shall see, so is life. But death comes first.

20

The J-Curve Calms a Quarrel

Creating a Path to Reconciliation

At the end of Philippians, we discover why Paul labors to connect the J-Curve with love. Two prominent women whom he loves and values as coworkers in the gospel are at one another's throats.

> I *beg* Euodia and I *beg* Syntyche to have the same attitude of mind in the Lord. Yes, I ask you also, true companion [or Syzygos], help these women, who have labored side by side with me in the gospel together with Clement and the rest of my fellow workers, whose names are in the book of life. (Phil. 4:2–3)[1]

This is a major meltdown. For starters, Paul *begs* two grown women to love one another. Notice also how carefully he avoids taking sides by repeating *beg* twice, addressing each woman separately.[2] Their quarrel warrants enough attention that he names them and their lack of love in a letter that will be read before the entire congregation on Sunday morning!

---

1. Following Peter T. O'Brien, *The Epistle to the Philippians*, The New International Greek Testament Commentary (Grand Rapids, MI: Eerdmans, 1991), 477–82, I've used the word "beg" in place of the typical "entreat" in this passage, and I have used "to have the same attitude of mind in the Lord" rather than "to agree in the Lord." O'Brien discusses (and sources) the possibility of *Syzygos* as a proper name, 480–81.
2. This is an unusual construction, since Greek seldom repeats verbs in this way.

Given the length of time it took for hand-carried letters to go from Philippi to Rome and back, this tension must have been festering for some time. Either the church has been frozen, unable to move toward them, or the two women have been resisting counsel, so Paul enlists the help of *a true companion* to help these women love one another. They don't lack faith—their names are written "in the book of life." They lack love.

Scholars have underestimated the significance of this quarrel, partly because it comes across as "not a big deal." Paul's words are simple and straightforward, with no hint of drama. That's surprising, since problems like this reek of drama. Drama functions as an intensifier: people talk and take sides, and soon the "fire" spreads. That likely explains why Paul is so brief. He's putting out a fire, so he wisely offers a simple, dramafree solution.

Why not send a private letter to these women? Usually in such situations, people have already gravitated to one of the sides, creating a congregationwide problem. Also, if these two leaders don't understand how the J-Curve applies to love, it's likely the entire congregation doesn't either. By outing the problem, Paul kills gossip, recruits a mediator, and holds everyone accountable. He puts his finger in the dike.

A Strategic Approach to Love

Notice Paul's fourfold strategy to help these two women.

First, Paul gives the church a clear goal, a vision of what they should be like: the perfection of unity (Phil. 2:1–4). You might call unity the skin of love, what people see. He appeals not only to their hearts, but also to their imaginations. Without a clear vision of the perfection of unity that Paul paints here, it's easy to get lost in the murkiness of the dispute over who's right and wrong, or in analyzing how the situation was mishandled. One of the worst aspects of our flesh is our fascination with other people's flesh. Put simply, we gravitate to the negative. That's why the upside of the J-Curve, the resurrection, is also critical to the work of love. By giving this vision to the congregation, Paul doesn't single these women out, which keeps the letter from having an unnecessary scolding tone.

Second, Paul peels back the outer skin and shows us the supporting structure of love, the J-Curve (2:5–8). Oneness or unity comes from pursuing the downward path of love. For a community of Jesus to look like Jesus, it has to enter the story of Jesus.

In Philippians 4, he links his rebuke back to the J-Curve in Philippians 2 by using similar language, calling them to be united and "to have the same attitude of mind in the Lord" (v. 2). By gently instructing them, Paul reduces the need for a lengthy rebuke. The J-Curve gives the congregation a worldview that makes reconciliation possible.

> For a community of Jesus to look like Jesus,
> it has to enter the story of Jesus.

The beauty of reliving the dying of Christ is that only one party of a quarrel needs to take the downward path of humility. So let's say Euodia "gets" the J-Curve, but Syntyche doesn't. Euodia says to Syntyche, "What have I done wrong? How can I make this better?" Euodia will get an earful. Some of what Syntyche says will be true, some will be unbalanced, and some will just be slights that Syntyche has created in her own mind. We did not invent touchiness. It's been around since the garden of Eden.

Euodia can repent and apologize for what she did wrong. In my experience, Syntyche will not ask Euodia the same question Euodia asked her because she sees herself as the victim. Has justice happened? No. Has love begun? Yes. When Euodia incarnates with Syntyche, she becomes a carrier of Christ, a Christ bearer. Jesus is beginning to glow in and through her. Resurrection has begun.

Third, Paul sprinkles examples of himself and his coworkers throughout the letter, giving concrete handles as to what love looks like. Embodying Jesus is the best thing a leader can do for his or her family or congregation. Without handles, love remains a sheer cliff. Only after Paul has laid this groundwork in Philippians 1–3 does he address the quarrel.

Finally, Paul wisely enlists Syzygos (or possibly an unnamed "true companion") to help these two women. A third-party peacemaker can protect Euodia in her downward descent and give space for her to speak honestly into Syntyche's life. Multiple times I've been in a tense situation where a "true yokefellow," like Syzygos, has helped me or others see things about ourselves. But it's not uncommon for someone like Syntyche to reject an appeal from Euodia to include a mediator to help her. I've also seen situations in which the mediator was biased in favor of one party. If the mediator favors Syntyche, that will only deepen Euodia's dying with Christ. But Paul forestalls this by openly commanding Syzygos to help the two women.

Each of these four elements gives these women and the church a positive vision for the work of love. Almost certainly, these women are struggling with pride and self-will. I've never seen a quarrel in which both weren't operating. It is appropriate at times to deal directly with these twin diseases, but they are enormously difficult to eradicate. Paul's strategy is counterintuitive. He deals with the Philippians by painting multiple alluring pictures of love, drawing them into a vision of *the good*. Embracing the J-Curve undermines the pride and self-will that lurk behind the women's quarrel.

Embodying Jesus is the best thing a leader can do for his or her family or congregation. Without handles, love remains a sheer cliff.

Notice how much richer Paul's approach is than a simplistic WWJD (What Would Jesus Do?) approach. Any imitation of Jesus should be prized, but if you reduce WWJD to only niceness, it collapses when confronted with the raw, unrelenting meanness our culture increasingly breeds. Mere kindness, when offended, eventually mutates into resentment and bitterness. We need to imitate the whole pattern of Jesus's life. The J-Curve provides the frame for love.

So Paul gives a goal (unity), a path (humility), an example (himself and his coworkers), and a person (Syzygos) to make the work of love possible. No one magic bullet makes it happen. Thus, Paul's opening prayer: "And it is my prayer that your love may abound more and more, with knowledge and all discernment . . ." (Phil. 1:9). We need to think in love.

Up till now, we've largely examined the downward or dying side of the J-Curve. In Part 4, we will turn upward with the J-Curve and discover what rising with Jesus looks like. We'll discover how dying and rising work together to shape us in the image of God's Son.

Mere kindness, when offended, eventually mutates
into resentment and bitterness. We need to
imitate the whole pattern of Jesus's life.

PART 4

RISING WITH JESUS

What Makes the J-Curve Go Up?

How Do We Re-enact the Resurrection
of Jesus in Our Daily Life?

How Does a Resurrection Lens Transform
How We View Life's Ups and Downs?

How Does a Resurrection Lens Defeat Cynicism?

21

Discovering the Power of Resurrection

What Makes the J Go Up?

What makes the J-Curve go up? What powers the resurrection? To discover Paul's answer, we need to first pause and look at how he defines the gospel.

If you ask most Christians, "What is the gospel?" they will say something like this: "Jesus died on the cross for my sins." That is good and proper. Paul says similar things:

Christ died for the ungodly. (Rom. 5:6)

Christ died for us. (v. 8)

But when Paul actually defines the gospel, he says something bigger. In his opening to Romans (1:1, 3–4), he divides the gospel into two stanzas; the first is Jesus's descent, his incarnation; the second is his resurrection and exaltation. The two stanzas parallel one another, line by line:

. . . the gospel of God . . . concerning his Son, (vv. 1, 3)	
who has come	who was appointed
from the seed of David	Son of God in power
according to the flesh, (v. 3)	according to the Spirit of holiness
	by his resurrection from the dead
	(v. 4).*

---

* Douglas Moo, *The Epistle to the Romans* (Grand Rapids, MI: Eerdmans, 1996), 45–50. Following Moo, I changed *declared* to *appointed*, and I have used his translation of Romans 1:3–4.

When Paul defines the gospel, he tells the story of Jesus's life, death, and resurrection in the form of a J-Curve. At its simplest, the gospel is a story of a person who loves deeply and gives himself completely. "For the history of Christ is the gospel in a nutshell."[1]

> At its simplest, the gospel is a story of a person
> who loves deeply and gives himself completely.

It is easy to miss this and make the gospel merely a formula. Formulas aren't bad; in fact, Paul gives us a formula here (Rom. 1:3–4). Pithy summaries make timeless truths memorable, but our modern formulas focus almost exclusively on the core of the gospel (forgiveness and justification by faith) and miss that the core is embedded in a story. If we miss the story of the person of Jesus, we depersonalize the gospel. We can never separate *story* from *person*—the two are completely intertwined. If I want to get to know you, I have to know your story.[2]

From the very beginning, the church described the gospel as the story of Jesus. Even Jesus, on his resurrection day, described the gospel in the shape of a J-Curve to the two disciples on the road to Emmaus:[3]

> And he said to them, "O foolish ones, and slow of heart to believe all that the prophets have spoken! Was it not necessary that *the Christ should suffer these things and enter into his glory?*" (Luke 24:25–26)

---

1. Richard B. Gaffin Jr., *Resurrection and Redemption: A Study in Paul's Soteriology* (Phillipsburg, NJ: P&R, 1987), 112–13. Gaffin points out the similarity between the J-Curve in Phil. 2:5–11 and Rom. 1:3–4.

2. See Alasdair MacIntyre, *After Virtue: A Study in Moral Theory*, 3rd ed. (Notre Dame, IN: University of Notre Dame Press, 2007), 204–25.

3. Jesus first articulated the J-Curve pattern (Luke 9:22; 24:46), which became the template for his disciples.

Fifty days later, at Pentecost, Peter described the same J-Curve pattern:

[*Life*:] Jesus of Nazareth, a man attested to you by God with mighty works and wonders and signs that God did through him in your midst, as you yourselves know—[*Death*:] this Jesus, delivered up according to the definite plan and foreknowledge of God, you crucified and killed by the hands of lawless men. [*Resurrection*:] God raised him up, loosing the pangs of death, because it was not possible for him to be held by it. (Acts 2:22–24)

This pattern of the gospel as the J-Curve punctuates almost every sermon in Acts.[4] I used to puzzle over the difference between the definition of the gospel in Acts and my own definition. My mistake was equating justification by faith with the gospel. But the gospel encompasses a larger picture. In Paul's famous gospel definition in 1 Corinthians 15:1, 3–8 (see Fig. 21A below), he weaves together the story of Jesus with the atonement by means of the phrase *for our sins*.

Fig. 21A. Paul's Gospel Definition

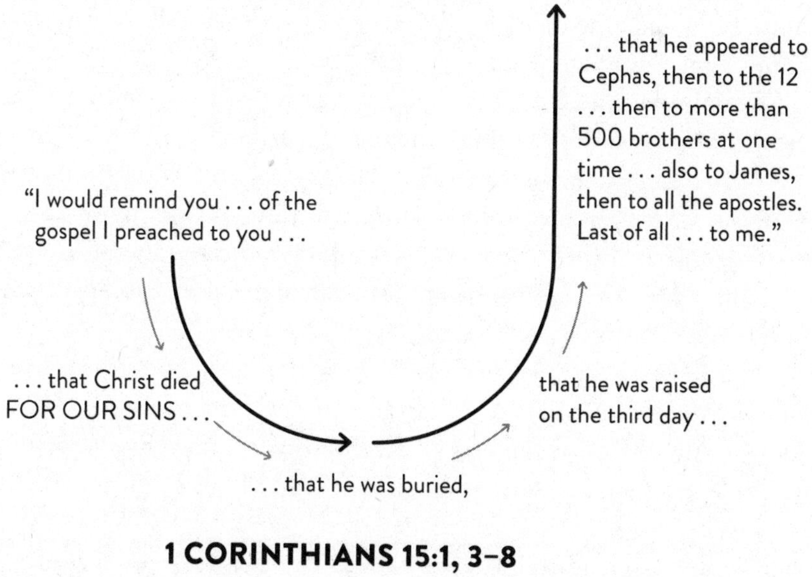

... that he appeared to Cephas, then to the 12 ... then to more than 500 brothers at one time ... also to James, then to all the apostles. Last of all ... to me."

"I would remind you ... of the gospel I preached to you ...

... that Christ died FOR OUR SINS ...

that he was raised on the third day ...

... that he was buried,

1 CORINTHIANS 15:1, 3–8

---

4. See the Virtual Appendix at www.seeJesus.net/J-Curvebook for a listing of Acts references.

His definition includes the entire gift of Jesus *for our sins* (sin's guilt and power), his taking on human form, dying for our sins, and rising for our justification. Jesus's death *for us* resides at the center of the gospel, but if you reduce the gospel to justification by faith, you depersonalize it.[5]

The Person Hidden in the Gospel

The gospel also includes the Spirit. In Paul's Romans 1 definition, the Spirit is the secret to the resurrection. The Spirit also appears in Paul's definition in 1 Timothy:

> He was manifested in the flesh,
>   vindicated by the Spirit,
>   seen by angels,
> proclaimed among the nations,
>   believed on in the world,
>   taken up in glory. (3:16)

In both gospel definitions, Paul uses language not typical of him, so the definitions likely predate him.[6] That means the entire early church, not just Paul, defined the gospel as the story of Jesus. Both definitions map on the J-Curve in Figure 21B below.

By telling us the gospel in the form of the J-Curve, Paul includes two things we normally don't include: resurrection and the Spirit. You can't have one without the other, because for Paul, the Spirit equals resurrection life. Jesus is "appointed Son of God in power according to the Spirit" (Rom. 1:4 AT) and "vindicated by the Spirit" (1 Tim. 3:16). The Spirit powers Jesus's resurrection. No Spirit, no resurrection.

The Spirit doesn't just give Jesus a new, improved body; Jesus lives now *by the Spirit*. Moment by moment, the incarnate Son of God is alive, ruling the universe, and exalted above all things by the power of the Spirit. Paul explains how this worked at Jesus's resurrection:

---

5. "The center of Paul's gospel-theology, its primary focus, is not one or other applied benefit of Christ's work—say, justification by faith or the work of the Spirit in believers—but that work itself." Richard B. Gaffin Jr., *By Faith, Not by Sight: Paul and the Order of Salvation*, 2nd ed. (Phillipsburg, NJ: P&R, 2013), 27. See also 46, 86.

6. See Gaffin, *Resurrection*, 98–99, and Douglas Moo, *The Epistle to the Romans* (Grand Rapids, MI: Eerdmans, 1996), 45.

Thus it is written, "The first man Adam became a living being"; the last Adam [Jesus] became a *life-giving Spirit*. (1 Cor. 15:45 AT)[7]

Fig. 21B. The Spirit and the Gospel

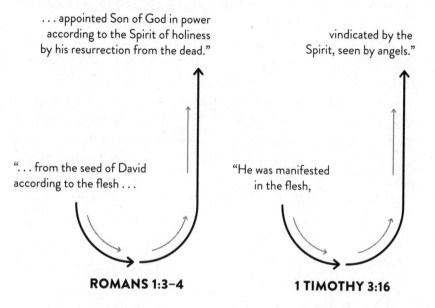

... appointed Son of God in power according to the Spirit of holiness by his resurrection from the dead."

vindicated by the Spirit, seen by angels."

"... from the seed of David according to the flesh ...

"He was manifested in the flesh,

ROMANS 1:3–4

1 TIMOTHY 3:16

On Easter morning, the Spirit transformed Jesus's lifeless body into *a Spiritual body* (1 Cor. 15:44 AT). The Spirit unites with Jesus so intimately that, without losing their separate identities, Jesus and the Spirit become functionally one.[8] They are so united that Paul easily interchanges "Spirit" and "Lord" or joins them in a single phrase, "the Spirit of the Lord." So Paul tells the Corinthians,

Now the *Lord is the Spirit*, and where the *Spirit of the Lord* is, there is freedom. And we all, with unveiled face, beholding the glory of the Lord, are being transformed into the same image from

---

7. Following Gaffin in *Resurrection*, 87, and Geerhardus Vos in *The Pauline Eschatology* (Grand Rapids, MI: Baker, 1979), 184, I have capitalized *Spirit* in this verse. When Paul says we are *spiritual*, he doesn't mean we are religious or pray easily; he means we are *in step with the Spirit* or *led by the Spirit*, that the third person of the Trinity brings us the incarnate Son of God. Vos writes about the word *spiritual* in 1 Corinthians 15:42–46, "In order to keep far such misunderstandings the capitalizing of the word ought to be carefully guarded both in translation and otherwise: πνευματικκα ["spiritual"] almost certainly leads on the wrong track, whereas Πνευματικκα ["Spiritual"], not only sounds a note of warning, but in addition points in the right direction positively." *The Pauline Eschatology*, 167.

8. See Gaffin, *Resurrection*, 89. Their union is not ontological (being) but economic (work).

one degree of glory to another. For this comes from the *Lord who is the Spirit*. (2 Cor. 3:17–18)

The Spirit now carries Christ's life to us. If Jesus lives by the power of the Spirit, so do we. Every time God brings life out of our deaths, that's the Spirit at work. He makes ongoing resurrection real.

As we've seen, Christ's life narrowed as he descended the J-Curve; likewise, our lives constrict as we love. The Spirit reversed the effect of the incarnation with the broadening of the resurrection. The incarnate Son of God, by the Spirit, became both exalted and universal. Jesus's resurrection life goes *up* and *out*, reversing the *down* and *in* of his dying life. Now in resurrection, life spreads and grows. The Spirit makes Jesus's embodiment universal, in effect, creating little Jesuses everywhere.[9]

Here's what this looks like in a diagram:

Fig. 21C. Dying and Rising by the Spirit

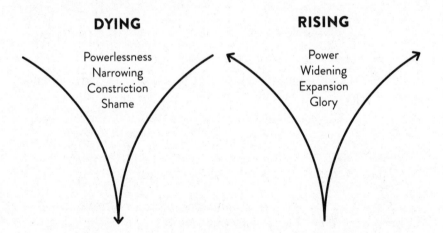

DYING

Powerlessness
Narrowing
Constriction
Shame

RISING

Power
Widening
Expansion
Glory

---

9. The Nicene Creed (AD 325) affirms that Jesus, as "very God of very God," fills the universe. The difference Paul puts his finger on has significant mystery in it, but I find it clarifying that (1) the preincarnate Son of God's universality did not extend to "the rebellion." We refused him as ruler. He was not enthroned in people's souls; and (2) Jesus is forever embodied. The Spirit now re-creates the incarnate Son of God, making him potentially personally universal to even the rebellion. Reflecting on 1 Cor. 15:42–45, Gaffin writes, "He [Christ] alone is the 'life-giving Spirit' . . . in his resurrection he has been so thoroughly transformed by the Holy Spirit and has come into such complete and final possession of the Spirit, that consequently they are one in the work of giving resurrection life, of bestowing eschatological life. The presence of the Holy Spirit in the church and as he indwells all believers is the indwelling presence of the exalted Christ in his resurrection life and power as Romans 8:9–11 . . . especially shows." *By Faith, Not by Sight*, 75.

To give you a feel for what the work of the Spirit looks like in everyday life, here's an update of a story about Kim that I shared in both *A Praying Life* and *A Loving Life*.[10]

Kim Pacing

For years, Kim paced in the early morning hours. She rose as early as 4 a.m. and started pacing upstairs, running out into the hallway and then back to her room. Jill and I took turns yelling at her to get back in bed, but like most yelling, it was ineffective. In mid-December 2007, just possibly because I was halfway through writing *A Praying Life*, I decided to go up and pray with her when she started pacing.

When I laid my hands on Kim to pray for her, I was surprised with a thought out of the blue: "I've underestimated Kim's ability to grow spiritually and own her own behavior." Over the next three months, I went upstairs weekly, sat on her bed, and prayed that God would quiet her spirit. Nothing happened until mid-March, when her pacing completely stopped. It stopped because we moved to a quieter neighborhood, where we'd found a house with an in-law suite for Kim. Only then did we realize that the diesel trucks from the meat factory across the street had been waking her up.

That seemingly random thought when I prayed for Kim gnawed at me. I thought I needed to do something to help her to grow, but I resisted for several months. Already my life felt constricted from all the Kim-care in the morning: combing her hair (I use puppets to entertain her since she dislikes having her hair combed), switching her clothes (usually something is on backward), checking her feet (they get cracks), making her breakfast, talking with her, cleaning up, brushing her teeth (which she hates), stretching her legs (she really dislikes this), cleaning her glasses, and helping her with her morning checklist (she loves this). But that prompt to nourish Kim's soul stuck with me, so that spring, I began having morning devotions with her.

After breakfast, we'd read a children's Bible story together, then I'd do the dishes while Kim briefly prayed on her speech computer.

---

10. Paul E. Miller, *A Praying Life: Connecting with God in a Distracting World* (Colorado Springs: NavPress, 2009); *A Loving Life: In a World of Broken Relationships* (Wheaton, IL: Crossway, 2014).

I knew I should sit with her as she prayed, but I balked at another constraint on my time. Then one day in the fall of 2008, I sat with her and watched her as she prayed. Instantly, her prayers blossomed. Thanksgiving poured out of her heart—for Disney, for her family, for her aides, for life. Now she thanks God for whatever event is coming up; Halloween or whatever holiday is next gets a hearty thanks from Kim.

Every few months, something new pops into Kim's praying. She has been telling people she will pray for them. She even puts her hands on people as she prays for them. She particularly enjoys praying for angry people, since she herself struggles with anger. Because she's not been particularly influenced by the eighteenth century Enlightenment philosopher Immanuel Kant, she's not aware that prayer should be kept in private "prayer times," so if she hears a need, she just starts praying in the middle of a conversation. How odd. How like Jesus.

Jill now joins us for Kim's morning prayer time—it's the highlight of our day. We have some heavy things weighing on our hearts, and by asking Kim to pray for them, it's like "going nuclear." If the key to faith is childlikeness, then Kim has that in spades.

Now that Jill and I are both over sixty and feeling the pull of old-age narcissism, we exercise self-discipline by limiting ourselves to asking Kim to pray for just one body part each. It's not unusual for Jill or I to debate whether to pray for our shoulder, knee, or back!

I think Kim has Pentecostal genes. She listens attentively to people as they pray, typing "yes" on her speech computer—although she has her limits. In Kim's opinion, a girl in her Sunday school class prays too long, so Kim started interrupting with her own prayer. Her teachers told Kim she needed to wait until the other girl said "Amen." Now, as soon as this girl starts praying, Kim holds her finger high in the air, poised to strike her speech computer at "Amen"!

One of our most memorable moments happened in an emergency room, where I took Kim because of an old break in her elbow. We weren't sure if she had reinjured it or if it was in her head. She had a meltdown in the waiting room—which got us very fast service—but nothing showed on the X-ray, so we went home. The next day, she typed out, "God spoke to me in the hospital." I was so surprised, I didn't ask her what he had told her. We seldom use that language in our home because it is often abused. The next day, I asked her what God had said. She typed, "To not be afraid. He was with me, and to be a Daniel."

Dying and Rising by the Spirit

What God did was so much wider than what I prayed for. I just wanted Kim to stop pacing; God wanted her to come alive spiritually. The Spirit worked in both of us.

Initially, the Spirit prompted me with the thought, "You've underestimated Kim's ability to grow spiritually." How do I recognize the Spirit? I'm never sure initially, and I'm cautious to label something "the Spirit," but he has a distinctive voice. If it's a call to love, to repent, or to go lower, it's usually him. After all, he's the Holy Spirit.

I thought Kim needed to repent. Instead, God wanted me to repent. My halting decisions to pray at her bedside, to have devotions, and to look at her as she prayed constricted and narrowed my life. The costs of doing these things were mild, but each step downward still had a slight sting as I went through a *repentance* J-Curve. In Romans 8, Paul links a *repentance* J-Curve to the work of the Spirit:

> For if you live according to the flesh you will die, but if by the Spirit you put to death the deeds of the body, you will live (v. 13).

When I put to death by the Spirit the deeds of the flesh (yelling at Kim, putting her into a spiritual box, multitasking), the Spirit created a multifaceted resurrection. To paraphrase Paul, "Death is at work in Kim's dad, but life in Kim" (see 2 Cor. 4:12).

The J-Curve consists of two miracles: the wonder of humility bringing us down and the wonder of the Spirit lifting us up. My life constricted slightly as I loved Kim better, but then the Spirit reversed that narrowing with a cascade of life in and through Kim.

The Spirit multiplies Jesus. He re-created Jesus's body on Easter morning, so Jesus now lives by the Spirit. He does the same work in us. He carries the incarnate Son of God, Christ Jesus, to us. He did that one morning when I stopped multitasking, sat down next to Kim, and watched her as she prayed.

I thought Kim needed to repent. Instead,
God wanted me to repent.

22

Repersonalizing the Resurrection

Discovering the Forgotten Half of the J-Curve

Now that we've seen how the Spirit powers and shapes resurrection, let's explore four key aspects of it. Each in its own way repersonalizes the resurrection. I say *repersonalizes* because we've lost a sense of how personal Jesus's dying and rising actually was. We are rediscovering what was always there. We begin with Good Friday.

1. Our Justification Is Hidden in Jesus's Justification

At the climax of his Jewish trial, when Jesus claimed to be the unique Son of God, the high priest had two choices: fall down and worship Jesus, or charge him with blasphemy. Matthew records the high priest's response:

> Then the high priest tore his robes and said, "He has uttered blasphemy. What further witnesses do we need? You have now heard his blasphemy. What is your judgment?" They answered, "He deserves death." (Matt. 26:65–66)

The charge is blasphemy, the verdict is guilty, and the sentence is death. At 3 p.m. that afternoon, the sentence is carried out, as Jesus breathes his last.

Let's say you are the most powerful person in Israel and you object to this judicial murder. You might be able to dismiss the charge and overturn the verdict, but you can't reverse the sentence. Jesus is dead. What good does it do to declare him innocent?

Surprisingly, that fact doesn't silence Jesus's disciples. On three different occasions, Peter rebukes Jewish men for their murder of Jesus. The first one is in his sermon at Pentecost:

> This Jesus, delivered up according to the definite plan and foreknowledge of God, *you crucified and killed* by the hands of lawless men. *God raised him up, loosing the pangs of death*, because it was not possible for him to be held by it. (Acts 2:23–24)

With our grace-only lens, we expect Peter to be more conciliatory, as in, "I know you killed Jesus, but really, we all killed him with our sin." Rembrandt captured this idea, which is so central to the gospel, in his painting of Jesus's crucifixion *The Raising of the Cross*: the man in blue helping the soldiers crucify Jesus is Rembrandt. It's true. We are all complicit in his death.

But this truth misses the moment. You see, the men of Jerusalem are complicit in the public, gruesome murder of the Son of God. The only truly good person who ever lived was tortured to death, and no one is repenting for it. The worst sin humanity ever committed, the murder of God, has to be confronted.

With our modern tendency to idolize compassion, we instinctively think Peter should incarnate with these men in a *love* J-Curve; instead, he tells them they need a *repentance* J-Curve. They need honesty, not compassion. (Because secular liberalism dismisses the law of God, it confuses J-Curves, substituting a *love* J-Curve—the need to incarnate—for a *repentance* J-Curve—the need to repent.) In other words, these men don't need to be understood—they need to understand themselves.

Peter parallels their sin with the Father's action. They accused Jesus of committing blasphemy by claiming to be the Son of God. By raising his Son from the dead, his Father reverses not only the verdict, but the sentence of death. The resurrection justifies Jesus. In the resurrection, the Father personally vindicates his Son. His Son is shamed, but now his Dad honors him.

Look how personal this makes justification by faith. Because we are hidden in the person of Christ, his justification becomes our justification. The *faith* J-Curve means we're not just united with Jesus in his death, but in his resurrection as well. As Paul says, Jesus "was delivered up for our trespasses and raised for our justification" (Rom. 4:25). In the words of Geerhardus Vos, "Christ's resurrection was the *de facto* [actual] declaration of God in regard to his being just . . . resurrection had annulled the sentence of condemnation."[1]

In the resurrection, the Father personally vindicates his Son. His Son is shamed, but now his Dad honors him.

The Father wasn't just "helping Jesus get back on his feet"; he was vindicating and honoring his shamed and murdered Son. You see, stoning Jesus would have been so much easier than crucifying him. But by having the Romans crucify him, he would be forever cursed (Deut. 21:22–23). The Jewish leadership wanted the method of his death to forever seal his reputation, which is exactly what happened. His dying forever proved he was the only obedient person who ever lived. Jesus was murdered because he *claimed* to be the Son of God. He was resurrected because his submission to that death *proved* he was the Son of God.

When Jesus humbled himself, his Father exalted him. Jesus's pithy saying, "Whoever humbles himself will be exalted" (Matt. 23:12b), is not only wise advice, but it also describes his life as a mini-J-Curve. Consider Jesus's comments on the humility of the tax collector who prayed for mercy:

> I tell you, *this man went down to his house justified*, rather than the other. For everyone who exalts himself will be humbled, but *the one who humbles himself will be exalted.* (Luke 18:14)

---

1. Geerhardus Vos, *The Pauline Eschatology* (Phillipsburg, NJ: P&R, 1994), 151.

Jesus, the obedient Son, humbled himself, and now, in the resurrection, his Father is exalting and justifying him. The Father hears his Son's cries of anguish from the cross, "My God, my God, why have you forsaken me?" (Matt. 27:46b) and "Into your hands I commit my spirit!" (Luke 23:46b). Resurrection, at its most basic, is simply answered prayer. The Son asks for a loaf, and his Father gives him a feast. The Father is vindicating his Son, shouting out in the resurrection and exaltation of Jesus, "That's my Boy!" Jesus's ongoing enthronement means that our justification is constantly being declared to the Father. What he did for Jesus, he does for us.

2. Our Rising Is Hidden in Our Dying

The Father responded to the purity and completeness of his Son's obedience by raising him. "The Father's act of exaltation is his reply to the Son's self-humiliation."[2] The sense of the Greek is that the J-Curve turns upward on "Therefore" (Phil. 2:8b–10):

Fig. 22A. Where the J-Curve Turns Upward

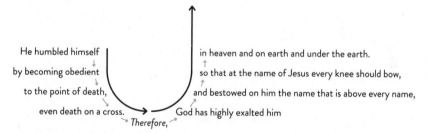

The instrument of Jesus's humbling (the cross) was the vehicle for his exaltation. Rising is embedded in dying.

If rising is embedded in dying, then not running from the customized dying that God permits in our lives is essential for resurrection. That's why endurance is the glue of the Christian life. To taste resurrection, we need to endure the death. An early exit cripples resurrection.

Probably my best resurrection was embedded in my worst death. At one point in my life, over a series of years, God stripped me of

---

2. "In response to this obedience, the Father has exalted the Son." Gerald Bray, *God Is Love: A Biblical and Systematic Theology* (Wheaton, IL: Crossway, 2012), 187.

everything I had loved and built in ministry. During this time, when I was reduced to simply enduring, to showing up for life, prayer became like breathing. Years later, my board encouraged me to write a book on prayer. I demurred, citing several good books on prayer. However, I lost the two-hour debate and wrote *A Praying Life*, which has helped hundreds of thousands of people to pray. Resurrection was hidden in death.

Just as an aside, it takes wisdom to know when to endure and when to exit. Usually, I find that the Spirit, the Word, and the counsel of mature friends make it clear. I suggest three principles:

1. Surprisingly, the default position is to flee. When Paul is beaten up in a city, he flees. He doesn't hang around for a second beating. We aren't Stoics, seeking suffering. Is there a way out?
2. If we are bound by a covenant of words (marriage, contract), we should stay. Words are sacred.
3. If we are bound by love or responsibility, we should stay. Martin Luther's pamphlet on the obligation of pastors and officials to stay in Wittenberg, Germany, during the Black Plague is a classic.

3. God Shapes and Controls the Resurrection

Resurrection isn't something we do—the Father does it through the Spirit. Earlier, we looked at seven verbs that describe Jesus's descent to death, but as Jesus goes up in resurrection, he does nothing. Jesus is active in death, but passive in resurrection.

They taunt at Jesus, "He saved others; he cannot save himself" (Matt. 27:42). Such taunting is at the heart of our fear of love. You see, it's true. You can save others, but you can't save yourself. In the work of love, you are often dying for others, but there is no one to die for you. That's where resurrection comes in.

We do the dying. God does the resurrecting. As one scholar put it, "Christ emptied Christ. God exalted Christ."[3] We will discover

---

3. J. A. Bengel, *New Testament Word Studies*, trans. C. T. Lewis and M. R. Vincent (Grand Rapids, MI: Kregel, 1971), 2:435, quoted in Gaffin, *Resurrection*, 64.

later that Paul is often active in his resurrections; he's alive to his desires and acts on them by rebuking, fleeing, and loving. Yet this fundamental structure remains—resurrection is from the outside. God saves Paul.

Knowing that I do the dying and God does the rising has helped me to be cautious in resurrection, to not grasp too quickly at seeming breakthroughs, but to wait for the story to unfold. It's easy to get ahead of the Spirit and think we see how the resurrection will go. It's a subtle form of impatience. For example, it was several years after *A Praying Life* came out that I connected the dots between the dying of years before with this rising of God's blessing on people praying. We see resurrection only in the rear-view mirror.

Attempting to create our own resurrections is a great temptation of the Christian life. For instance, if someone has slandered me, I'm tempted to create a mini-resurrection by boasting. They deflated me, so I inflate me. Silence keeps me on the dying side of the J-Curve. It's an act of surrender to let my Father vindicate me rather than to try to do so myself. His resurrections are always better than mine. We wait for his wonders.

4. Jesus Christ Is Lord!

Earlier, we saw that Jesus's descent had a two-part structure: first, incarnation, from heaven to the manger, and then from the manger to his death. His ascent, likewise, has a two-part structure: resurrection → exaltation.

Not only do we forget resurrection, we also forget exaltation. In Philippians 2, Paul is so transfixed by the reality of the exalted Christ, he doesn't even mention the resurrection; he implies it. The resurrection is subsumed into the larger reality of the Father's exaltation of Jesus:

> Therefore God has highly exalted him and bestowed on him the name that is above every name, so that at the name of Jesus every knee should bow, in heaven and on earth and under the earth, and every tongue confess that Jesus Christ is Lord, to the glory of God the Father. (Phil. 2:9–11)

Fig. 22B. Jesus's Descent and Ascent

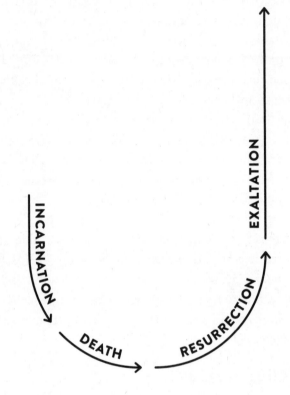

When Paul declares that *every knee will bow*, he participates in the exaltation and enthronement of Jesus. This all-encompassing vision of all creation bowing before the exalted Christ consumes Paul. It's his vision, job description, and strategy. In every sermon he preaches in Acts, Paul announces some aspect of Jesus's resurrection or enthronement. Paul wants knees to bend.

Paul's language about Jesus's exaltation is striking. For him, as a good Jew, the name above all names is *Yahweh*. God says through Isaiah, "I am the LORD [Yahweh]; that is my name" (42:8a). In other words, "That's my name and no one else's." Yahweh is not a tribal deity or the "top god" among many gods—you see, there are no other gods.

For I am God, and there is no other. By myself I have sworn; from my mouth has gone out in righteousness a word that shall not return: "*To me every knee shall bow, every tongue shall swear allegiance.*" (45:22–23)

In Philippians 2, Paul takes Isaiah's language about God and applies it to Jesus. Jesus's exaltation declares him to be the unique, only-begotten Son of God.

The oldest, simplest confession of the early church is "Jesus Christ is Lord." That's not just a general statement about Jesus—it describes his resurrection and exaltation. When we say "Jesus Christ is Lord," we participate in the enthronement of Jesus as Lord of the universe. The early Christians greeted one another by saying, "Christ is risen." The response was, "He is risen indeed." The oldest Christian confession and the oldest Christian greeting both focus on the upward side of the J-Curve, the exaltation of Christ.

Up to this part of the book, we've emphasized the dying side of the J-Curve and neglected the rising. We are not alone. The Western church has been strong on Jesus's death for us, but weak on his resurrection for us.[4] We affirm the resurrection, of course, but tend to trot it out just at Easter. Even when we tell others about the gospel, we tell people about his death and not his resurrection. We think of the resurrection as the cleanup, the tidying up of his death, but for Paul and the early church, the resurrection was everything.

> The Western church has been strong on Jesus's death for us, but weak on his resurrection for us.

Our lack of emphasis on resurrection is one reason why even mature Christians can go on endless idol hunts, looking ever deeper into their hearts for roots of sin. It's one reason we are shy about celebrating goodness or get ensnared by cynicism. We can get stuck in death and don't have a vision for either the power of God to bring real-time resurrections or a vision for the beauty of Jesus God wants to imprint on us. We participate in his death, but not his resurrection.

---

4. "Western theology since the time of Anselm . . . has concentrated heavily, if not exclusively, upon the death of Christ." Richard B. Gaffin Jr., *Resurrection and Redemption: A Study in Paul's Soteriology*, 2nd ed. (Phillipsburg, NJ: P&R, 1987), 15.

Rediscovering Resurrection

Repersonalizing Jesus's resurrection was on my mind when I took a day trip down to Washington, DC, to talk to Heather, who was dying of cancer. She'd grown up in a strong Christian home, but she had lost her faith at a Christian college when a speaker introduced her to a compassionless God. She rejected her parents' faith, and like so many of her generation she embraced the world of secular-liberalism. She rejected the Reformation view of *the good* and embraced a secularized Jesus view of *the good*. Her job, her friends, and her family were all deeply embedded in the world of secular liberalism.

I went because her mom, a friend, had asked me to pray for Heather some eight years before, so I had some skin in the game. I wasn't sure if she could meet for more than five minutes, partly because of lack of interest and partly because her cancer was in its final stage. Partly just to please her mom, she agreed to meet. I suspected she had reacted negatively to a depersonalized gospel, so my goal—even if we had only five minutes—was to repersonalize the gospel for her.

I wanted to convey three things: (1) the gospel is a person, (2) the resurrection is real, and (3) I love a living Jesus, thus embodying the first two truths. I knew concentration was extremely hard for her, so I couldn't argue, but I could paint. I could create for her a vision of *the good* that lay at the heart of our faith. He is altogether lovely.

As I looked at her gaunt and frail body, I told her I thought we agreed on one thing: she could use a new body. She smiled faintly. We both looked down at her infant daughter playing on the floor to whom she was about to say goodbye. I told her all of Christianity hinged on the resurrection. She'd not thought about that. She'd lumped all the miracles together—at the same level of importance.

Using my immersion in the person of Jesus over the last twenty-five years, I told her the story of Jesus's first conversation after his resurrection outside the garden tomb. He deliberately hid himself from his two favorite disciples, then showed himself to a woman, Mary Magdalene. In typical Jesus fashion, he created a hint of mystery by not introducing himself to her but letting himself be discovered. He asked her two questions: "Why are you weeping?" and "Whom are you seeking?"

(John 20:15a). It's just like him to draw another person out, to leave her space to emerge.

And Mary emerged. Thinking he was the gardener, she asked him, "If you have carried him away, tell me where you have laid him, and I will take him away" (v. 15b). We discover a take-charge woman, quick to solve problems, resourceful, like so many of her Hebrew ancestors—Deborah, Ruth, and Abigail.

Jesus's single-word response to her, "Mary" (v. 16a), is pure poetry, almost elegant. He was understated, at the edge of the story, letting the mystery unfold. Hearing her name on his lips shattered her grief—"It's him. He's alive!" That single word pierced her heart, and she lunged for Jesus, likely falling at his feet. The last time she had let him out of her sight, they had murdered him. Jesus had to tell her to stop clinging to him. He wanted her to go tell the disciples (v. 17).

I told Heather, "It's him. It's Jesus. It's his cadence. I could recognize him anywhere. That's how he talks. That's how he relates to people." And yes, Mary was half right in thinking he was a gardener. Jesus deliberately re-enacted a garden scene with a man and a woman. In the first garden, a woman introduced man to forbidden fruit; now the resurrected Jesus commissions a woman to introduce men to him.

Heather and I talked for an hour and a half; I could see her heart warm to Jesus. A week later, she died. Her mom told me later, "I was amazed at her appearance after your conversation. She was erect, her eyes were bright, and she was smiling—in stark contrast to the terrible pain she'd been in just before you arrived—lying in a fetal position. She was visibly affected by seeing the person of Jesus."

In an increasingly hopeless world, the hope of the resurrection is everything. I won't know till heaven if Heather experienced that hope. We shouldn't mute by one iota our emphasis on the cross, but we need to rediscover what Paul lived and inhabited—"the power of his resurrection" (Phil. 3:10b).

23

Looking through a Resurrection Lens

The J-Curve Transforms Our Vision of Life

Jesus's resurrection transforms how Paul processes life. His reaction to being imprisoned with a death sentence hanging over his head reveals a remarkable vision of life, one that promises to undermine our modern commitment to anxiety and to free us for a life of reflexive joy.

Paul gives us two cryptic descriptions of his imprisonment that I call "stories." Of course, these aren't just stories. Paul wants the Philippians to imitate him as he embodies the gospel: "Brothers, join in imitating me, and keep your eyes on those who walk according to the example you have in us" (Phil. 3:17). So let's keep our eyes on Paul and watch how Jesus's story shapes his story.

Story No. 1: Seeing Resurrection in "Mean" Places

To understand Paul's first story of viewing life through the resurrection, imagine that you have a difficult boss (or coworker) who takes credit for your work and mocks you openly in meetings. He can't fire you because your work is valuable to the company, but he can keep you from getting a raise and generally make your life miserable. You can't quit because you have a family to feed. You are trapped.

Here's how you might explain your prisonlike experiences to your friends:

"I hate going to work."

"My boss is the pits."

"I don't know how much longer I can take this."

In the right setting, any of these responses would be appropriate. In fact, all of them could be prayers. Likewise, it would be entirely fitting for Paul to write this about his imprisonment:

> I'm thankful for your prayers. The chains have been digging into my wrists, creating open blisters, but the Lord has given me endurance. Some of the guards are bullies, but most are relatively kind.

However, notice the difference in Paul's actual "prayer letter" from prison:

> I want you to know, brothers, that what has happened to me has really served to advance the gospel, so that it has become known throughout the whole imperial guard and to all the rest that my imprisonment is *in Christ*. And most of the brothers, having become confident in the Lord by my imprisonment, are much more bold to speak the word without fear. (Phil. 1:12–14 AT)[1]

Paul views his imprisonment through the dying and rising of Jesus, which causes four remarkable perspectives to emerge.

First, Paul isn't focused on himself. He has things to complain about—the word *imprisonment* actually means "chains." He's chained as he dictates this letter, but he has so embodied the mind of Christ that he takes no thought of himself.

Second, Paul is entirely focused on Jesus and the advance of the gospel—the story of Jesus's dying and rising for us. Paul never stops boasting, but he shifts from boasting about himself to boasting about Jesus.

---

1. Following Moisés Silva, *Philippians*, Baker Exegetical Commentary on the New Testament (Grand Rapids, MI: Baker Academic, 2005), 62, I've changed *for Christ* to *in Christ*. Silva translates 1:13b as "I bear my chains by virtue of my union with Christ" to bring out this point. Silva, *Philippians*, 61.

Third, notice Paul's strange way of describing his imprisonment: "my imprisonment is *in Christ*." We expect Paul to say *for Christ*. One scholar translated it, "It has become clear throughout the whole palace guard I am in chains because of my *union with Christ*."[2]

Paul never stops boasting, but he shifts from boasting about himself to boasting about Jesus.

Remarkably, the imperial guard has some sense that Paul is not just in chains, but *in Christ*. Paul sees his imprisonment through the lens of Christ's dying and rising. We can easily picture Paul's guards puzzling over his joy. He is not shy about connecting his joy with his being in Jesus as opposed to in chains. Guards always learn the character of their charges.

Notice the symmetry in Paul's life between what he says and who he is—he talks the gospel and embodies the gospel. In a cynical world, nothing is more powerful than our inner and outer worlds matching.

Fourth, the Philippians evidently are concerned that Paul's imprisonment will stop the gospel. "Not only is the gospel not hindered," Paul says, "but the entire imperial guard knows my imprisonment is in Christ. In addition, Christians are bolder." Instead of limiting the gospel, Paul's imprisonment accelerates it. Similarly, in the early 1990s, the murders of several leaders of the Iranian church by the leaders of Iran emboldened the church to speak even more openly.[3] Rising is embedded in dying.

Paul's prison *dying* opens the door to *eternal life* for the Roman guards. Evil becomes a launching pad for good.[4] Paul, however, does not forget this. In the midst of his own dying, he's on the lookout for resurrections. But it's not a "happy lens." He hunts for resurrection-like activity because he experiences the Spirit bringing life out of death.

Paul's location in Christ's dying and rising shapes how he views his chains cutting into his wrists and ankles. He looks at his dying (chains) through the lens of resurrection (the gospel going out even more). Dying no longer has the last word.

---

2. Silva, *Philippians*, 61.
3. Based on a conversation with Will Longenecker, a former worker in Iran.
4. See Richard B. Gaffin Jr., "The Usefulness of the Cross," *Westminster Theological Journal* 41, no. 2 (Spring 1979), 240.

If you don't view your circumstances through a resurrection lens, even low-level, persistent evil, such as an arrogant boss or a critical spouse, can bend your soul to the pain. Like a stubbed toe, evil rivets you, fixing your gaze in its direction. Initially you resist, but eventually evil's tenaciousness can wear you down. Even if you forgive, evil can seize and hold your attention, like a claw in the back of the brain. The chains dig into your soul, creating open blisters of the heart. Unwittingly, you become caught in its web and give in to cynicism or bitterness.

You cannot be passive in the face of evil. If you are, it will eventually eat you alive. When Aleksandr Solzhenitsyn was imprisoned in Siberia, he initially responded with hatred to his persecutors. Then he realized that the line dividing good and evil wasn't between him and them, but down the middle of his own heart. He, too, had become a murderer, in need of grace. He wasn't passive; he actively repented for his own hatred and then forgave the men abusing him.

Nik Ripkin tells the story of Dimitri, a pastor imprisoned for his faith, who survived seventeen years in a Soviet prison. Every morning, Dimitri stood by his bed with arms outstretched and sang his Heart Song (his favorite worship hymn) as loudly as he could. The other fifteen hundred hardened criminals mocked and jeered him. After fifteen years of thinking that all his family was dead, he first offered to sign and then refused to sign a confession. In a final act of defiance, he posted a page of Bible verses on a pillar. As the angered prison officials led him away to what appeared to be his execution, all fifteen hundred prisoners stood and sang his Heart Song. The stunned guards asked him, "Who are you?" Dimitri answered, "I am Jesus in your midst." They returned him to his cell. Soon afterward, he was released.[5] Dimitri's resurrection lens gave him a new way of seeing, fixing him on resurrection.

We instinctively want to understand evil, to get our minds around it, but evil is irrational at its core. A resurrection lens frees us from evil's ability to cling to our souls. Watching for real-time resurrections destroys evil's narrative web. The J-Curve map allows Paul to

---

5. Nik Ripkin with Gregg Lewis, *The Insanity of God: A True Story of Faith Resurrected* (Nashville: B&H, 2012), 158. I've paraphrased some.

see rising where we might get stuck in dying. As John Calvin put it so simply, "The fact that afflictions always have a happy end is a consolation that much mitigates their bitterness."[6]

Story No. 2: Seeing Resurrection with Mean People

In the second cryptic "story," Paul views his coworkers' jealousy through a resurrection lens:

> Some indeed preach Christ from envy and rivalry, but others from good will. The latter do it out of love, knowing that I am put here for the defense of the gospel. The former proclaim Christ out of selfish ambition, not sincerely but thinking to afflict me in my imprisonment. What then? Only that in every way, whether in pretense or in truth, Christ is proclaimed, and in that I rejoice. (Phil. 1:15–18)

Here Paul "dies" as he endures old-fashioned jealousy, that mother of all sins. Jealousy always masks itself, especially to the jealous person. I've seen jealousy tear apart churches, missions, and families, and yet it's seldom the focus of any teaching.

Since the gospel always disturbs the status quo, possibly these other evangelists are hoping to stigmatize Paul as a rabble-rouser by making the gospel more prominent. Paul's resurrection lens allows him to see God using jealousy to push the gospel out even more.

When Paul says "Christ is proclaimed," he has a larger vision in mind than witnessing. He longs for all creation to see what he sees— the exalted Christ. To *proclaim Christ* is to call all of creation to bend the knee. Every day, as he tells everyone he meets about Jesus, Paul participates in the resurrection and exaltation of Christ.

We could paraphrase Paul like this: "What about these jealous men trying to get me into trouble? Who cares! God is using even their evil motives to get the news of the resurrection rule of Jesus the Messiah out. When they proclaim the resurrection rule of Jesus, that's a resurrection for me!" Paul's whole life is an extension of the resurrection and exaltation of Jesus.

---

6. John Calvin, *Commentaries on the Epistles to Timothy, Titus, and Philemon* (Eugene, OR: Wipf & Stock, 2007), 243.

Once again, dying (jealous men) is the place of rising (Jesus proclaimed). Death is the launching pad for resurrection. That's why enduring through the deaths is so crucial. When we escape the dying, we miss the resurrection. Without our presence in the story, there's no room for the surprise.

Don't confuse Paul's resurrection optimism with modern "happy-thought therapy," as in Deepak Chopra's statement: "Death ended nothing; it opened up limitless adventures."[7] Such meaningless word spinning would not have snookered the ancients. They knew death ruled life. The most common tombstone in the Roman era declared, "I was not. I was. I am not." Death holds no magic. It's a terrible, evil thing. But in Jesus's resurrection, where death once ruled, the Father creates life through the Spirit.

Seeing Resurrection in the Middle of Death

As I was writing this chapter, two men I know attended weddings on the same weekend. Matt's daughter was getting married. After his wife left him twenty years ago, he remained faithful to the Lord and poured himself into the lives of his daughters. Matt shared tears of joy and sadness with his third and last daughter as he walked her down the aisle. He felt joy over her new life and sadness at their separation. Matt's ex-wife, now on her third husband, ended up sitting in the wrong row, next to Matt. He is not in the least bitter, but I still encouraged him to look at that accidental seating through the lens of the resurrection. That is, in the midst of the joy of resurrection, God permitted a moment of dying. That protects Matt from slipping into a victim narrative, in which he might say to a friend, "It was a wonderful wedding, except for my ex sitting next to me. She almost ruined it, like she does so many other things." Alertness to resurrection dethrones the victim narrative and keeps dying from having the last word.

My other friend, Tim, who is wheelchair-bound because of multiple sclerosis, had poured his heart and soul into an excellent ministry, building a regional office from the ground up. But when others listened to and believed charges against him, he was demoted without

---

7. Deepak Chopra, "What Happens after We Die?" *Today*, October 16, 2006. http://www.today.com/popculture/what-happens-after-we-die-wbna15291472.

being told why. His sensitive conscience deepened his pain because he kept reviewing his past, wondering how he had contributed to this outcome.

At a wedding reception, Tim happened to sit next to a former co-worker. Hearing the coworker say this year would be "the best ever" grieved Tim because the ministry had been entrusted to him, but also because he realized he used to talk that way. So while he was fighting to forgive, his past pride was also exposed. Tim was in a double J-Curve—the suffering of being sinned against and the suffering of actively putting to death the sin of boasting. I encouraged him to see this fellowship of his suffering as God's way of purifying him, imprinting him with the image of Jesus. When we embody the story of Jesus, we begin to look like him.

A year after Tim went through this, I asked him, "Which was harder, forty years of struggling with MS or betrayal?" He replied without any hesitation, "Betrayal." His quick response showed evil's stickiness.

I pray that Tim will realize that "the seed that dies will bear much fruit" (see John 12:24), that he will taste resurrection, even in the midst of death. The key we've seen in this chapter is that we must keep an eye out for it—as we watch the story unfold, we must do so with an eye of hope.

Joining Jesus in his death liberates us from bitterness; joining Jesus in his resurrection frees us from joylessness. Dying with him removes the negative; living with him gives us a positive vision. A resurrection lens creates a new way of looking at life:

- We live expectantly, watching for God to work.
- We pray expectantly for God to work.
- We focus on the good and not the bad.

Joining Jesus in his death liberates us
from bitterness; joining Jesus in his
resurrection frees us from joylessness.

24

The Secret of an Irritation-Free Life

The J-Curve Cures Grumbling

When talking about his imprisonment and his jealous coworkers in Philippians 1, Paul does "all things without grumbling." The Spirit who creates resurrection life is so present, so real for Paul that he sees good in the midst of evil. He makes no mention of the repeated injustices that put him in prison and doesn't even hint at the bad food or the sores on his ankles and wrists. He's "without blemish in the midst of a crooked and twisted generation." He'd been falsely imprisoned four years earlier in Judea, when *crooked* men slandered him and *twisted* the truth. His resurrection lens allows him to "shine as [a light] in the world," to shine with the beauty of Jesus, and he invites the Philippians to have that same outlook:

> Do all things without grumbling or disputing, that you may be blameless and innocent, children of God without blemish in the midst of a crooked and twisted generation, among whom you shine as lights in the world, holding fast to the word of life, so that

in the day of Christ I may be proud that I did not run in vain or labor in vain. (Phil. 2:14–16)

The words I've italicized above highlight Paul's call to live a relentlessly cheerful, grumpy-free life. He says, "Do all things without grumbling." He doesn't say, "We all struggle at times with crankiness"; he says we are to be "without blemish in the midst of a crooked and twisted generation." Paul calls us here to a *pristine purity*. He dares to order us (it's a command, not a suggestion) to be pure in this semisacred area of modern life: the right to be irritated at rude drivers, bothersome phone salesmen, or call centers in India. He actually thinks we can aim for purity.

I've detected a return to pagan fatalism among Christians, as if the spirit of this age were stronger than the Spirit of Jesus. After the Supreme Court affirmed same-sex marriage in 2015, a young dad who loves the Lord wondered out loud to me if we would need to anticipate our children exploring same-sex attraction. In response, I said, "The Roman world was far more openly perverted than ours. In Pompeii, wall murals are covered with sex scenes; doorknobs were male phallic symbols. When the Parthian cavalry cut off a Roman army, the Romans had to abruptly abandon their camp. The Parthian general was so appalled by the pornography left behind, he sent a mocking message to the retreating Romans.[1] In the midst of all this perversion, the church demanded and maintained incredibly high standards of purity. It didn't give in one inch to the spirit of the age."

I've detected a return to pagan fatalism
among Christians, as if the spirit of this age
were stronger than the Spirit of Jesus.

We also live in an increasingly "crooked and twisted generation," but in the midst of that, we can be "without blemish." Paul expects us to live cheerfully, as he did in prison. If this were mountain climbing, he would be showing us a sheer cliff and telling us, "Climb this cliff.

---

1. John Warry, *Warfare in the Classical World: An Illustrated Encyclopedia of Weapons, Warriors, and Warfare in the Ancient Civilizations of Greece and Rome* (New York: St. Martin's Press, 1980), 156–57.

By the power of the Spirit, you can do it." A weakness of a grace-only lens (for sanctification) is thinking that the purpose of the cliff is to show you how much you need Jesus. But here Paul is not describing the means of salvation, but the goal. He's calling us to image Jesus. Of course, you can't do that unless you are "holding fast to the word of life."[2] *Word of life* is one of Paul's many phrases for the gospel.

Paul wants to create an object of stunning beauty that reflects the loveliness of Jesus Christ. The church has lost this vision of *the good*.

Here's a point from a hypothetical "good sermon" on this passage:

> Paul's background to this passage is the Israelites' grumbling in the wilderness. It is important not to grumble. We all struggle with complaining at times. [Here, the pastor inserts a story of another driver causing him to grumble this week]. When you grumble, you are asserting your own will against God. God can give us the grace not to grumble.

Every single line in the above paragraph is true and appropriate. But the "good sermon" misses how Paul's words in Philippians 2 shimmer with love. He is not just giving advice or moralizing, he's carving the church into *The Pietà*—Michelangelo's stunning sculpture of Mary holding the dead body of her son. The "good sermon" misses the clarity of Paul's vision of what we are moving toward. It is blinded to beauty, so imagination dies.

A hypothetical "gospel sermon" also misses this passage. The pastor begins with a story about his own grumbling, then says:

> We all struggle with grumbling. In fact, as our world gets worse, there is more to grumble about! The key to this passage is the gospel. If you try not to grumble in your own strength, you will fail. Only as you keep returning to the gospel are you able to endure in an increasingly cranky world.

Again, every single line is true and good, but this gospel sermon imposes Martin Luther's vision of *the good* (faith and repentance) on

---

2. Scholars generally accept that *word of life* and other similar Pauline phrases mean "gospel" and not "Bible," although Paul has an equally high view of Scripture.

a text focused on the beauty God wants to fashion in us. It's the right sermon for the wrong text.

The Hidden I-Beam for Love

We're watching Paul, the master builder, create a cathedral of love. The J-Curve functions like the steel I-beams hidden behind the outer shell. If you weaken the I-beams, as happened at the World Trade Center on 9/11, the building collapses. Likewise, consciously re-enacting the story of Jesus sustains the outer shell of Christian behavior—the purity of love. You see, the problem with grumpiness is you've become too important. The J-Curve kills your self-importance.

Paul frames his *love* J-Curve (Phil. 2:5–11) with two visions of the purity of love. The first text, "In humility count others more significant than yourselves" (2:3b), comes just before the J-Curve and focuses on humility as the secret to unity. The second text, "Do all things without grumbling . . . in the midst of a crooked and twisted generation" (2:14–15a), comes just after the J-Curve and focuses on purity. The J-Curve functions like a hidden I-beam that "supports" the specific application of the gospel to our lives. Together, the two texts give us a complete building—the first text focuses on the inside, how we relate to one another; the second text on the outside, how we relate to the world. These two visions of *the good*—unity and purity—are possible only when sustained by the beaten path of the J-Curve.

The I-Beam for Both Dying and Rising

The J-Curve functions like a hidden I-beam for both sides of Christ formation. In Colossians 1, Paul links stopping bad behavior with Jesus's dying and starting good behavior with his rising:

> If then you have been *raised with Christ, seek the things that are above*, where Christ is, seated at the right hand of God. *Set your minds on things that are above*, not on things that are on earth. *For you have died*, and your life is hidden with Christ in God. . . . *Put to death* therefore what is earthly in you: sexual immorality, impurity, passion, evil desire, and covetousness, which is idolatry. (Col. 3:1–3, 5)

The twofold combination of stopping/dying and starting/rising touches on the two sides of goodness. Think of dieting: I need to stop eating lasagna and start eating salads. I can't merely add the positive (salad) to the negative (lasagna). I've got to *get rid* of the negative and *put on* something positive.[3] Most Philadelphians have not figured this out. It's not uncommon to see someone eating a Philly cheesesteak with a Diet Coke, thinking a 0-calorie Coke cancels out a 1300-calorie cheesesteak!

But Paul isn't talking about abstract goodness or mere self-improvement, like dieting. By embedding our obedience in the J-Curve, he wants to imprint us with the image of Jesus. His image drives Paul's pristine visions of goodness that make the pagan Stoic visions of goodness pale in comparison. Paul's vision of *the good* reflects the sheer, unbelievable beauty of Jesus. The ongoing process of dying and rising with Christ imprints his image on us:

> You have put off the old self with its practices and have put on the new self, *which is being renewed in knowledge after the image of its creator.* (Col. 3:9b–10)

Participating in the J-Curve creates a new person who looks like Jesus.

Then, in the next breath, Paul gives us another stunning vision of *the good*—the beauty of Jesus imprinted on us, the end game of the Christian life. We need new clothing for our new selves:

> Put on then, as God's chosen ones, holy and beloved, compassionate hearts, kindness, humility, meekness, and patience, bearing with one another and, if one has a complaint against another, forgiving each other; as the Lord has forgiven you, so you also must forgive. And above all these put on love, which binds everything together in perfect harmony. (Col. 3:12–14)

Paul's opening phrase, we are "God's chosen ones, holy and beloved," applies justification by faith to our identity as sons and daughters of God. Then comes the "other half of Paul"—his vision of *the*

---

3. This helpful insight comes from Jay Adams, *Competent to Counsel* (Phillipsburg, NJ: Presbyterian and Reformed, 1971), 151.

good, an overflowing effervescent cascade of love. Both visions together allow us to flourish in "a crooked and twisted generation."

Of course, beauty formation "comes from the Lord, who is the Spirit." The upward move of the J-Curve, powered by the Spirit, shapes us into the image of Jesus.

> And we all, with unveiled face, beholding the glory of the Lord, are being transformed into the same image from one degree of glory to another. *For this comes from the Lord who is the Spirit.* (2 Cor. 3:18)

Nothing could be more alien to *feelism* than Paul's vision of *the good* here. *Feelism*, with its commitment to the care and revelation of the authentic self, recoils from the work of love because it focuses on its own feelings, its own reaction to its environment. It feels the chains, the jealous evangelists, and the lack of freedom that Paul experienced in prison. So Paul's command to put on "compassionate hearts, kindness, humility, meekness, and patience" seems impossible because you feel none of those things. All your compassion is turned inward into self-pity. Paul's vision exposes the utter bankruptcy of *feelism*. It has no goal, no narrative structure, no vision of *the good* outside of itself. It's just me on steroids.

But the I-beam structure allows Paul to build a skyscraper of love that—unlike *feelism's* house of straw—can hold tremendous weight. Paul fearlessly hangs our obedience on the J-Curve. The Christ story calls for and supports extraordinary Christ formation. Dying with Jesus eliminates the negative; rising with him embraces the positive. In our pilgrimage, the J-Curve is our map, the application passages describe our goal, Paul's stories are our travelogue, and the Spirit is our guide. The J-Curve makes for a complete pilgrim!

Participating in the J-Curve creates a
new person who looks like Jesus.

25

Resurrection Realism

The J-Curve Protects Us from Cynicism

Joy permeates Paul. In fact, he is so joyful, we might be inclined to think he's an optimist, one of those incorrigibly happy people who live in the borderland of denial.

Some Christians have made Paul's incessant rejoicing into a new law that says we should always be rejoicing. There's no room for discouragement or fear. Some spread their legalistic cheer by blithely encouraging depressed people to rejoice. That's not Paul. He does tell the Philippians to "rejoice always" (Phil. 4:4), but he describes a time when he "despaired of life itself" (2 Cor. 1:8). When so many abandon him as he nears his final J-Curve, his martyrdom (2 Tim. 4:9–17), we can feel his discouragement.

Mere optimism is blind to the dark side of life and thus collapses in the face of evil. That's not Paul. He talks openly about his chains and other people's jealousy of him.

Paul is neither an optimist nor a pessimist—he's a realist. He sees a wider reality, a "deeper magic"—the resurrection of Jesus the Messiah from the dead. Jesus's resurrection by the Spirit dwarfs everything else.[1] It's the elephant in the room, the overwhelming truth all other truths bend toward.

---

1. "Deeper magic" is what the White Witch missed in C. S. Lewis's *The Lion, the Witch and the Wardrobe* (New York: HarperCollins, 2008), 156.

Because Paul sees all of life through this reality, his chains and others' jealousy become "light and momentary afflictions" (2 Cor. 4:17). Any thought of self-pity or a victim narrative dies in light of this reality. The Spirit re-created Jesus's lifeless body (past); he will re-create our lifeless bodies (future); and he is re-creating our lifeless situations (present). Because the Spirit continually makes resurrection a present reality for Paul, he overflows with joy.

> What then? Only that in every way, whether in pretense or in truth, Christ is proclaimed, and *in that I rejoice. Yes, and I will rejoice.* (Phil. 1:18)

In the next breath, Paul explains why he is rejoicing: "for I know that through your prayers and the help of the Spirit of Jesus Christ this will turn out for my deliverance" (v. 19). As we saw, the Spirit is the secret to the resurrection—he makes the J go up. "Through your prayers" is not pious jargon. Not only does the Spirit transform our prayers, but prayer activates the Spirit, creating real-time resurrections. Paul doesn't just die daily, but he rises daily. That is the stuff of joy.

The Spirit is the secret to the resurrection—
he makes the J go up.

Paul encourages the Philippians to pray for him by telling them that "it is my eager expectation and hope that I will not be at all ashamed, but that with full courage now as always Christ will be honored in my body, whether by life or by death" (v. 20). Because Paul's realism is rooted in the active, present work of the Spirit, he says elsewhere, "Hope does not put us to shame" (Rom. 5:5), or, as another translation puts it, "Hope does not disappoint us" (NRSV). He's not embarrassed by the possibility of failure, because "Christ will be honored in my body, whether by life or by death." You can't flip Paul, because his goal is not avoiding death but revealing Jesus.

The expected goals of justice (a fair trial), freedom (release from prison), and health (his body staying connected to his head!) are missing. If Paul's head is severed from his body, then Christ will be revealed as Paul follows Jesus into death. Paul's only fear is being ashamed of Jesus in front of others. That would shame him. That would be failure.

Paul's goal of the image of Christ being revealed in him shapes his values, so self-pity and self-awareness are stripped of their narrative foundation—the story of the revelation of me becomes the story of the revelation of Jesus in and through me. Paul's hopeful way of looking at life is not rooted in an inherent optimism, but in the ongoing resurrection work of the Spirit that results in Christ being revealed through him.

A Brief History of Optimism

We are watching how Paul processes life, the birth of hope. The upward part of the "J" is all about hope.

Stage 1: Paganism—Realistic Despair

Paul's seeming optimism would have stood out starkly because paganism was deeply realistic. The ancients were realists—they saw death everywhere: in nature, in their own lives, and even in nations and empires. Everyone knew the path of life was birth, growing old, and then death. Death had the final word.

Fig. 25A. Paganism

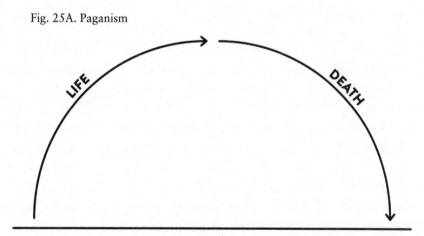

"Life sucks and then you die" describes paganism perfectly. Life seldom disappointed pagans because they expected little. The world was a dangerous place—hope was sure to disappoint—so paganism valued stability, caution, and, above all else, one's tribe. The goal was to stay with your tribe and keep your head down. A good motto for paganism would be "Don't make waves." Pagans knew that hoping led to needless disappointment and shame.

Stage 2: Christianity—Realistic Hope

Christianity replaced the realistic despair of paganism with the realistic hope of the Spirit of Jesus Christ, who is alive in our hearts and situations, bringing resurrection out of death. This hope permeated Western civilization, the civilization most affected by Christianity for the longest period of time. That spirit of optimism, based on the ongoing experience of God bringing dead things to life, meant we could do life cheerfully and boldly. It created the spirit of adventure and courage that characterizes the Western mind. Hope permeated the mind-set of Western explorers, inventors, and scientists. You don't just build castle walls, but you send ships around the world. You create telescopes to search the skies and microscopes to discover bacteria. Life becomes an adventure.

Stage 3: Secular Liberalism—Unrealistic Hope

When secular liberalism dethroned Christianity in the West in the 1800s and 1900s, it retained hope, but jettisoned the basis of hope. It threw out the kernel and kept the husk. That left us with the rising J based not on the power of the Spirit, but on the power of humanity to resurrect itself. So in *The Sound of Music*, Julie Andrews sang about having "confidence in confidence alone" and "confidence in me." Franklin Roosevelt, in his fireside chats, talked about having "faith in faith." If you remove the Spirit from the J-Curve, you are left with a hollow core. Faith, apart from a living relationship with God based on the atonement, is a passing human emotion that wilts in the face of evil and death.[2]

Stage 4: Contemporary Culture—Cynicism

The naive optimism of secular liberalism creates cynicism, because optimism rooted in the goodness of humanity collapses. Left to

---

2. This insight comes from my dad, Jack Miller, and his 1970 course at Westminster Theological Seminary, "Calvinism and American Literature."

ourselves, we are not good. But in elementary school, popular culture, and the media, secularized Christian hope lingers on. That sets people up for repeated failure. Instead of preparing us for life, our culture first offers unrealistic hope and then crashes us on the rocks of human depravity.

Take the journey of a young woman, Emma, who begins life dreaming she "can be anything she wants." As a young girl, she imagines becoming a Disney princess and finding "true love." She begins her pilgrimage by auditioning with multiple princes in high school, and in her twenties, she moves in with several boyfriends. She hopes the offer of sex will draw a young man to commit to her, but all she finds are multiple sex partners—no lovers; lots of "buds," but no men.

By her early thirties, Emma's dreams are dying. Fear and insecurity have replaced what she now realizes was an empty hope. Disney betrayed her. She has experienced the grittiness of life. So she begins to shut down emotionally. She has her own little tribe of friends, but many of them feel the same as she does. She's come full circle and entered the despair of ancient paganism, but because she was offered a dream as a child, she feels betrayed. Her life is a reverse J-Curve—she began with hope and is ending with death. She's not just discouraged; she's cynical. Hope has died. It would have been easier not to have hoped.

Emma's reverse J-Curve is shown in Figure 25B below (p. 204).

Emma's life goal from childhood was a tantalizing combination of beauty and relationship. Like Paul, her goal shaped her values. She freely offered her beauty along with sexual intimacy, because it offered a sure path to a lifelong relationship—or so she hoped. She never consciously chose this goal; she just inhaled it from her culture. Yet she is no victim. Her life goal is focused on herself and her pleasures.

So how do we love Emma? We take the downward path of the J-Curve and, like Jesus, enter her world, care for her, and love her. I love to befriend the Emmas of this world, to get to know them in the midst of their dying, to help and encourage them, and to point them to a hope that does not disappoint.

Paul's resurrection *realism* avoids the depression of *pessimism* and the denial of *optimism*. A resurrection lens allows us to live truly victorious lives that can look any enemy in the face—cancer, slander, or depression. Jesus's past resurrection means we experience present real-time resurrections as we wait for the future *big one*, when all creation will be resurrected.

> A resurrection lens allows us to live truly victorious lives that can look any enemy in the face—cancer, slander, or depression.

Fig. 25B. A Modern Pilgrimage

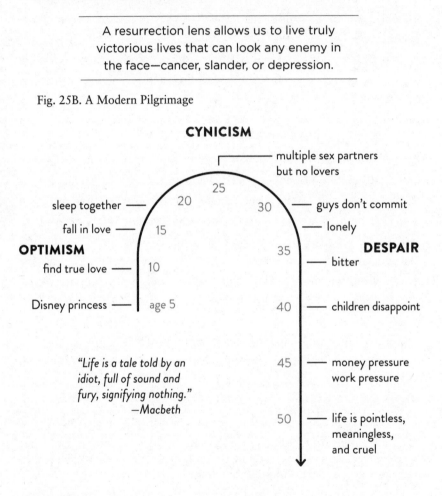

CYNICISM

multiple sex partners but no lovers

sleep together — 20   25   30 — guys don't commit

fall in love — 15   — lonely

OPTIMISM   35   DESPAIR

find true love — 10   — bitter

Disney princess — age 5   40   — children disappoint

"Life is a tale told by an idiot, full of sound and fury, signifying nothing."
—*Macbeth*   45   — money pressure work pressure

50   — life is pointless, meaningless, and cruel

26

Delaying Resurrection for Love

Saying No to Good Desire

After Paul updates the Philippians on his situation, he contemplates two possible outcomes from his trial:

> For to me to live is Christ, and to die is gain. If I am to live in the flesh, that means fruitful labor for me. Yet which I shall choose I cannot tell. I am hard pressed between the two. My desire is to depart and be with Christ, for that is far better. (Phil. 1:21–23)

Paul is deliberating between two possible resurrections: (1) life and freedom or (2) death by execution that will lead him to heaven. Each option is a J-Curve. Paul's current "death" (prison) could lead to either of these resurrections. If Paul chooses this life, his resurrection will be "fruitful labor" for the church. If he chooses the next life, death will allow him to "depart and be with Christ."

Here's a paraphrase of Paul's slogan, "For to me to live is Christ, and to die is gain":

> *For to me to live is Christ* formed in you. If I stay alive, you will see more of Christ. *To die is gain*, because if I die, I will be with the love of my life; I will see more of Christ.

Fig. 26A. Paul's Choices

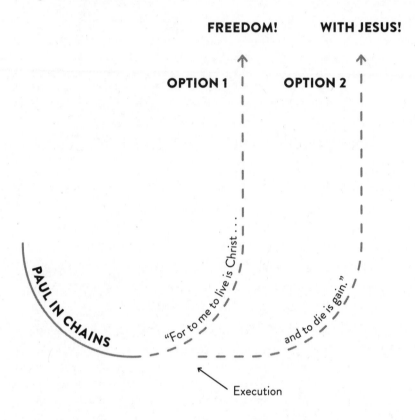

The first resurrection is for others. The second is for Paul. Neither is wrong, but the narrative of Jesus's descent shapes Paul's decision-making. Like Jesus, Paul doesn't grasp at his right to be with the Father. He leaves heaven behind. He substitutes his joy at the prospect of being with Jesus for the needs of the churches. Look at the symmetry of Paul and Jesus:

4 Steps of Love	Jesus (Phil. 2:6-8)	Paul (Phil. 1:23)
1. My Right	He [who] was in the form of God,	My desire is to depart and be with Christ. . . .
2. My Choice	did not count equality with God a thing to be grasped	But to remain in the flesh is more necessary on your account.

4 Steps of Love	Jesus (Phil. 2:6–8)	Paul (Phil. 1:23)
3. My Love	*but emptied himself, by taking the form of a slave . . .*	Once released, Paul endures in love.
4. My Cost	*becoming obedient to the point of death, even death on a cross.*	He delays the inexpressible pleasure of being in the presence of Jesus.

At first glance, "for to me to live is Christ, and to die is gain" seems like two equal options, but remaining alive is death for Paul, while death by execution is life. Paul is dying to die!

His love for Jesus—for the person—colors Paul's life goals. Jesus's enthronement, his physical presence in heaven, is as real for Paul as the book you are holding. He longs "to depart and be with Christ, for that is far better." A translation that captures the Greek is "far, far better" or "by far the best."[1] Paul's overwhelming desire is to go to heaven and be with Jesus, where he will finally be in complete, unfiltered union with Christ, the love of his life. Paul wants to go home.

While Paul can't "choose death," he can, like Jesus at his trial, choose to be silent. He is "hard pressed" between these two choices. Luke uses the same word that is translated as "hard pressed" when he describes Jesus's anxiety as he awaits his death (Luke 12:50). One scholar says that Paul is torn "like a traveler on a narrow road with walls of rock on both sides, unable to turn either way."[2]

In this battle between the two great loves of Paul's life, the church wins:

> But to remain in the flesh is more necessary on your account. Convinced of this, I know that I will remain and continue with you all, for your progress and joy in the faith. (Phil. 1:24–25)

Paul dies for the Philippians' rising. "So death is at work in us, but life in you" (2 Cor. 4:12) captures this idea. Paul calls this the "law of Christ"—dying to self for the sake of love.[3] He submits his

---

1. Peter T. O'Brien, *The Epistle to the Philippians*, The New International Greek Testament Commentary (Grand Rapids, MI: Eerdmans, 1991), 130–31.

2. O'Brien, *Philippians*, 129.

3. Michael J. Gorman, *Cruciformity: Paul's Narrative Spirituality of the Cross* (Grand Rapids, MI: Eerdmans, 2001), 174, makes the case that the "law of Christ" in Paul (Gal. 6:2; 1 Cor. 9:21) is the J-Curve of Phil. 2:5–11.

personal desire to the needs of the churches. He suppresses his desire to enter the unimaginable pleasure of being united with Jesus forever. Love trumps desire. Love shapes the dying side of the J-Curve; it also shapes the rising side.

Love shapes the dying side of the J-Curve;
it also shapes the rising side.

In contrast, our modern world merges desire and love. After falling in love, we desire intimacy, so we have sex. But merging desire with love kills intimacy, because in any close relationship, we are called to suppress personal desire for the sake of love.

The narrative of the manger, the cross, and the empty tomb defines Paul's life. He preaches a gospel of substitutionary love and lives a life of substitutionary love. The message and the man are identical. That's authenticity at its best.

Spirit-Led Wisdom in Decisions

What's fascinating is *how* Paul makes this decision. You'd expect that with all his visions, the Spirit would lead him the way I've heard people say the Lord led them to get married (to someone they barely knew) or to get divorced (because the feelings were gone). They mask their self-will with God talk, taking God's name in vain (the Third Commandment).

But Paul, who made an actual journey to heaven, shapes his decision-making on the model of Jesus's death. Dying with Christ for the sake of love trumps his own desires and provides a map out of the maze of his personal feelings.

Paul is relatively certain he will be released from prison (Phil. 1:25), but later he qualifies that, saying that he will send Timothy "as soon as I see how it will go with me" (2:23). Paul is cautious in resurrection, waiting for the story to unfold, not presuming he knows the shape of the story.

We can try to avoid death by claiming to know the shape of the resurrection. When our hoped-for resurrection fails us, we can turn our anger on God, even though the problem is our own self-will. Things didn't turn out as we wanted.

It's not us but the Spirit of Jesus that shapes our resurrections. If my tribe of Presbyterians can be overly cautious, not expecting or anticipating resurrection, Pentecostals face the opposite danger of at times seeing resurrection under every bush. Both can kill the work of the Spirit: the Presbyterians through unbelief, the Pentecostals through self-will. We both need the Spirit. The Spirit's best, clearest work is to lead us into a life of dying love. That's easy to discern but impossible to do unless the Spirit breathes the life of Jesus into us.

> The Spirit's best, clearest work is to lead us into a life of dying love.

Affirming Desire

In Paul's first two prison stories (chap. 23), he's in a *suffering* J-Curve— evil comes at him from the outside. He doesn't chose suffering; it chooses him. Now, as he grapples with either life or death, he chooses suffering in this life out of love for the church. It's a *love* J-Curve. In the table below, Paul says yes to option 1. His love for the church trumps his personal desire.

Two Possible Scenarios	Paul's Desire	Who Gets Resurrection?
1. Staying alive for the church	For the church to look like Jesus	The church
2. Execution leading to heaven	To die and be with Jesus	Paul

Notice that Paul sees option 2 (doing something for himself) as a legitimate choice. Caring for his own desires is not wrong. We can tell that because he agonizes over this decision. That is, even with all his wisdom, what he should do isn't instantly clear to him. He's no Buddhist or Stoic suppressing desire; he's alive to good choices that will benefit him. In his missionary journeys, whenever he's beaten, he chooses something good for himself by fleeing. He wisely chooses safety. He doesn't seek suffering. He works to avoid it.

I say this cautiously because our culture is obsessed with materialism and hedonism; "doing something for ourselves" is almost a religion. But we can go in the opposite direction and suppress all desire. We saw in Francis of Assisi and Mother Teresa the danger of pursuing suffering for its own sake. "Love trumps desire" does not mean that all desire is bad. In other words, in resurrection, God gives us good gifts—life, friendship, and joy.

Paul closes these three stories by appealing to the Philippians to enter a life of dying love:

> For it has been granted to you that for the sake of Christ you should not only believe in him but also suffer for his sake. (1:29)

That's Paul's central message to the Philippians: "Don't just believe the gospel, but enter this life of suffering love that I'm modeling for you." The Philippians don't need to believe the gospel more—as important as that is. They need to become like the gospel. The church today needs to do the same—to enter into the dying and rising of Jesus in everyday life.

Finding Hope in the Patterns of the Resurrection

In closing, let's reflect on two areas of resurrection: me and you. You see, Jesus's resurrection (the template for our resurrections) was for him (he was dead) and for us (we were dead in our sins). We'll look at four different ways we can be resurrected: our *spirits* (emotions), our *seeing* (perceptions), our *obedience* (morals), and our *situation* (environment).

The first category is me—how I participate now in Christ's resurrection:

1. My *spirit* is resurrected; joy fills my heart. This is the present emotional state of feeling Christ's resurrection now. Each of us can carry Easter in our hearts. This resurrection is the reset button that really works. It's often the earliest touch of the *Spirit*, who brings resurrection.

2. My *seeing* is resurrected; I see God use dying to produce rising. Paul sees that his imprisonment opens more doors to the gospel.

3. My *obedience* is resurrected; the dying of repentance produces new holiness in me. We've seen this in Joni, when she receives her wheelchair as a gift, and in Paul, when he receives his thorn in the flesh. This is the upside of both the *repentance* and the *suffering* J-Curve.

4. My *situation* is resurrected. Paul is still in prison. His situation hasn't been resurrected. He still has his thorn in the flesh. And Joni is still in a wheelchair. Nevertheless, resurrection, actual deliverance from pain, is what God promises and we all long for. This longing is good.

Second, here's how resurrection affects you. The dominant feature of this category is the central pattern of the gospel: my dying is for your rising. As Paul says, "So death is at work in us, but life in you" (2 Cor. 4:12).

1. Your *spirit* is resurrected. My discomfort leads to your comfort.

2. Your *seeing* is resurrected. When I *embody Christ* in my dying and rising, you get a template for how to live your life, which encourages you (2 Cor. 1:3–7).[4]

3. Your *obedience* is resurrected. That's the point of Colossians 3 and Romans 8.

4. Your *situation* is resurrected. My dying delivers you from a *problem.* So my slight discomfort in checking on Ed the sheep or in taking Kim to Florida relieves Jill's stress.

These four ways of being resurrected interact in multiple ways. For example, if my spirit is resurrected and I'm filled with joy, that lets me see my situation differently. Likewise, if I obey in a new way, that fills me with joy and lets me see life differently. Resurrection goes viral.

---

4. Christ's dying and rising are intimately linked in Paul. Even as I focus on rising here, notice that dying is closely linked. John Calvin reflects, "So then, let us remember that whenever mention is made of his death alone, we are to understand at the same time what belongs to his resurrection. Also, the same synecdoche applies to the word 'resurrection': whenever it is mentioned separately from death, we are to understand it as including what has to do especially with his death." *Institutes of the Christian Religion*, ed. John T. McNeill, trans. Ford Lewis Battles, The Library of Christian Classics, vols. 20–21 (Philadelphia: Westminster, 1960), 521.

Now let's mix in dying as well. My honesty to you (dying) might lead to new obedience in you (rising), which then transforms your spirit (rising). As we saw, Paul's dying (choosing not to go to heaven) leads to the church's rising.

To recap, sometimes resurrection is for me. Sometimes it's for you. In either case, our resurrections are based on and re-enact Jesus's resurrection. He is the vanguard, or, to use Paul's language, the "first-fruits" (1 Cor. 15:20). We experience his resurrection now as his Spirit inhabits our *spirits*, helping us to see all of life through a resurrection lens. Because it's his resurrection that we are participating in, we can enjoy resurrection now as we wait for the final resurrection of our bodies along with all of creation. Resurrection is the final word.

27

Becoming Human Again

The Emotional Life of the J-Curve

For Paul, Jesus's example isn't enough. For Jesus to be formed in us, we need to see *little Jesuses* who embody his story. We need to see Jesus in 3D. A story gives us a richer view. We "catch" what it means to be fully human again. So in this chapter, we're going to look at what dying and rising look like embodied in a team.

In Philippians 2, Paul tells a story of Timothy and Epaphroditus, who embody the descent of love, but first he refers to his unfinished J-Curve—the possibility of his own martyrdom:

> Even if I am to be poured out as a drink offering upon the *sacrificial offering of your faith*, I am glad and rejoice with you all. Likewise you also should be glad and rejoice with me. (vv. 17–18)

He wants the Philippians to know he doesn't control his J-Curve story. None of us do. Like an Old Testament drink offering of wine, Paul might be poured out on the sacrifice of the Philippians' faith. Paul uses sacrificial language to connect the possibility of his death with the sacrificial service of the Philippians, that is, their faith.[1] Paul's

1. See F. F. Bruce, *Philippians* (Peabody, MA; Hendrickson, 1983), 63–65, 88, and Peter T. O'Brien, *The Epistle to the Philippians*, The New International Greek Testament Commentary

J-Curve will enhance their J-Curve. Jesus uses the same imagery of being poured out as a drink offering when he describes his death at the Last Supper, saying, "This cup that is poured out for you is the new covenant in my blood" (Luke 22:20).

For the next 250 years, thousands of martyrs would *pour out* their lives on the *sacrifice of the church's faith*. Martyrs were the celebrities of the early church.

Next, Paul turns his attention to two mini-celebrities who live a life of dying/resurrection love. Since he mentions them here, instead of at the end of his letter, he clearly wants the Philippians to look at them.

Almost Martyrs

Paul's story of his two coworkers is filled with tantalizing details, but we are left in the dark as to what actually happened. So you don't get lost in the story, I've written this imaginary, but historically accurate, scenario:

Since a fair trial is impossible in Judea, Paul uses his Roman citizenship to appeal to Caesar. After a shipwreck, Paul, along with Luke and Aristarchus, arrives in Rome in March, AD 60. Paul learns he needs a large sum of money to pay a lawyer to represent him before Caesar because a delegation from the Sanhedrin has arrived from Jerusalem to slander him. Without a lawyer, Paul faces execution as a "troublemaker."

Timothy, Paul's right-hand man, arrives in Rome in May to help Paul. This allows Aristarchus to return to Greece with news of their deliverance, as well as Paul's critical need for money. The Philippians immediately take a generous collection and send it to Rome with Epaphroditus (one of their leaders) and Aristarchus.

During their three-week journey, Epaphroditus becomes violently sick with the "Roman fever" (malaria), which is particularly bad in the summer. He refuses Aristarchus's advice to rest and instead sends a message back to Philippi by an eastbound traveler while they press on to Rome. Epaphroditus knows that without this gift, Paul could die.

(Grand Rapids, MI: Eerdmans, 1991), 272, 306, who translates v. 17, "Yes, even if my life is to be poured out as a drink-offering in addition to your sacrificial service—that is, your faith—I am glad and rejoice with all of you."

Epaphroditus arrives in Rome near death, and Paul and his team nurse him back to health. Epaphroditus's sacrifice moves Paul deeply. The gift allows Paul's case to be heard in court and silences Paul's internal debate about whether he should even bother defending himself.

Meanwhile, word gets back to Philippi that Epaphroditus is near death, and the Philippians fear he may have died on the way to Rome. To make matters worse, two of the prominent women, Euodia and Syntyche, have been quarreling, paralyzing the whole congregation.

The Philippians describe their plight in a letter to Paul sent via one of Lydia's merchant ships. When the letter arrives, Paul and his team are distraught because of the Philippians' problems. Timothy is especially eager to go to help the Philippians.

Paul dictates his letter to the Philippians, which Epaphroditus carries back via Lydia's ship. Paul would love to send Timothy as well, but prisoners are totally dependent on their friends. Timothy is crucial for his survival. Paul tells the Philippians that as soon as he knows how his case will go, he will release Timothy. Paul will follow shortly thereafter.

Here's Paul's actual story:

I hope in the Lord Jesus to send Timothy to you soon, so that *I too may be cheered* by news of you. For I have no one like him, who will be genuinely concerned for your welfare. For they all seek their own interests, not those of Jesus Christ. But you know Timothy's proven worth, how as a son with a father he has worked like a slave with me in the gospel. I hope therefore to send him just as soon as I see how it will go with me, and I trust in the Lord that shortly I myself will come also.

I have thought it necessary to send to you Epaphroditus my brother and fellow worker and fellow soldier, and your messenger and minister to my need, for *he has been longing* for you all and has been *distressed* because you heard that he was ill. Indeed he was ill, near to death. But God had mercy on him, and not only on him but on me also, lest I should have *sorrow upon sorrow*. I am the more eager to send him, therefore, that you may *rejoice* at seeing him again, and that I may be *less anxious*. So receive him in the Lord with all *joy*, and honor such men, for he nearly died for the work of Christ, risking his life to complete what was lacking in your service to me. (Phil. 2:19–30 AT)[2]

Paul holds up Timothy and Epaphroditus as Christ bearers who model the dying and rising of Jesus (Phil. 2:5–9). Timothy is "genuinely concerned for your welfare"; he doesn't seek his own interests. As Jesus took the form of a slave, so Timothy has "worked like a slave" with Paul for the gospel. Likewise, Epaphroditus nearly died for the work of Christ, risking his life for Paul. Both embody a dying love. Paul celebrates how these Christ bearers reflect the other-centeredness of Christ.

The Passions of Dying and Rising

By telling a story, Paul shows us how dying and rising with Jesus shapes his, Epaphroditus's, and Timothy's emotions. Christlikeness, the art of looking like Jesus, doesn't flatten you. Instead, it makes you come alive as a person. Look at the range of emotions expressed in this story.

First, Paul begins with joy. As he contemplates being "poured out as a drink offering," he says, "I am glad and rejoice with you all" (Phil. 2:17). He juxtaposes the sadness of his possible death with the joy of resurrection, and then invites the Philippians to join him in joy: "Likewise you also should be glad and rejoice with me" (v. 18). Dying and rising, sadness and joy, are joined at the hip.

Christlikeness, the art of looking like Jesus, doesn't flatten you. Instead, it makes you come alive as a person.

Second, Paul wants to send Timothy to the church at Philippi "so that I too may be cheered by news of you" (v. 19). Paul trusts Timothy, a proven Christ bearer, to facilitate reconciliation in the Philippian church, which in turn will cheer Paul. Paul goes on to say that when Epaphroditus arrives in Philippi, he (Paul) will be "less anxious" (v. 28). Paul's emotions rise and fall on good or bad

---

2. Following O'Brien, I've substituted "worked like a slave" for "served." See O'Brien, *Philippians*, 315.

news. The path of Christ doesn't lift these Christ bearers above life; it sweeps them into life's currents, fully alive to both their exterior world and their interior response. They don't manage their emotions; their emotions reflect their full and honest participation in Jesus's life. Joy is not a rule. Like sadness, it reflects Paul's grip on reality.

Third, Paul affirms other people's emotions. Epaphroditus "has been longing for you all and has been distressed because you heard that he was ill" (v. 26). When Epaphroditus hears that people are distressed over him, he feels distress. The word *distress* here is the same word used to describe Jesus's feelings at Gethsemane, the anxiety that follows great shock.[3] Paul and Epaphroditus feel stress because they've dared to love. As C. S. Lewis says, if you don't want to feel sad, then don't love anything, not even a dog.[4]

Fourth, when God healed Epaphroditus, Paul realized God was delivering him (Paul) from "sorrow upon sorrow" (v. 27). Epaphroditus's death on top of his imprisonment and the Philippians' struggles would have been sorrow upon sorrow. Paul is fully alive to the good desire to avoid deep grief.

Fifth, Paul works so that others may experience joy. Speaking of Epaphroditus, he says, "I am the more eager to send him, therefore, that you may rejoice at seeing him again" (v. 28). He sends Epaphroditus on a risky, twenty-day journey just so the church can rejoice. Paul facilitates resurrection. He works to create hope.

Many people fear that if they become more Christlike, they will become stilted as a person; but no, these three men become more human, more in tune with life.

A Jesus Community at Work

What fuels all this passion? We are watching a real-life, first-century Jesus community at work. It's a virtual community—the Philippians and these three men are separated by a twenty-day journey—yet everyone incarnates with everyone else. They descend into one another's lives, their love weaving a seven-step tapestry:

---

3. O'Brien, *Philippians*, 334. Cf. Matt. 26:37; Mark 14:33.
4. C. S. Lewis, *The Four Loves* (New York: Harcourt, Brace & Company, 1988), 121.

1. The Philippians incarnate with Paul by sending Epaphroditus with a gift.
2. Epaphroditus incarnates with Paul by risking his life.
3. When the Philippians hear of Epaphroditus's illness, they incarnate with him in their anxiety.
4. Then Epaphroditus incarnates with the Philippians' anxiety.
5. Timothy responds by incarnating with the Philippians.
6. Then Paul incarnates with Epaphroditus and the Philippians in their anxiety.
7. Paul plans to send Epaphroditus and Timothy later to encourage the Philippians and increase his own joy.

Paul, Epaphroditus, and Timothy give us a living, breathing example of what Jesus looks like embodied—an entire community swept up in a symphony of love. In every sense of the word, they are both *in* Christ and *in* one another.

The J-Curve lies at the heart of this virtual community. We have already seen that the key to oneness, to unity (Phil. 2:1–4), is reenacting the dying life of Jesus (vv. 5–8). Now we visualize that truth in a cascade of love: Paul suffers for the gospel in prison → the Philippians join him in his suffering with their gift of money and Epaphroditus → Epaphroditus almost dies for Paul → the Philippians experience anxiety because of their love for Epaphroditus → he responds with anxiety over their suffering.

Figure 27A below captures the multiple ways this virtual community is bound together in love. Each arrow represents "love."

Notice the sheer emotional richness of this passage: grief, sadness, anxiety, stress, longing, and joy. Our flesh, which Calvin called a "perpetual factory of idols," creates idols out of emotional states.[5] An older, fundamentalist Christianity tended to deny emotions, particularly sadness and grief, and made joy absolute, demanding that others have joy, making "Rejoice in the Lord always" (Phil. 4:4) into a law. Not Paul. He experiences anxiety. Love feels.

On the other hand, a newer, therapeutic Christianity, influenced by *feelism*, exalts emotions, especially grief. Because emotional states are

---

5. John Calvin, *Institutes of the Christian Religion*, ed. John T. McNeill, trans. Ford Lewis Battles, The Library of Christian Classics, vols. 20–21 (Philadelphia: Westminster, 1960), 1.11.8.

sacred, therapeutic Christianity cringes at Paul's command to "Rejoice in the Lord always." Both the fundamentalist and the psychologist can depersonalize you, creating narrow rules that keep love from flourishing. As our world gets crazier, our need to see love embodied has never been greater.

Fig. 27A. A Community Bound by Love

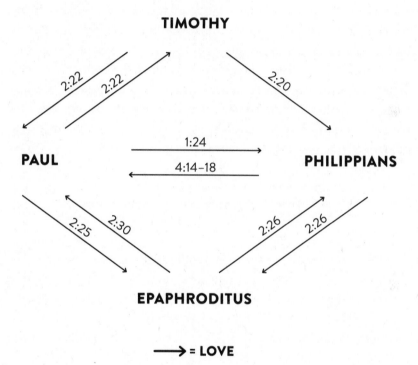

Modern Church "Characters"

Paul's way of being human would not make sense to our two characters, the manager and the therapist. Every culture, according to the philosopher Alisdair MacIntyre, embodies its morality not only in a narrative, but also in characters.[6] Both the manager and the therapist focus not on the goals of Christlikeness and Christ glorification, but on a good, safe process. They focus on reducing

---

6. Alasdair MacIntyre, *After Virtue: A Study in Moral Theory*, 3rd ed. (Notre Dame, IN: University of Notre Dame Press, 2007), 30.

stress and error—thus, our modern obsession with safety and a mistakefree life.

The therapist would question the Philippians' initial gift to Paul: "Given how frequently Paul is in prison, aren't you enabling him?" The manager would question Epaphroditus's decision to push on in the midst of illness; he would be bothered by the tremendous waste of resources involved in sending Epaphroditus back home just to encourage the Philippians. What kind of metric is a twenty-day trip just to encourage someone? The therapist would be concerned about the unnecessary anxiety caused by people worrying about things they can't control. Paul worries about Epaphroditus; the Philippians worry about Epaphroditus; and Epaphroditus worries about the Philippians. "This community clearly has significant issues with boundaries," the therapist thinks. Blah, blah, blah. I get weary of the blather of our modern characters. These guys are community killers.

Both the manager and the therapist focus not on the goals of Christlikeness and Christ glorification, but on a good, safe process.

The character that previously embodied Christlikeness for the church was the missionary. I remember as a boy sitting at our dining room table in California listening to Bruce Hunt, a missionary to Korea, tell why he didn't flee to safety and endured prison when the Japanese invaded Korea in World War II. He said, "I couldn't tell them to endure in suffering and then leave."

Now, in a broad spectrum across the church, missions conferences are dying. Celebrating Christlikeness is either dead or dying in most evangelical churches. Instead, the American church honors these two characters:

The celebrity pastor. Fame is not a sin; it's a responsibility. Many famous pastors reflect a genuine Christlikeness, but I find them to be an exception. Celebrity culture dominates the church. One famous pastor illustrated his leadership style at a pastors' conference by telling how he fixed a glitch in the media on Sunday morning. Between services, he discovered who'd made the mistake and fired the person on the spot. So what's the narrative? A celebrity pastor ends the career of a lowly tech person because the tech ever so slightly pulled the pastor down the Failure-Boasting Chart. Instead of embodying the dying of Christ, this celebrity pastor killed this tech's career.

The worship leader. I love contemporary worship, but at times, worship leaders focus on performance. At one church, prospective worship leaders line up to lead from the front, and yet the church struggles to get someone to lead worship in a Sunday school class for people affected by disabilities. The teachers in that class limp along playing YouTube worship videos. Disabilities provide no path to human glory—the audience is small, hidden, and off key, but it is in touch with heaven.

Celebrating Christlikeness is either dead or dying in most evangelical churches.

Honoring Modern Christ Bearers

It's not enough to give someone a moral program, even one as exalted as the narrative of Christ's dying and rising. Dying and rising must be embodied. That's why Paul tells the Philippians, "Honor such men" (Phil. 2:29)—hold them up, talk about them, watch them.

Christ bearers provide conduits to the life of Jesus. That's why Jill and I love going to Joni Camp every year—to see the narrative of Jesus's life in person. There's Ralph and Isabelle, who care for their beautiful daughter, Cindy, who is crippled with cerebral palsy. They are getting up in years and need to be thinking about Cindy's long-term care after they are gone, but they can't bear to part from their daughter. When I mentioned this to Jill, she said, "Could you leave Kim?" I said, "Of course not." So Ralph and Isabelle head into an unknown future with a dying love.

There's feisty Carren and her faithful son, Gerard, who gave up a career to move home to help his mom with his brother Luke, who's wheelchair-bound with severe cerebral palsy. Carren's husband walked away when things got tough. Last summer, I watched her and Gerard struggle to feed Luke when his feeding tube got blocked. Carren glowers at me every time I smile at her as I walk by her table; "Here comes trouble," she says.

Jill and I are in awe of Roger and Jane, who adopted three severely disabled adults: Dusty, a wannabe policeman who has been working me to buy him another US Marshall badge (he has dozens); Felicia, who has struggled with relating—and yet, Roger loves her to death; and Timmy, who wears large earphones because of his autism. Although Roger has done well in his air-conditioning business, he and Jane did not grasp at the privilege of wealth, but lowered themselves in love.

One of the difficulties of honoring Christ bearers is that they are often exhausted—or just plain busy at the work of love. They aren't showy people, but they are good at showing up for life. Like Jesus, their glory is hidden. Ralph and Isabelle, Carren and Gerard, and Roger and Jane are gifts to the church. Let's honor people like them!

28

The Art of J-Curve Living

Dying and Rising in Twenty-Four Hours

When you are learning a trade, such as house painting or marketing, there comes a point when you stop attending classes and begin an apprenticeship, where you watch an actual master at work. There at the feet of the master, you pick up little things you'd never learn in a book. Now, let's watch Paul, the master lover, through the eyes of Luke, his traveling companion, to see what we can learn about inhabiting the life of Jesus. We aren't hunting for one big insight, but for the small insights that come from watching an experienced master in the art of J-Curve living.

Dying in Philippi

In one remarkable twenty-four-hour period during Paul's first visit to Philippi, Paul and Silas re-enact the dying and rising of Jesus.[1] When Paul arrives, he finds the Jewish place of prayer and shares the gospel with a God-fearing businesswoman named Lydia, who becomes a believer along with the rest of her household. Then trouble starts:

---

1. Paul's first visit was in AD 50. The letter to the Philippians was written about AD 62, assuming it was written from Rome.

As we were going to the place of prayer, we were met by a slave girl who had a spirit of divination and brought her owners much gain by fortune-telling. She followed Paul and us, crying out, "These men are servants of the Most High God, who proclaim to you the way of salvation." And this she kept doing for many days. Paul, having become greatly annoyed, turned and said to the spirit, "I command you in the name of Jesus Christ to come out of her." And it came out that very hour. (Acts 16:16–18)

So far, so good. To understand what happens next, know that Philippi was a Roman colony, proud of its Roman heritage. For Romans—and pagans in general—public order was everything. Romans valued stability the way Americans value freedom. In a world teetering on the brink of invasion, disease, and famine, that made sense. In addition, the Emperor Claudius had expelled the Jews from the city of Rome the year before because of fights over a man named Crestus.[2] Most scholars think this name means "Christ." So Jewish identity was at a low point in the empire. All these factors are in play as trouble starts:

But when her owners saw that their hope of gain was gone, they seized Paul and Silas and dragged them into the marketplace before the rulers. And when they had brought them to the magistrates, they said, "These men are Jews, and they are disturbing our city. They advocate customs that are not lawful for us as Romans to accept or practice." The crowd joined in attacking them, and the magistrates tore the garments off them and gave orders to beat them with rods. And when they had inflicted many blows upon them, they threw them into prison, ordering the jailer to keep them safely. Having received this order, he put them into the inner prison and fastened their feet in the stocks. (Acts 16:19–24)

Look how skillfully these owners weave a false narrative, saying, in effect, "These despised Jews are disrupting our public order and bringing in new, non-Roman ideas." The real narrative? Evil men have

---

2. See Acts 18:2 and Seutonius (AD 69–122), *The Lives of the Twelve Caesars: Volume II*, trans. J. C. Rolfe, Loeb Classical Library 38 (Cambridge, MA: Harvard University Press, 1914), 51.

enslaved and abused a young woman for money. When Paul disrupts their corrupt system, they retaliate. Paul and Silas enter into a *fellowship of his sufferings* as they are seized, dragged, attacked, stripped, beaten, and finally thrown into prison, where stocks spread their feet apart to extend the pain.

At first glance, Paul's silence over his Roman citizenship is puzzling. Several times in his life, he willingly plays his Roman citizenship card. The reason is the false narrative. This is a highly charged and violent scene. People's passions are inflamed. In the crowd's mind, Paul and Silas have trampled on the Roman flag. This pro-Roman narrative controls the public mind. Nothing Paul can say will change the false narrative. If he plays his Roman card, he will save his skin, but the false narrative will oppress the budding church. It will be "that church that disrupts Roman order and then uses Roman citizenship to escape." So Paul takes a beating for the sake of the church.[3]

Fig. 28A. Paul at Philippi

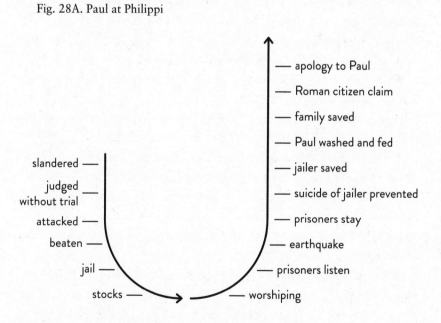

3. Insight from Eckhard J. Schnabel, *Acts*, Zondervan Exegetical Commentary on the New Testament (Grand Rapids, MI: Zondervan, 2012), 687.

Rising in Philippi

Now comes resurrection:

> About midnight Paul and Silas were praying and singing hymns to
> God, and the prisoners were listening to them, and suddenly there was
> a great earthquake, so that the foundations of the prison were shaken.
> And immediately all the doors were opened, and everyone's bonds
> were unfastened. When the jailer woke and saw that the prison doors
> were open, he drew his sword and was about to kill himself, suppos-
> ing that the prisoners had escaped. But Paul cried with a loud voice,
> "Do not harm yourself, for we are all here." And the jailer called for
> lights and rushed in, and trembling with fear he fell down before Paul
> and Silas. Then he brought them out and said, "Sirs, what must I do
> to be saved?" And they said, "Believe in the Lord Jesus, and you will
> be saved, you and your household." (Acts 16:25–31)

Paul and Silas's resurrection begins in their hearts. By worshiping,
they look at their imprisonment through a resurrection lens. Worship
keeps Paul from collapsing in the face of evil. As a "resurrection guy,"
he anticipates a real-time resurrection. It's easy to put Paul's worship
into a religious category and miss that he is boasting in Jesus just like
he used to glory in the law and in himself.

By focusing on the goodness of God in the face of evil, Paul and
Silas have an effect on the other prisoners who are listening. Those
prisoners must be wondering, "Who are these strange men who aren't
cursing, but are filled with joy?" Resurrection is catchy.

Then God acts. An earthquake shatters the prison doors and loos-
ens everyone's bonds. If the prisoners escape, the jailer will have failed
in his duty and thus dishonored his name and Rome. Honor was
everything to an ancient Roman. The reason for failure will make no
difference. He gave his word, and if the prisoners escape, he will not
have kept it.

Either Paul and Silas's singing calms the prisoners or Paul urges
them to stay. In any case, he shouts to the jailer from the back of the
prison, "Do not harm yourself, for we are all here." The stunned jailer
rushes in and falls down before Paul and Silas, trembling. He must be
asking himself, "Who are these strange resurrection-men, who rejoiced

in the midst of their suffering, calmed the prisoners, and have saved my life?" Stunned, the jailer asks, "Sirs, what must I do to be saved?" Paul has completely disrupted his world. Not only has Paul saved the man's life, but he has also shown him a new kind of person, one who forgives, worships, and loves in the face of evil.

The earthquake has done more than rescue Paul. His God has spoken through it. Because of the eighteenth-century Enlightenment, we think of disasters as purely physical events. But the ancients lived in an integrated universe where the physical and spiritual worlds intertwined in a moral whole. The Roman historian Tacitus writes that immediately after the Emperor Nero's gay wedding, a fire swept through Rome (AD 64). Nero tried to blame the Christians, but the Roman elites knew that Nero had angered the gods.[4]

The earthquake exposes the false narrative of Paul and Silas as "troublemakers." The entire city knows that Paul's God has shamed their magistrates. They put him in jail, but his God has released him, justifying him. Now a new narrative takes shape: Paul and Silas are peacemakers, quieting the riot by receiving the beating, calming the prisoners with their worship, preventing a prison escape, and saving the jailer's life. They uphold Roman order. In a city of about ten thousand people, news like this travels.

Now we can understand the behavior of the two magistrates the next morning.[5] Like good bureaucrats the world over, they are in damage-control mode, hoping this whole thing ends quietly without tarnishing their image any further. Luke describes the charming scene:

> But when it was day, the magistrates sent the police, saying, "Let those men go." And the jailer reported these words to Paul, saying, "The magistrates have sent to let you go. Therefore come out now and go in peace." But Paul said to them, "They have beaten us publicly, uncondemned, men who are Roman citizens, and have thrown us into prison; and do they now throw us out secretly? No! Let them come themselves and take us out." The police reported these words to the magistrates, and they were afraid when they

---

4. Jerry Toner, *Roman Disasters* (Malden, MA: Polity Press, 2013), 112.

5. Magistrates (*stratego* in Greek; *duumviri* in Latin, meaning "two men") were two wealthy men elected by the council. Wealthy men always had a retinue of "clients" or followers.

heard that they were Roman citizens. So they came and apologized to them. (Acts 16:35–39a)

Paul's brilliant move of demanding the magistrates apologize in person displays their foolishness to the whole city and prevents them from sweeping the whole incident under the rug. These men who prided themselves on following Roman law have to publicly apologize for breaking the law. Picture the two magistrates parading through town, arrayed in their purple robes and followed by a small retinue. They apologize, red-faced, to Paul and Silas. Paul's resurrection vindicates him and his message, putting the gospel on display for everyone to see. So he writes about Jesus:

> He stripped all the spiritual tyrants in the universe of their sham authority at the Cross and marched them naked through the streets. (Col. 2:15 MESSAGE)

By accepting the death and waiting for the resurrection, Paul strengthens the young church in multiple ways:

- The false narrative of the slave owners is exposed.
- The earthquake sends the message that Paul and Silas's God is not to be trifled with.
- The jailer, his family, the slave girl, and the prisoners all have stories to tell. Since this incident is the talk of the town, the church will be honored.
- The church sees Paul and Silas demonstrate the dying and rising of Jesus.
- The three "stars" of the show cross gender (businesswoman), ethnic (jailer), and social (slave girl) barriers creating a true Jesus community.[6]

Master Artists at Work

So what do we learn from this story?

First, notice the pattern of a *love* J-Curve followed by a *suffering* J-Curve. When Paul goes after evil (freeing the girl), evil comes after

---

6. Darrell L. Bock, *Acts*, Baker Exegetical Commentary on the New Testament (Grand Rapids, MI: Baker, 2007), 536.

Paul. His willingness to take a beating comes from twin loves: love for the girl and love for the church. Like Jesus's, Paul's love is substitutionary. He substitutes his well-being for the Philippian church by not grasping at his rights of Roman citizenship to protect himself from a beating. He not only protects the church, but models for them what it looks like to participate in Jesus's life. *Love always works at two levels—caring for the person in need and embodying Jesus.* The world is watching.

Love always works at two levels—caring for the person
in need and embodying Jesus. The world is watching.

Second, observe how Paul's grip on reality shapes his behavior. The overshadowing reality for him and Silas as they lie in prison with their feet spread apart and their bodies aching is the enthronement of Jesus. So they respond to what is true and good by worshiping and praying. Focusing on Jesus's enthronement deprograms them from evil's shock value, which can leave us disoriented, dazed, and doubting. By worshiping, they seize the high ground as they participate anew in Jesus's resurrection. *You can't be passive when assaulted by evil. Satan creates a false narrative and uses that to destroy. Worshiping in the face of evil resets the false narrative.*

Third, notice that God's action alone doesn't overturn the false narrative. Paul and Silas are active in the resurrection: worshiping, calming the prisoners, and rescuing the jailer. Paul is not passive; he's fully alive to the opportunities God gives him. His resurrection lens first transforms how he reacts internally, which in turn transforms the jail.

Fourth, notice that Paul isn't by himself. He seldom goes through dying and rising alone. He almost always has a companion, and often a whole team in the J-Curve with him. Here it's Silas, although Luke and Timothy are also with him. *We die and rise in community.*

In addition, by watching Paul and Silas, we discover seven simple insights on the art of J-Curve living. These are the kinds of insights we can gain only if we are apprentices watching a master.

- If you've lost the narrative, don't fight it. You'll wear yourself out. (Paul doesn't fight the public slander.)
- Avoid shouting matches. Don't react emotionally to someone else's passion. (Paul silently receives the beating.)

- Think in love. (When Paul thinks about his total situation—"I've lost the narrative. If I save my skin, I'll hurt the church."—he "dies" for the church.)
- Sing in prison. It kills the victim narrative.
- Don't try to control either your death or your resurrection. Follow Jesus in it. (As this story is unfolding, Paul doesn't know what will happen next. He's riding the wave of the Spirit.)
- Hidden things are always revealed. It just takes time. (Paul's peacemaking slowly emerges.)
- Pursue justice if you can. (Paul does that by publicly shaming the magistrates.)

Modern False Narratives

Let's take a moment to listen to our modern characters, the therapist and the manager, as they visit Paul in jail (before the earthquake) to help him make sense of this troubling incident. The therapist probes, "Were you upset, Paul, when you cast out this demon? Should you have been working out of anxiety?" The manager has equally penetrating questions: "Why did you confront the slave girl so directly? Look at the mess it got you in. Maybe if you'd first talked to her owners, there wouldn't be such a mess. Did you pray enough about this before you cast out the demon? Are you aware that you could have prevented your punishment by saying you were a Roman citizen?"

This chart compares the victim and the manager narratives with the Jesus narrative. (For this chart, I've focused on the "victim," since the therapeutic tends to create a victim mind-set.)

	Victim Narrative	Management Narrative	Jesus Narrative
What is the *main* focus?	Me. My feelings. Protecting *the self.*	Order. Safety. Work. How could this have been prevented? How do we fix this?	Declaring and reflecting the beauty of Jesus.
What is the master narrative?	How other people have hurt me.	Efficiency and effectiveness.	Jesus's story.

	Victim Narrative	Management Narrative	Jesus Narrative
What do I think or feel?	Depressed. Angry. Everything is always going wrong.	How could we have done this better? Guilty. Anxious. Pressured.	A whole kaleidoscope of emotions based on where I am in the J-Curve: irritated, angry, joyful, satisfied.
What do I do?	Cultivate self-pity and a like-minded community.	Solve problems. Prevent problems.	A *fellowship of his sufferings* frees me to grieve, worship, love, rebuke, and witness.
Result?	Self-pity. A self-entangled life that never dares to love an enemy.	A carefully managed life, never in touch with the Spirit, never dreaming big— just the careful, safe thing. Joy is manufactured through pleasure seeking.	A joy- and hope-filled life that bounces back from deaths. Knowing resurrection is coming keeps me from getting lost in my suffering.
What's the worst scenario?	I get hurt.	A mess. Problems.	I betray Jesus by rejecting my suffering.
Motto	"I'm the victim!"	"This was not well managed."	"Jesus's beauty was revealed through my suffering!"

The therapist and manager possess Stoic-like wisdom, but their essentially selfish goal (what's best for me) distorts their insights. Neither know anything of love.

Waiting for the Story to Unfold

Many years ago, something similar to what happened to Paul happened to me (but on a much smaller scale). During a study leave, a subordinate accused me of something I'd not done. When I returned, I discovered this person was my new boss, and I'd been demoted. At first, I recoiled from the injustice. When I met with the person, he apologized, but the deed was done. I appealed to the people who had approved this decision, thinking that honest dialogue would set things right, but it made it worse. I'd lost the narrative.

I was overwhelmed and fighting bitterness, yet the Spirit kept nudging me, reminding me, "The seed that dies bears much fruit" (see John 12:24) and "Take the lower place" (see Luke 14:10). I'd recently discovered the *fellowship of his sufferings*, so I knew God wanted me to enter the story of his Son. I resisted the victim narrative and received the dying by quietly accepting the demotion and beginning to learn to do my new job: raise funds. Helping fund the salaries of people who I felt had betrayed me stripped my ego. Not grasping my right to justice and honesty preserved the unity of our mission. To paraphrase Paul, *death was at work in me, but life was at work in our mission* (see 2 Cor. 4:12). My small act of dying created oneness.

As happens with most resurrections, I realized only in retrospect what God was doing. I needed to master the skill of fundraising in order to do the work I am doing now. So my Master demoted me so I could master fundraising so that I could do a work that, by God's grace, would help the church see its true Master. Sometimes you have to wait for the story to unfold to see the Father's hand.

Sometimes you have to wait for the story
to unfold to see the Father's hand.

29

Seeing the Big Picture

Multiyear Dying and Rising

Americans love the quick, the efficient, the short. We love formula and dislike apprenticeships. But apprenticeships are similar to J-Curves—you need to slow down, watch a master, and submit to him. In the same way, you can't learn how to inhabit the dying and rising of Christ quickly. It takes time.

By continuing to watch Paul, particularly in the events surrounding his imprisonment in Jerusalem, we'll deepen our apprenticeship in the art of J-Curve living. Up until now, we've focused on single J-Curve narratives over a relatively short span. Let's switch to a wider and longer lens, and look at multiple J-Curves over a longer time.

Here's the story (as found in Acts 21–23): at the apex of Paul's career, after he and his team have planted hundreds of house churches throughout Asia and Greece, he decides to make one last attempt to reach the heart of Judaism by traveling to Jerusalem during Passover. He's repeatedly warned that he will be imprisoned, but he sets his face to go to Jerusalem.

The Jerusalem church warmly welcomes him, but encourages him to take several fellow Jews through a seven-day rite of purification to show he is a practicing Jew, following the law of Moses. Paul is happy to comply. At the end of the seven days, he visits the temple.

Passover was a passionate time, when Jerusalem's population swelled to over a million. To keep a lid on the crowds, the Romans brought a full cohort (six hundred soldiers) to the Antonia Fortress, which overlooked the northwest corner of the Temple Mount. Signs on the temple platform warned Gentiles not to pass a low barrier wall surrounding the temple on pain of death.

However, some Jews see Paul in the temple and accuse him of bringing a Greek past the low wall. They shout,

> Men of Israel, help! This is the man who is teaching everyone everywhere against the people and the law and this place. Moreover, he even brought Greeks into the temple and has defiled this holy place. (Acts 21:28)

All hell breaks loose. Thousands of people rush to the Temple Mount as the mob drags Paul out of the temple, screaming, "Away with him!" Only the quick action of the Roman SWAT team prevents Paul's murder. Luke's mention of a tribune and several centurions (vv. 31–32) tells us that several hundred soldiers descend on Paul to get him out of the riot. When they reach the steps to the Antonia Fortress, the mob becomes so ferocious that the soldiers raise Paul up on their shoulders.

The next scene is charming. As Paul rides on their shoulders with the mob screaming, he introduces himself to the tribune, tells him where he's from, and asks if he can speak to the crowd. The tribune, thinking he has nothing to lose, likely orders his centurions to form a wall with their massive two-handed shields. Luke describes the scene:

> Paul, standing on the steps, motioned with his hand to the people. And when there was a great hush, he addressed them in the Hebrew language. (v. 40)

Using the natural acoustics of the steps, Paul shares his testimony with upward of one hundred thousand fellow Jews. It is an unbelievable opportunity to speak of the risen Christ in the heart of Judaism.

Paul is *in Judaism* so the crowd can be *in Christ*. This moment is the climax of his life. Paul couldn't ask for a better resurrection.

The Jews listen attentively—until he mentions including Gentiles in the kingdom. Then the crowd goes crazy again, and the tribune brings Paul into the fortress. Here's the Jerusalem J-Curve.

Fig. 29A. Paul in Jerusalem

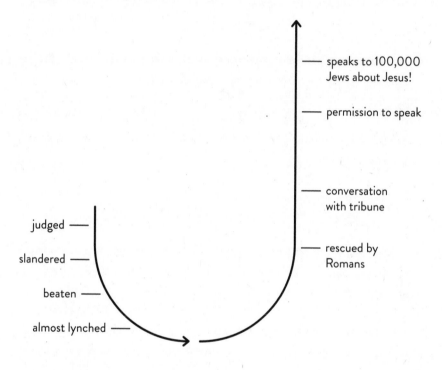

Let's reflect on what Paul's actions here can teach us about the art of J-Curve living.

What Happens When You Lose the Narrative?

The similarities between Paul's Philippi and Jerusalem J-Curves are striking. In both cases, Paul loses the narrative (he is slandered), which opens the door to suffering (he is beaten).

The American church has also lost the narrative. Evangelicals don't control the media, the schools, the universities, or entertainment. So the media regularly paints evangelicals as narrow, backward,

reactionary, old-fashioned, and women-hating, while painting themselves as bright, open-minded, inclusive, accepting, and compassionate. The mob is screaming, "Away with them." We evangelicals are
doing a lot of hand-wringing, wondering how we can regain the cultural narrative, but we can't. We've lost.

The map of the J-Curve orients us—we are on a corporate downward path that we don't control. The story of Jesus's dying and rising
isn't just for us as individuals; it's for the church as a whole. That's
his best gift.

Knowing we are in a corporate death keeps us from fighting the
wrong battles or focusing on wins and losses. It keeps us from returning to the macho Christianity of the past, where we are going to "Take
the hill." We are going through a corporate humbling in which we
need to relearn the basics of Christianity in new and fresh ways. Dying
is the place of knowing.

> The story of Jesus's dying and rising isn't just for
> us as individuals; it's for the church as a whole.

Our loss of control means that suffering is increasing at multiple
levels in our families and churches. But we don't have to be frozen. As
we've seen, the Spirit comes alive in weakness. As we descend into this
corporate death, the map of the J-Curve guides the way. Resurrection
is coming, and even though we don't know the timing or nature of it,
like Paul, we can seize Spirit-led opportunities for rising even in the
dying.

It's possible that this corporate death we are entering will be so
severe that the final resurrection for the church will be the return of
the Lord Jesus. Remember, each of us will end this life with a death.
Our final resurrection will come on the other side of death. Several
times, Paul expected to die prematurely (Acts 27:20; 2 Cor. 1:8–9).
Our willingness to die, to receive the death God has given us, keeps
us from running from suffering. We outfox evil by receiving what it
threatens us with.

Knowing we are dying in him guards us from being overly critical
of the church. Just because the church is struggling to adjust to living

without a voice doesn't mean we become the church's judge. We need to give space for the church to receive this death.

Also, we must be careful not to inhale the mob's false narrative of Christians. It's easy to get caught up in our culture's narrative and assume that the church is narrow and judgmental. Paul never caves in to the false narrative that others construct about him. He's irrepressible, always alive to opportunities, acting as if he has already won the war. And he has won—the reality of the enthronement of Jesus makes Paul relentless in battle. So in the midst of absolute chaos, he starts chatting with the tribune, which leads to the opportunity of a lifetime. Paul isn't interested in his own vindication—that's already happened in Christ—he's interested in announcing Jesus's vindication and victory. So instead of making it our main goal to get out of suffering, we make it our goal to reveal Christ in the suffering.

Let's continue Paul's story, but with an even wider view.

J-Curves within a J-Curve

Over the next three days, Paul goes through a series of J-Curves—one a day. When the tribune takes him into the fortress to be flogged (Romans didn't trust you until you were tortured[1]), Paul pulls a resurrection out of his hip pocket, telling the tribune that he's a Roman citizen.

The next day, he's brought before the Sanhedrin, where he's struck by the high priest's servant. Knowing his audience is divided between the conservative Pharisees who believe in the resurrection and the secular Sadducees who don't, Paul cries out, "I am on trial for the resurrection." It's a brilliant move that leads to these two groups arguing, with the Pharisees siding with Paul. As Paul is being pulled apart, the Romans come to the rescue again.

That night, a group of Jewish zealots makes a pact not to eat or drink until they murder Paul. Paul's nephew overhears this and tells Paul, who in turn has his nephew tell the tribune, who orders a detachment of 270 soldiers to take Paul that night to Caesarea, the Roman provincial capital on the Mediterranean.

---

1. See Pliny, *Letters* 10.96–97, http://faculty.georgetown.edu/jod/texts/pliny.html.

Here's an overview of these four J-Curves:

Fig. 29B. Paul in Prison

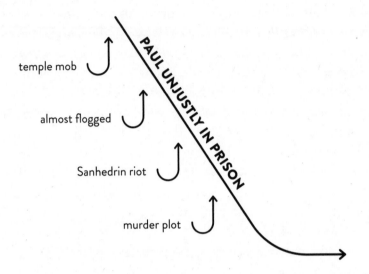

I offer three observations about Paul's four J-Curves. First, notice that they are embedded in the larger J-Curve of Paul's imprisonment. So in the midst of these daily dyings and risings, he is in one long dying—prison. Paul doesn't know that his imprisonment will last four more years. Mini-resurrections help us see the present work of the Spirit even though we are still in a bigger death. Seeing small J-Curves helps us rest as we wait for bigger ones. It's easy to lose perspective and to focus on the big death, thinking God isn't for me.[2]

Almost everyone I've seen who has been trapped by bitterness has focused on the big dying and been blind to multiple mini-resurrections in their lives. Almost counterintuitively, the most thankful and happy people I know are confined to wheelchairs. The very deep J-Curves, in my experience, force you (if you take that path) so deeply into Christ that you emerge from them *singing in prison*. During some of my lowest years, I tuned myself into the "resurrection channel" by

---

2. This pattern of dyings and risings embedded in a larger J-Curve can be found all through Acts, especially in the sections on Paul's sea journey.

beginning the early morning habit of reviewing the previous day and thanking God for little mercies, little resurrections. When everything was dark, the Spirit prompted me to hunt for life. People cultivate bitterness by retelling the story of what life has done to them. We can cultivate joy by watching for the Spirit to re-enact the story of Jesus's dying and rising.

The very deep J-Curves, in my experience,
force us so deeply into Christ that we
emerge from them *singing in prison.*

Second, for some people, the word *spiritual* means "weird, discon-nected, out of touch," but dying and rising are not mystical. Paul's four mini-deaths are physical: he is attacked by a mob, almost flogged, hit by the high priest's servant, and targeted for murder. The resur-rections are equally concrete: he is rescued by a Roman SWAT team, reveals his Roman citizenship, cries out, "I'm on trial for the resurrec-tion," and receives the help of a nephew and a quick-acting tribune. Some have made a *fellowship of his sufferings* into a purely mystical experience. It's not. The J-Curve doesn't float you above life; because it is so true, so good, it helps you come alive in your deaths.

Third, whether Paul is dying or rising, he's attentive to his audience and his situation. Once again, he's not passive. Like practitioners of the martial arts self-defense system Krav Maga, who are trained to see everything as a potential weapon, Paul seizes whatever resources are at hand: the tribune, his citizenship, a divided audience, and a listening nephew. Paul isn't cynical, mystical, or passive. He's hopeful, concrete, and active.

Re-enacting Jesus's Passion

Let's pull back and look at this series of events through another lens. Luke (and likely Paul as well) notices a remarkable similarity between Paul's final trip (Acts 21-26) and Jesus's Passion (Luke 22-23). Luke draws a dozen parallels:[3]

---

3. See the Virtual Appendix at www.seejesus.net/J-Curvebook for Scripture references. These parallels are taken from Charles Talbert, *Literary Patterns, Theological Themes* (1974), quoted in Michael Barber, "Acts of the Apostles: Luke-Acts Parallels (Part 3)," *The Sacred*

1. Seven times Luke mentions that Paul and Jesus are going to Jerusalem.
2. Both trips are made under divine necessity, and neither Paul's nor Jesus's disciples understand.
3. Both Paul and Jesus are welcomed by the people or church.
4. Both visit the temple.
5. Both are opposed by Sadducees but acknowledged by scribes.
6. Both are seized by a crowd.
7. Both are slapped by the high priest's assistants.
8. Both have two Jewish trials and two Roman trials.
9. Both are falsely accused.
10. Both are thrice declared innocent by Gentile authority.
11. Both appear before Herod.
12. The ruler (Pilate for Jesus, King Agrippa and Festus for Paul) is set to release them.

Paul and Luke see that our lives are designed to look like Jesus's life; we often have life events that resemble his Passion. All Christ followers have a master passion story they inhabit.

I think of my wife's passion: the gift of Kim. Jill entered into a passion close to thirty-seven years ago. That is, the main suffering (Kim's disability) is still with Jill, but God has repeatedly done mini-resurrections in Kim's life: learning to walk; learning sign language at a school for the deaf; learning to use her speech computer; getting a job. Kim's resurrections were also Jill's. But the biggest resurrections were the ones that God did in Jill and me: Jill surrendering her will; me learning to love Jill in new ways.

I also think of my friend Julie, who was deserted and divorced by her husband, an elder in the church at the time. For twenty years now, she has lived with the consequences of his desertion, but again and again I've seen God do mini-deaths and mini-resurrections in her life: she saw a Muslim woman converted in her Bible study on the person of Jesus, which led to work with seeJesus and an international teaching ministry.

Page blog, April 22, 2010. http://www.thesacredpage.com/2010/04/acts-of-apostles-luke-acts-parallels.html.

Fig. 29C. Mini-resurrections

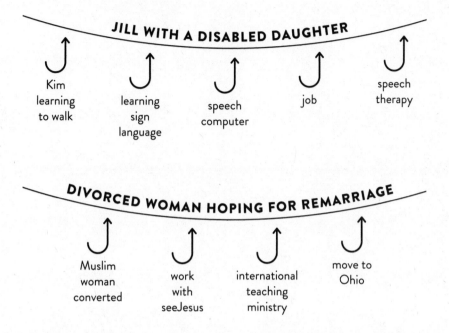

Seeing little victories, mini-resurrections like these, encourages us when "the big thing" still hangs over our head. Overlapping J-Curves fill our life. J-Curves are daily, weekly, monthly. So study your life thoughtfully, like Paul and Luke did, and watch for the dying and rising. His Passion is your passion. Your life makes sense when seen through Jesus's narrative.

Your life makes sense when seen
through Jesus's narrative.

PART 5

FORMING A J-CURVE COMMUNITY

How Does the J-Curve Create
a Loving Community?

How Do You Create Unity When Everyone
Is Organized into Their Own In-Groups?

How Do You Break Down the Barriers between
Jew and Gentile, Rich and Poor, Black and White?

What Is the Danger of Idolizing Community?

When Does the J-Curve Help Us to
Actually Divide a Community?

30

The Power of Weakness

How the J-Curve Defeats Tribalism

Paul's vision of *the good* encompasses three distinct visions. As we've emphasized, each vision involves a distinct task and needs our attention.

The first task, rediscovered by Martin Luther, is the simplicity and beauty of faith. Luther put his finger on the problem—medieval faith in Jesus for salvation was not pure. It was corrupted with our own futile doing.

The second task focuses on love, especially the J-Curve. We can be pure in the midst of a *crooked and perverse generation.*

Now, in Part 5, we introduce a third vision, formed by the first two visions: a unified and loving Jesus community. This vision focuses on the final "product"—the leveling and uniting effect of our union with Christ, which brings together all the polarities of this world: male/female, rich/poor, black/white, slave/free, healthy/disabled, and Greek/Jew.

These three visions are tightly linked. A pure faith creates a pure love, which forms the beauty of Jesus in community.

A pure faith creates a pure love, which forms
the beauty of Jesus in community.

Creating a loving community is extraordinarily difficult. We all
long to be part of an accepting community we can call home, but even
in a family, where we share common genes and a common upbringing, the task is daunting. What many struggle to do in their families,
the apostle Paul wants to do with the Corinthians, who share neither
common DNA nor similar upbringing. He's determined that they will
all be one.

You see, anyone can form a community. Just get like-minded people together and presto—you have a tribe. Thus, the rise of tribalism
in our culture. Paul repeatedly turns to the pattern of Jesus's dying
and rising as a way of shaping the Corinthians and their tribes into a
true body of Christ. In Philippi, Paul presented a positive vision of a
Jesus community; now, in Corinth, he goes after a negative vision. In
all Christ formation, you need to put off (remove the negative) and put
on (add the positive). First and Second Corinthians make an excellent
primer for forming a Jesus community, because they give us multiple
concrete examples of what *not* to do!

Let's take a look at the extent of the problem Paul is facing in Corinth.

The Corinthians' Way of Community

Corinth was a large, bustling boomtown in southern Greece, much
like San Francisco during the 1849 gold rush. Its strategic location on
a narrow strip of land meant it controlled the east-west trade in the
Mediterranean. The wealth it accumulated from trade made Corinth
an upwardly mobile society, filled with the newly rich and the always
poor.

Paul traveled south through Greece to Corinth in the spring of
AD 50. Walking down the longest colannaded sidewalk in the ancient
world, he passed under a majestic triumphal arch with two gilded
chariots and into the forum or marketplace. "The forum itself was
a vast open space thronged with merchants, street-hawkers, travel-
lers, and local residents. Varicoloured tents covered the market stalls.
He would see works of public art: paintings, marble sculpture, and

works of bronze, shrines, sanctuaries and temples, shops . . . dazzling colours."[1]

As Paul entered the forum, off to his far right was a monument that recently had been erected by a man named Babbius, with this epigraph:

> Gnaeus Babbius Philinus, commissioner and overseer of religion, had this monument erected at his own expense, and he approved it in his offical capacity of mayor.[2]

We can tell a lot about Babbius from this inscription. He was one of the two purple-robed mayors. He likely became wealthy from trade since he also built a temple to Poseidon, the god of the sea. Since he didn't mention his father (Babbius, the son of . . .), he was likely a freedman, a slave who had bought his freedom. He was a self-made multimillionaire.

Babbius's monument promoted Babbius.[3] To make sure no one missed it, he wrote his inscription twice. This was his solution to a problem I've wrestled with—if you are humble, no one notices you! Babbius reflected the mind of Corinth:

> Corinth was a city where public boasting and self-promotion had become an art form. The Corinthian people thus lived with an honor-shame cultural orientation, where public recognition was often more important than facts. . . . In such a culture a person's sense of worth is based on recognition by others of one's accomplishments, hence the self-promoting public inscriptions.[4]

In short, Corinth was a celebrity culture. But what's a celebrity without fans? So wealthy people or patrons like Babbius would essentially "buy" their fans. The more fans, the higher Babbius went up the Failure-Boasting Chart, which in turn helped his fans move up.

---

1. D. Engels, *Roman Corinth: An Alternative Model for the Classical City* (Chicago: University of Chicago Press, 1990), quoted in Anthony C. Thiselton, *The First Epistle to the Corinthians* (Grand Rapids, MI: Eerdmans, 2000), 20.

2. Quoted in Thiselton, *First Corinthians*, 8.

3. Plutarch, *Moralia*, 805.E–F, quoted in Andrew Clarke, *Secular and Christian Leadership in Corinth* (Eugene, OR: Wipf & Stock, 2006), 141. Clarke mentions that Babbius was magistrate AD 9–11.

4. Ben Witherington, *Conflict and Community in Corinth: A Socio-Rhetorical Commentary on 1 and 2 Corinthians* (Grand Rapids, MI: Eerdmans, 1995), 21.

Fig. 30A. Honoring Babbius

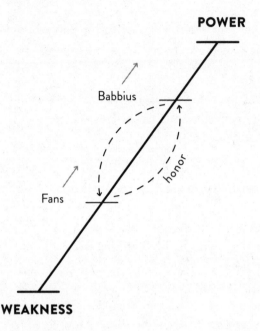

Plutarch (AD 46–120) said that as a young vine twines itself around a strong tree to gain height, so an obscure person will seek a connection with a person of reputation to be "under the shelter of his power and grow great with him."[5] A simple exchange occurred: patrons gave their fans money, and the fans gave their patrons honor in the forum and assembly. The fans were the patron's cheerleaders, PR men, or whatever the patron needed. An ambitious young man like Augustine climbed the patronage ladder, leaving his patron in Carthage and finding a more prominent one in Rome. Babbius needed his fans because there is only so much room at the top. In the competition for glory, we need allies.

Babbius's quest looked like this: Money → Friends → Honor → Power.

A Celebrity Culture Invades the Church

After eighteen months planting the church in Corinth, Paul moves across the Aegean Sea to Ephesus, where he hears reports of the celeb-

---

5. Plutarch, *Moralia*, 805.E–F, quoted in Thiselton, *First Corinthians*, 125.

rity culture invading the church and creating factions. Paul confronts this head on:[6]

> I appeal to you, brothers, by the name of our Lord Jesus Christ, that all of you agree, and that there be no divisions among you, but that you be united in the same mind and the same judgment. For it has been reported to me by Chloe's people that there is quarreling among you, my brothers. What I mean is that each one of you says, "I follow Paul," or "I follow Apollos," or "I follow Cephas," or "I follow Christ." (1 Cor. 1:10–12)

The Corinthians have created celebrities (Paul, Apollos, Cephas, and Christ), complete with rival fan groups. Instead of a Jesus community, they have formed competing clubs or tribes. They know the center of the gospel (justification by faith), so Paul barely mentions it in his letters to them. What they don't know is how to re-enact the gospel, how to participate in the dying and rising of Jesus. In Corinth, justification by faith sits like a shroud over an essentially pagan power structure. The Corinthians don't know that the normal Christian life is not about gaining power, but about losing power for the sake of love. In short, they don't know the J-Curve or the community it forms.

Marketing 101: Four Ways to Promote Yourself

To understand Paul's response, let's see the four ways the Corinthians moved up the Failure-Boasting Chart.

Money was the best way up. Babbius, like other hardworking freedman, converted his wealth into honor by gifting the city with at least four temples and monuments.

Lacking money, another path up was cultivating "wisdom." We've already encountered bits of wisdom in Babbius and Plutarch:

- Let others know of your accomplishments. Market yourself.
- Buy your way up the ladder of success. Money is power.
- Display your generosity to move you up the ladder of others' esteem.

---

6. See Thiselton, *First Corinthians*, 29–32, on dating. These dates are estimates, accurate to within one to two years.

- Manipulate your friendships to get a good patron.
- Get in the right group.
- Use people as stepping-stones to your glory.

But people needed to appreciate your wisdom. That's where the third path came in: oratory or fine speech. Eloquence was the ultimate Facebook—it put you on display like nothing else. Plutarch gives us some first-century wisdom:

> How then is it possible that a private person of ordinary costume and appearance who wishes to lead a State may gain power and rule the multitude unless he possesses persuasion and attractive speech?[7]

Finally, having the right connections moved you up. Right connections were the glue that held this all together.

These four things (money, wisdom, oratory, and connections) worked together. The result? You not only moved *up*, but *in*. What was at the top? Power and honor. Thus, there is a universal allergy to weakness and shame.

The Power of Weakness

Yet, Paul is able to form a Jesus community out of this toxic mix of human pride and power. In a brilliant three-pronged opening attack in 1 Corinthians 1, he unmasks the underpinnings of their celebrity culture.

Notice that he doesn't say "stop fighting." That would be like pulling the top of a weed. He goes after the root. Factions are embedded in a system that maximizes human glory and power. Paul goes after the Corinthians' DNA, their allergy to the downward move of the J-Curve.

Paul's opening salvo is "Look at the cross!" (1 Corinthians 1). He wants the church to see that the weakness and foolishness of the cross (dying) is the secret to power and knowledge (rising). (In the passages below, I've italicized *dying* and underlined rising.)

> For the word of *the cross is folly to those who are perishing*, but to us who are being saved it is the power of God. . . . But *we preach Christ crucified*, a stumbling block to Jews and folly to Gentiles, but to those

---

7. Plutarch, *Moralia*, 801.E, 802.E. quoted in Clarke, *Secular and Christian Leadership in Corinth*, 37.

who are called, both Jews and Greeks, <u>Christ the power of God and the wisdom of God</u>. For the *foolishness of God* is <u>wiser than men</u>, and *the weakness of God* is <u>stronger than men.</u> (vv. 18, 23–25)

In other words, while the cross appears to define weakness, it's really the power of God. It appears foolish, but it's really the path of wisdom. Next, Paul says, "Look at yourselves!"

For consider your calling, brothers: not many of you were wise according to worldly standards, not many were powerful, not many were of noble birth. (v. 26)

In effect, Paul says, "Don't be ridiculous. Why try to be at the top of the Failure-Boasting Chart when you are clustered at the bottom? Why try to join 'in groups' when you're 'out'?"

The weakness of our lives mirrors the weakness of the cross. Look at the familiar cadence of dying and rising:

But God chose what is *foolish in the world* to <u>shame the wise</u>; God chose what is *weak in the world* <u>to shame the strong</u>; God chose what is *low and despised in the world, even things that are not,* <u>to bring to nothing things that are</u>, so that no human being might boast in the presence of God. (vv. 27–29)

Weakness is the place of wisdom and power. God uses our weakness as a launching pad for his strength. He loves to use low and despised things to defeat human pride.

Paul's third salvo is "Look how I embody the weakness and power of the gospel":

And I, *when I came to you, brothers, did not come proclaiming to you the testimony of God with lofty speech or wisdom. For I decided to know nothing among you except Jesus Christ and him crucified. And I was with you in weakness and in fear and much trembling, and my speech and my message were not in plausible words of wisdom,* <u>but in demonstration of the Spirit and of power,</u> so that your faith might not rest in the wisdom of men but <u>in the power of God.</u> (2:1–5)

Paul deliberately weakens himself to guard the integrity of the gospel. He doesn't grasp at eloquence, which would elevate him. Skilled oratory would send a double message, since the cross is all about weakness. He can't preach weakness while living in human power. The narrative of his life must match the narrative of the cross.[8] So when Paul speaks about Jesus losing power for the sake of love (the gospel), Paul loses power by muting his own eloquence.

Paul's weakness protects the Corinthians from relying on "the person of Paul," thus rooting their faith in *the power of God*. A community of Jesus must be grounded in the person Jesus. Because they have rooted their faith in a person other than Jesus, the Corinthians have created a culture hungry for celebrity pastors.

> A community of Jesus must be
> grounded in the person Jesus.

Fig. 30B. Examples of Weakness

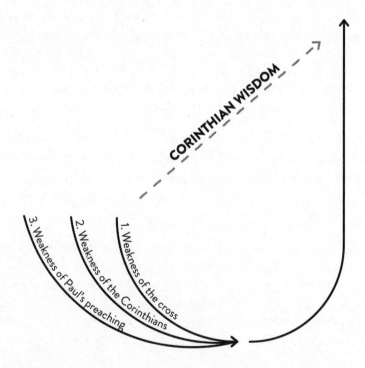

---

8. "In Paul's theology, the cross is more than (but not less than) a remedy and atonement for past sins. It provides the basis for Christian identity and his transformative power to reshape Christian existence in the present and the future." Thiselton, *First Corinthians*, 147.

Paul's weakness plants their faith not in him but in a "demonstration of the Spirit and of power." His "much trembling" pushes them away from him to Jesus. Because Paul does not grasp at eloquence in the same way Jesus didn't grasp at the privileges of divinity, the congregation's faith sinks its roots into the grace of God. So Paul's weakness not only models Jesus's dying and rising for others, but it also embeds the Corinthians in Jesus. Paul's dying is for their rising. So he writes to them later to say, "So death is at work in us, but life in you" (2 Cor. 4:12).

A summary in diagram form of Paul's three examples of weakness is shown above (Fig. 30B).

A Jesus Résumé

Paul's best, most charming example of his weakness is in 2 Corinthians 11. Under the influence of the Judaizers, the Corinthians charge him with having an inferior résumé (he's not one of the "original twelve") and boast of their own résumé.

Paul counters their boasting with his own boasts, but true to his pattern of inhabiting the dying and rising of Jesus, he boasts in his weaknesses:

> If I must boast, I will boast of the things that show my weakness. The God and Father of the Lord Jesus, he who is blessed forever, knows that I am not lying. At Damascus, the governor under King Aretas was guarding the city of Damascus in order to seize me, but I was let down in a basket through a window in the wall and escaped his hands. (2 Cor. 11:30–33)

I can imagine the Corinthians' smiles when they hear this read on Sunday. Let me explain. The most challenging combat in ancient warfare was breaching a city wall. The defender condensed his forces on the wall and assaulted the enemy with projectiles, boiling water, and boulders from a superior height. Even if an attacker was able to "crack" the wall, it took superhuman force to hold it because a defender could reinforce more quickly using his interior lines. This is why it took four of Rome's finest legions (seventy thousand men) six months to break Jerusalem's defenses in the Jewish Revolt (AD 70).

But once the attacker took the wall, for all practical purposes, he had won. Consequently, the Romans honored the man who breached the wall with their highest honor, the Wall Crown, a gold crown shaped like the walls of a city. The peculiar shape of European crowns with little turrets comes from the Wall Crown. To get this coveted award, a soldier had to take and hold the wall by planting his legion's standard on it.

The Roman soldier went up the wall, boldly killing his enemies, while Paul went down the wall, hiding in a basket, fleeing his enemies. Paul is making fun of himself, boasting in his weakness. He mocks the Failure-Boasting Chart—just as the cross mocks our foolish boasts.

You see, for Paul, life is grace-saturated; he's puzzled with these Corinthians, who live as if they've earned or merited blessing.

> What do you have that you did not receive? If then you received it, *why do you boast as if you did not receive it*? (1 Cor. 4:7b)

Paul argues, "If all of life is gift, then why are you acting as if you are special, as if you earned it? Why are you trying to move up the Failure-Boasting Chart?"

By the way, when faith increases, so does our ability to laugh at ourselves. Not surprisingly, as faith dims in our culture, people are struggling to laugh at themselves. Several popular comedians are avoiding college campuses because college students are not able to laugh at themselves.[9]

The Cell Phone Seminar

The Failure-Boasting Chart haunts the American church. Here's an example of this from one of our seeJesus prayer seminars. We open our seminars with a time of personal prayer on Friday evening. After five minutes, we debrief the participants at length by asking, "What was hard about that prayer time?" It's almost always encouraging for people to see that others are struggling with the same things in prayer.

I say "almost" because several years ago I led a seminar for the leadership team of a prominent church. The discussion after the open-

---

9. Caitlin Flanagan, "That's Not Funny: Today's college students can't seem to take a joke," *The Atlantic*, September 2015. https://www.theatlantic.com/magazine/archive/2015/09/thats-not-funny/399335/.

ing prayer time was unbelievably awkward. I couldn't get anyone to talk—about a third of the people in the group were openly on their smartphones. The others must have been intimidated, so they were silent too. Eventually, when I shifted to lecturing, they started putting their phones down, and we ended up with a great evening. On Saturday morning, the executive pastor apologized to me and asked the participants to put their phones away. I was thankful for his intervention.

When I debriefed with Bob Allums, the director of our prayer ministries, he was incredulous. He'd led hundreds of prayer seminars, but he'd never seen anything like this. I started laughing and said, "Bob, it isn't that complicated." I shaped my arm like a Failure-Boasting Chart and said, "They were up here, and I was down here. I was below them, and thus not deserving of their full attention." Bob said, "Yes, but why pay seeJesus to bring in someone who can equip them to pray, and then not pay attention? What an incredible waste of an opportunity." While still chuckling over Bob's shock, I said, "You're right, Bob, but it shows you how powerful celebrity culture is in the church. In their eyes, I lacked gravity."

I laughed without a trace of resentment, because I didn't live in that leadership team's narrative. At least in this seminar, we were in different locations: they were on the Failure-Boasting Chart; I was in the J-Curve. I was *in Jesus* and they were *in work* or *in efficiency*. They were just relating to me as someone who was outside of and beneath their tribe.

I don't mean to imply for a moment that I'd arrived at a permanent state of Christian maturity. Far from it. In fact, as I've grown in Christ, I've become much more aware of my flesh, of how frequently I am living on the Failure-Boasting Chart. Yet, the frequent *fellowship of his sufferings* in my life had begun to train my soul to not recoil from the downward drift of dying with Christ that is often offered to us by others. The J-Curve had become familiar territory for me.

Their inattentiveness made union with Christ come alive for me in a fresh way by drawing me ever so briefly into the dying of Jesus. Their treatment of me, as mild as it was, weakened me, making me helpless, so I had to pray my way through a prayer seminar. I'd led hundreds of prayer seminars, but I didn't know how to lead one with people who didn't interact.

Knowing I was in a mini-fellowship of his sufferings freed me to love them even as I endured their momentary lowering of me. Not only does humility absorb pride, but resurrection follows death. As a result of that seminar, and others' input as well, I had the joy of seeing their congregation become more of a praying church.

I'd led hundreds of prayer seminars, but I didn't know
how to lead one with people who didn't interact.

These leaders knew and loved the gospel, but in this particular instance, it sat on the surface of their lives. I was sympathetic to their struggle because I fight pride and boasting in my heart every day. Only the gospel-lived-out can destroy the toxic mix of pride and power that thwarts the forming of a Jesus community. In order to form a community that embodies his life, we need dying leaders who embody a dying Savior.

31

The Spirit at the Center

Learning Wisdom Down Low

The Corinthians messed up both sides of the J-Curve. They recoiled from going down, and they tried going up in their own strength and wisdom. They saw no need for the Spirit's resurrection power and wisdom.

Paul's third salvo against the Corinthians' factionalism, which we touched on in the previous chapter, introduces the Spirit:

> My speech and my message were not in plausible words of wisdom, *but in demonstration of the Spirit and of power*, so that your faith might not rest in the wisdom of men but in the power of God. (1 Cor. 2:4–5)

Paul deliberately weakens himself, thus imitating the dying of Jesus and opening the door to the Spirit's power and wisdom. As we see here, our weakness is the Spirit's womb. The Spirit recoils from human strength and wisdom, but dwells in brokenness. Just as the Spirit lives at the center of his life, Paul wants the Spirit at the center of the Corinthian community. The Spirit is the beating heart of a Jesus community.

The Spirit is the beating heart of a Jesus community.

Corrupting the Spirit

True to form, the Corinthians used the Spirit to promote themselves by creating a spiritual Failure-Boasting Chart with a self-appointed inner circle of mature people who possessed "secret wisdom" and looked down on mere infants, thus creating a spiritual tribe.[1]

Paul flips their spiritual Failure-Boasting Chart on its head, calling the mature mere infants:

> But I, brothers, could not address you as *Spiritual* people, but as people of the flesh, as *infants* in Christ. . . . For while there is jealousy and strife among you, are you not of the flesh and behaving only in a human way? (1 Cor. 3:1, 3 AT)

Paul counters their desire to be in an elite in group with *the foolishness of the cross*. Because the Corinthians separated Christ from the cross in their daily lives, effectively severing Jesus from the J-Curve, Paul repeatedly links Christ with the cross. That's where knowledge begins:

> . . . lest the *cross of Christ* be emptied of its power. (1 Cor. 1:17b)

> We preach *Christ crucified*. (v. 23a)

> For I decided to know nothing among you except *Jesus Christ and him crucified*. (2:2)

So what does the cross have to do with wisdom? How can weakness be wise? Reflect on the Cell Phone Seminar, where the cross's wisdom eventually trumped the flesh. My mini-death allowed me to persevere and not take the group's inattentiveness personally, freeing me to love and even laugh. Maturity comes when we begin to look like a God who reveals himself in the humiliation of the cross. I didn't push the humiliation away, forming an alternative tribe of *the downtrodden*. Jesus's DNA resists tribalism. That's wisdom.

---

1. They "were teaching that they had the potentiality of becoming *spiritual* within themselves by virtue of the spiritual nature given them by God, and that by a cultivation of Wisdom they could rise above the earthly . . . level of existence." Birger A. Pearson, *The Pneumatikos-Psychikos Terminology in 1 Corinthians: A Study in the Theology of the Corinthian Opponents of Paul and Its Relation to Gnosticism*, Society of Biblical Literature Dissertation Series 12 (Missoula, MT: Scholars Press, 1973), 40, quoted in Anthony C. Thiselton, *The First Epistle to the Corinthians* (Grand Rapids, MI: Eerdmans, 2000), 269.

May the Force Be with You!

Notice the capital "S" above in *Spiritual* (1 Cor. 3:1 AT).[2] A *Spiritual* person is not someone who is religious or prays easily. A *Spiritual* person is in *step with the Spirit* and *led by the Spirit*. Deepak Chopra and Mahatma Gandhi are *spiritual*, but they are not *Spiritual* people whose life, like Jesus's resurrected life, is sustained by the Spirit. The Spirit possesses us in the same way he possesses Jesus. The Spirit carries the mind of Jesus into our lives, allowing Jesus's fruits (Gal. 5:22–23) to become our fruits. Dropping the capital "S" depersonalizes the Spirit.

Following the mind of the age, some Corinthians viewed the Spirit as a semi-impersonal force, like "The Force" in *Star Wars*.[3] Oprah Winfrey would have been completely at home with their ideas. If *God* is within me, then change from within is completely possible. Here's C. S. Lewis's response to the idea of "God as a force":

> An "impersonal God"—well and good. A subjective God of beauty, truth and goodness, inside our own heads—better still. A formless life-force surging through us, a vast power which we can tap—best of all. But God Himself, alive, pulling at the other end of the cord, perhaps approaching at an infinite speed, the hunter, king, husband—that is quite another matter. There comes a moment when the children who have been playing at burglars hush suddenly: was that a *real* footstep in the hall? . . . Supposing we really found Him? We never meant it to come to *that*! Worse still, supposing He had found us?[4]

Notice how different a mindless force feels from a real person— "hunter, king, husband." A life force poses no threat and makes no

2. Geerhardus Vos, *The Pauline Eschatology* (Phillipsburg, NJ: P&R, 1994), 164–67; Richard B. Gaffin Jr., *Resurrection and Redemption: A Study in Paul's Soteriology* (Phillipsburg, NJ: P&R, 1987), 80–92; and Thiselton, *First Corinthians*, 1258, 1283–85 actually capitalize the word *spiritual* to emphasize the connection to the Holy Spirit.

3. Some of the Corinthians saw "God as a kind of animating world-soul or immanental spirit of the world." Thiselton, *First Corinthians*, 260. Epictetus, a Stoic philosopher (AD 55–135), said: "Our souls are so bound up with God . . . as being parts and portions of His being." Epictetus, *The Discourses as Reported by Arrian, the Manual, and Fragments. Volume 1*, trans. W. A. Oldfather (Cambridge, MA: Harvard University Press, 1926), 103. Epictetus also commented that at death a person passes "back to that from which you came, to what is friendly and akin to you, to the physical elements. What there was of fire in you shall pass into fire, what there was of earth into earth, what there was of spirit into spirit, what there was of water into water." Epictetus, *The Discourses as Reported by Arrian, the Manual, and Fragments. Volume 2*, trans. W. A. Oldfather (Cambridge, MA: Harvard University Press, 1929), 93.

4. C. S. Lewis, *Miracles* (New York: Harper Collins, 2001), 150.

demand, and yet how vulnerable the children feel at the thought of a real footstep, a real burglar.

Wisdom from the Spirit

Paul also confronts the Corinthians' confusion about the nature of wisdom and the Spirit:

> These things God has revealed *to us* through the Spirit. (1 Cor. 2:10a)

Wisdom is not an esoteric knowledge available to only a few *spiritual* ones. God has revealed himself *to us*—to all of us. Notice the flatness of Paul's third vision of *the good* (a Jesus community): we are all sinners, all saved by grace, all taught by the Spirit.

This insight shapes how I lead prayer meetings. I take time at the beginning to hear people's hearts. I do that to care for them, but also to give space for the Spirit to speak through even "the least of these." Like the mature believers at Corinth, my propensity as the leader, author, and all-around expert is to fill the verbal space. That's why I call my phone's mute button the "Holy Spirit button." When I press "Mute," I leave space for him.

The Spirit himself is a gift—"the Spirit who is from God" (1 Cor. 2:12). He's not part of a world soul—he's a person, a personal gift from a personal God. So at every level, gifts lie at the heart of the church (1 Cor. 4:7).

With the gift of the Spirit, we can "understand the things freely given us by God" (1 Cor. 2:12b). That's why "the Spirit searches everything, even the depths of God" (v. 10b). Only God can reveal God. So wisdom comes from outside us. The wisdom of the cross is so alien to our spirits that we need his Spirit to talk to our spirits. God lavishes on us these three interlocking gifts: wisdom, the cross, and the Spirit.

In the modern church, some Pentecostals have disassociated the Spirit from the wisdom of the cross and the work of love. The wealth that some preachers have accumulated is at odds with Paul's vision of the Spirit helping us to see that the heart of wisdom is a dying Savior and thus our dying love. They use the Spirit to move up the Poverty/Wealth Chart. Some Reformed (my heritage) have marginalized and depersonalized the Spirit, thus creating a vacuum that we've filled with a passion for order, rationalism, and prayerlessness. We desperately need the Spirit of Jesus to breathe fresh life into his church.

Here's an overview of Paul's teaching in 1 Corinthians 2:

	The Corinthian Errors	Paul's Correction
Spirit	A force that permeates life.	A person, a gift from God.
Wisdom	A way to get power. The mature possess a secret, insider knowledge.	True wisdom is the wisdom of the cross.
Maturity	Mature Christians are part of an elite inner circle.	Maturity comes when our lives reflect a God who reveals himself in the humiliation of the cross.

Why does Paul focus on the Spirit when trying to form this third vision of *the good*—the church? The Spirit is the functional CEO of the church. Ignore him, and you merely create a tribe. When we depersonalize or marginalize the Spirit, we leave him without a job. Of course, we give him a theological job description: always proceeding from the Father as he sustains the universe. But he's functionally unemployed when it comes to our daily lives.

Now let's see what this means.

Living by the Spirit

One of the first times I saw clearly what it means to *be in step with the Spirit* was when my daughter Courtney, a high-school senior, came home late from youth group. We had a job list on our refrigerator with fifteen-minute jobs (five minutes of work and ten minutes of complaining). That night, Courtney had to sweep the kitchen. I hadn't said anything, but when she came in the door, she was angry that I was making her do her job even though she was tired. I volunteered to help her, but that only made it worse. She was just mad.

I was about to say, "I'm not sure why you are mad at me. We agreed on these jobs; we talked about this as a family." But I didn't trust myself, so I hesitated. I recall fighting to be weak and not lecture her. I asked, "Courtney, what's wrong?" When she snapped back, "Nothing! I don't want to talk about it!" I got a clue. Something else was going on. Finally, I said, "Sit down." To my surprise, she did. I sat next to her and asked again, "Courtney, what's wrong? What's upsetting you?" She said that her youth group leader had ridiculed her in front of her friends, and she felt shamed. As I listened, I realized I'd been struggling with similar problems. We shared our problems with one another for about ten minutes. Then we did her job together.

I remember consciously waiting for the Spirit to help me love. During Courtney's ranting, I prayed because I was confused, uncertain. I lacked wisdom. I knew our rules were important, but I also knew the tendency of my flesh to correct and lecture. The Spirit helped me to shut my mouth. Plus, I'd recently noticed in the Gospels how much Jesus looked at people. The Spirit didn't operate in a vacuum; the body of Christ and the Word were his language, helping me to listen.

I knew our rules were important, but I also knew
the tendency of my flesh to correct and lecture.
The Spirit helped me to shut my mouth.

We are inside the J-Curve, seeing how the parts fit together. The path of *weakness → prayer → Spirit of Jesus → wisdom → love* was working even in this small incident. Listening to Courtney when she was angry involved a mild "descent" as I didn't grasp at clarity, justice, or respect. From that emerged a resurrection in our relationship: genuine closeness. The gospel lived out created a small reconciliation, breaking down the Parent-Child dividing wall and creating a Jesus community.

But it wasn't the mere application of principles—the Spirit, not I, was in the center. He helped me value and care for Courtney. I found myself caught up in a dance, one I was not leading. By waiting and praying, I discovered the wisdom and reconciling power of the cross acted out.

Unless the Spirit repeatedly brings the *mind of Christ* into our hearts, our ever-present flesh will recoil from the wisdom of the cross. Only the Spirit can continually make the cross fresh. He made the J-Curve happen in Jesus, and he makes it happen now in us.

The table below traces these two alternative paths in the story of Courtney: the flesh and the Spirit. The only thing these two paths have in common is that initially they have identical data, but then everything changes.

	Wisdom of the World (Flesh)	Wisdom of the Cross (Spirit)
Data	*Courtney is mad about doing her jobs.*	
What do I see?	An angry, rebellious teenager	I'm not sure.
Who's at the center?	Me. No need for the Spirit. All is clear.	The Spirit. I am at the edge of the story. I need to wait on the Spirit, to give him space.
What do I do?	Talk, correct Courtney's errors.	Wait, pray, ask questions.
What do I say?	"Courtney, we agreed you'd do this."	I wonder, "What is wrong? What should I say?" I say to Courtney, "What's wrong?"
My attitude	Nice, but demanding.	Wondering, watching, waiting.
Feel of activity	Clear, confident, quick.	Messy, slow, uncertain.
Feel of time	Initially quick, but in time, slow.	Initially slow, but in time, quick.
Feeling of safety	Good	Risky
The effect on community	I divide by gossiping, "Courtney is driving me nuts."	I unite with Courtney by moving toward her.
My heart cry	"Do your jobs!" ("Do this and live.")	"Abba, Father" (Gal. 4:6)—the cry of the confused and vulnerable.
Final result	Separation	Reconciliation

Notice how messy and uncertain love is. As soon as we begin to love someone, we are confronted with our lack of wisdom. Loving people quickly gets complicated. Our dislike of the uncertainty and the fog of love leads to pulling back. Not surprisingly, the Corinthians did not like the complexity of love, the subject of our next chapter.

To summarize: a Jesus community can work only if Jesus, by the Spirit, is at the center. Staying in step with the Spirit is not nearly as complex as we might think. We aren't trying to read spiritual tea leaves—as we embrace Christ in the dying and rising, the Spirit always shows up!

We aren't trying to read spiritual tea leaves—
as we embrace Christ in the dying and
rising, the Spirit always shows up!

32

Love Treads Softly

Entering the Complexity of Love

At the Cell Phone Seminar, I experienced distance that comes from pride. Put simply, the participants felt "above" me. Pride separates. That's why Paul links pride and factions:

> I have applied all these things to myself and Apollos for your benefit, brothers, that you may learn by us not to go beyond what is written, *that none of you may be puffed up in favor of one against another.* (1 Cor. 4:6)

But sometimes it's simply true we *are* above the other person. How do we create community when some people are wise and insightful, and others less so? How do we become one when differences are real? Paul faced that challenge with two very different groups at Corinth: the *weak* and the *strong*. The sticking point between these two groups was eating meat that had been sacrificed to idols.

Dining Dilemmas

Meat was expensive and thus rare in the ancient world—except during religious festivals, when temples served sacrificial meat at their attached restaurants. Archaeologists have uncovered a restaurant with three dining rooms built on the east side of the courtyard at the temple of Asclepius in Corinth.[1] Below is an actual invitation to a temple restaurant in Egypt. The meat must have been particularly good, because five invitations to this restaurant have been discovered!

> Apollonius requests you to dine at the table of the Lord Serapis (a Greek god) on the occasion of the coming of age of his brothers in the temple of Thoeris.[2]

Paul describes two kinds of diners at Corinth: *strong* Christians, who eat meat sacrificed to idols, and *weak* Christians, who believe it's wrong to do so. Keep in mind that most of the meat in the market had been sacrificed to idols.

Paul doesn't try to eliminate the division between the *weak* and the *strong*; in fact he recognizes it. The factions we saw in the last chapter were sinful divisions based on pride, power, and a desire to get into an in group. Here the division is real, between more mature Christians and a less mature group.

Paul first incarnates with the *strong* Christians by agreeing with them that it is OK to eat sacrificial meat:

> Therefore, as to the eating of food offered to idols, we know that "an idol has no real existence," and that "there is no God but one." (1 Cor. 8:4)

Then he invites the *strong* to incarnate with the *weak* by explaining where the *weak* are coming from:

> However, not all possess this knowledge. But some, through former association with idols, eat food as really offered to an idol, and their conscience, being *weak*, is defiled. (v. 7)

Because of their past, the *weak* recoil at the thought of eating meat sacrificed to idols. It's easy to imagine them shrinking back from eating at a temple as they recall the sights, the smells, and the memories of worshiping there. Before J. I. Packer was a Christian, he played

---

1. Jerome Murphy-O'Conner, *St. Paul's Corinth: Text and Archaeology* (Collegeville, MN: Liturgical Press, 2003), 187.
2. Quoted in Anthony C. Thiselton, *The First Epistle to the Corinthians* (Grand Rapids, MI: Eerdmans, 2000), 619.

the saxophone in a jazz band. When he became a believer, he walked away from playing sax for many years because it had so many negative associations for him. Proximity to old flesh patterns was dangerous.

Paul's problem isn't with the beliefs of the *strong*, but with their behavior:

> But take care that this right of yours does not somehow become a stumbling block to the *weak*. For if anyone sees you who have knowledge eating in an idol's temple, will he not be encouraged, if his conscience is weak, to eat food offered to idols? And so by your knowledge this *weak* person is destroyed, the brother for whom Christ died. Thus, sinning against your brothers and wounding their conscience when it is weak, you sin against Christ. (vv. 9–12)

Here's Paul's concern: the *weak* are eating meat because of the influence and example of the *strong*. They want to get *in* with the *strong*. The *weak* sin because they go against their conscience in order to get *in*.

Later, Paul describes another scenario in which someone invites one of the Corinthian Christians to his home and serves sacrificial meat from the marketplace for dinner.[3]

> If one of the unbelievers invites you to dinner and you are disposed to go, eat whatever is set before you without raising any question on the ground of conscience. But if someone says to you, "This has been offered in sacrifice," then do not eat it, for the sake of the one who informed you, and for the sake of conscience—I do not mean your conscience, but his. (10:27–29b)

Paul says, "If you sense you are with a *weak* person, don't eat the meat."

This is beginning to feel a little galling for the *strong*. In his next breath, Paul anticipates their reaction:

> For why should my liberty be determined by someone else's conscience? If I partake with thankfulness, why am I denounced because of that for which I give thanks? (vv. 29b–30)

---

3. Thiselton, *First Corinthians*, 783.

The *strong* want to know, "Why should I become a codependent? Why do I need to be controlled by your hang-ups?" The modern person fears being trapped in a relationship where we lose our identity.

Along with the apostle Paul, I say, "Welcome to love!" Let me explain.

Paul calls the *strong* to not grasp their rights out of love for a *weaker* brother or sister. Just before this, he writes, "Let no one seek his own good, but the good of his neighbor" (1 Cor. 10:24). He wants the *strong* not to grasp at the privilege of being right, just as Jesus did not grasp at his divinity. Earlier Paul writes,

> But take care that this right of yours does not somehow become a stumbling block to the weak. . . . Therefore, if food makes my brother stumble, I will never eat meat, lest I make my brother stumble. (8:9, 13)

When the *strong* die to their rights, they strengthen the faith of the *weak*. When powerful people lower themselves in love, they create a Jesus community.

The Complexity of Love

Imagine what it feels like to be invited to a non-Christian's home. You've been looking forward to this dinner all week. It's not too likely that other Christians will be there, so you'll be able to enjoy your meat. As you enter, you smell the meat sizzling. As the servant approaches with the meat dish, your mouth starts watering. Just then someone across the table says, "That's sacrificial meat." Inwardly you groan as you motion the servant away. You got stuck sitting across from a *weak* Christian. Love is inconvenient.

Look how complicated life has become in this situation for the *strong*:

- I need to be alert to other Christians and their opinions.
- I have to eliminate an innocent pleasure from my life because other Christians are confused and legalistic.
- I can't complain.

The problem with eating idol meat illuminates how common the *love* J-Curve is for a follower of Jesus. It is not a big, dramatic death, just lots of mini-deaths. When you love like this, you lose your identity, but take on Christ's identity. When his path becomes your path, his image becomes your image. Like him, you don't grasp at privilege. When you lower yourself in love, allowing your behavior to be shaped by someone else's weakness, you've entered the world of love, and you form a Jesus community. Your mini-death creates oneness.

> When you love like this, you lose your
> identity, but take on Christ's identity.

Knowledge Is Toxic

The *strong* run roughshod over the *weak* because the *strong* have a narrow view of knowledge:

> Now concerning food offered to idols: we know that "all of us possess *knowledge*." This *"knowledge" puffs up*, but love builds up. If anyone imagines that he *knows* something, he does not yet know as he ought to *know*. But if anyone loves God, he is *known* by God. (1 Cor. 8:1–3)

The *strong* Corinthians *know* idol meat is harmless, but they use that knowledge to *puff* themselves up. The Greek fables described a frog that puffed itself up with air. When the Corinthians depersonalize knowledge and separate it from love, they become puffed up. They are using knowledge to move up the Failure-Boasting Chart.

Knowing for Paul requires entering into a person's life. Recall that Paul wants to *know Christ in the fellowship of his sufferings* (see Phil. 3:10). He *knows* Jesus by participating in his life, by learning the cadence of dying and rising. Not eating meat, then, becomes a way of *knowing* the *weak*, of participating in their life, of accepting them and their weak knowledge.

Learning to love my daughter Courtney by slowing down and knowing her was a turning point for me. Normally I operated like the *strong* Corinthians, who knew idol meat was harmless. I knew Courtney had committed to doing her chores and that she was angry with me for making her do them. I knew that because she said so. But like the *strong* Corinthians, I had missed Courtney, the person. For me, that meant slowing down, being aware of her, wondering, and asking questions. Knowing the other person and the pattern of dying as the center of love leads the *strong* into a life of love and deference for the *weak*. The cross re-enacted is wisdom.

The Seduction of the Inner Ring

Unlike the factions we considered in the previous chapter, the *weak* and the *strong* Corinthians aren't divided. In fact, that's the problem—the *weak* so want to get *in* with the *strong* that they are willing to sacrifice their integrity. Their desire to be *in the strong* robs them of being *in Jesus*.

The *strong* are likely those with "social power, influence, political status and wealth," but also include "a traditional Roman value of ability or competence in a variety of areas," while the *weak* are not only "of low social standing," but part of a nondescript "mass of undifferentiated citizens" who crave identity and acceptance by the *strong*.[4]

C. S. Lewis, speaking to his Oxford students, captured the toxic power of our desire to be in an in group. Every community has a hidden in group, says Lewis.

> You discover gradually, in almost indefinable ways, that it exists and that you are outside it. . . . People think they are in it after they have in fact been pushed out of it, or before they have been allowed in; this provides great amusement for those who are really inside.
>
> I believe that in all men's lives . . . one of the most dominant elements is the desire to be inside the local Ring and the terror of being left outside. . . . Unless you take measures to prevent it, this desire is going to be one of the chief motives of your life.
>
> [What many young people want is] the sacred little attic or studio, the heads bent together . . . and the delicious knowledge that we—we four or five all huddled beside this stove—are the people who know. In short what the Inner Ring . . . offers is precisely what

---

4. Khiok-khng Yeo, *Rhetorical Interaction in 1 Corinthians 8 and 10: A Formal Analysis with Preliminary Suggestions for a Chinese Cross-Cultural Hermeneutic*, Biblical Interpretation 9 (Leiden: Brill, 1995), 90, quoted in Thiselton, *First Corinthians*, 644.

the serpent offered Eve . . . the knowledge that makes mere people into Gods. Your genuine Inner Ring exists for exclusion.[5]

This dynamic can be seen when a dirty joke is told among friends. If you don't laugh, you are an outsider and might be cast out. Likewise, gossip creates a shared group of sympathizers who are in the know about someone else. If you say something good about the person who is the focus of the gossip, you disrupt the quiet union of feasting on someone else's blood and risk becoming an outsider yourself. Whatever you are *in* radically shapes who you are.

The Obligations of the Strong

Paul doesn't call the *strong* to stop being *strong*, but to use their privilege to enter the world of the *weak*. We can do that only when we see that the church is Jesus's body.

As Paul lowers himself in love by not eating meat, he enters not just the lives of the *weak*, but Christ. He bluntly tells the *strong* that by "sinning against your brothers and wounding their conscience when it is weak, you sin against Christ" (1 Cor. 8:12). Ever since Jesus accosted Paul on the Damascus Road by asking, "Why are you persecuting me?" (Acts 9:4b), "Paul can't look on the face of the weak without seeing the face of Jesus."[6]

When the *strong* learn to love the *weak*, it creates a Jesus community. By inviting the *strong* to follow the path of Jesus by surrendering their rights, Paul flattens the *weak/strong* hierarchy and closes the distance between the two groups. When the *strong* re-enact Jesus's death by lowering themselves to the *weak*, the body of Christ is created:

> For he himself is our peace, who has made us both one and has broken down in his flesh the dividing wall of hostility . . . that he might create in himself one new man in place of the two, so making peace, and might reconcile us both to God in one body through the cross, thereby killing the hostility. (Eph. 2:14–16)

---

5. C. S. Lewis, "Commemoration Oration at King's College," December 1944, quoted in Alan Jacobs, *The Narnian: The Life and Imagination of C. S. Lewis* (New York: Harper San Francisco, 2005), 178–180.

6. J. A. T. Robinson, *The Body: A Study in Pauline Theology* (London: SCM, 1952), 58, quoted in Thiselton, *First Corinthians*, 655.

Paul does not rebuke the *weak* other than in his brief opening comment that the *weak* are incorrect. He empowers the *weak* by putting the onus on the *strong* to lower themselves. Living the J-Curve collapses the social hierarchies that prevent friendship between different classes. It unites differences without erasing them.

Living the J-Curve

Each of us is surrounded by *weak* people with ill-formed or bad opinions. My obligation as a *strong* person is to treat them with respect. I don't have to endorse their views, but I must treat them with dignity.

This has enormous practical implications for my interactions with people who are different or distant from me. It means, for example, that my "white privilege" is real and obligates me to love across social and cultural barriers. So where do I begin? Even though I lived and ministered in the inner city for ten years, I'm not sure. But I do know how to start. Five years ago, I started praying regularly and seeking opportunities to love. Small things are beginning.

To love another person, I begin with "I don't know . . ." That's where wisdom begins, with knowing you don't have wisdom (Prov. 3:6–8). To care for the person means going through a dying—not grasping at my right to eat in a temple, not grasping at the comfort of my in group. That's why prayer and the Spirit are so important. Without the Spirit of Jesus, I either remain distant or I love from above—that's called *paternalism*. When I do that, I forget the person.

To love another person, I begin with "I don't know . . ."

A common place to learn the complexity of love is in our families, where we experience the fragility of the *weak*. In most relationships, if things get a little dicey, we aren't "trapped." That is, there is space to stay away or distance ourselves. But family is sticky, which means hurt can build up. Now that our culture has turned judging into an art form, we might feel at times that we are walking on eggshells at family gatherings. From the apostle Paul, we learn that that's OK. In a fallen world, love treads softly.

When we say *community* or *intimacy*, people instinctively think of a warm group of loving friends. Don't confuse that with the body of Christ. The nonwarm, nonloving people—*the weak*—require my ongoing death. Jesus died to make us one. We die to make that a present reality.

Jesus died to make us one. We die to
make that a present reality.

33

Leadership Goes Low

Re-enacting Jesus in Community

We've repeatedly seen that Paul embodies the gospel. Instead of using the privileges of leadership to escape suffering, he descends the J-Curve. We can sustain a Jesus community only when the leaders continually re-enact the gospel.

After telling the *strong* to lower themselves to the *weak*, Paul reminds them that he didn't take their money, but instead provided for his needs by his tentmaking (his descent). Following Jesus's pattern of not grasping at his rights, Paul first affirms his right to be paid, then immediately renounces it:[1]

> The Lord commanded that those who proclaim the gospel should get their living by the gospel. *But I have made no use of any of these rights.* (1 Cor. 9:14–15a)

Paul's refusal to take money seems strange. It's like Billy Graham moonlighting at McDonald's during a crusade. Let me explain.

We can sustain a Jesus community only when
the leaders continually re-enact the gospel.

---

1. Michael J. Gorman, *Cruciformity: Paul's Narrative Spirituality of the Cross* (Grand Rapids, MI: Eerdmans, 2001), 183. I am indebted to Gorman for the main thought of this chapter.

In the Roman world, a traveling teacher such as Paul would be-friend a wealthy person, who would support the teacher financially. In turn, the teacher would give honor and wisdom to his patron. Paul is no mere traveling teacher—he is a highly educated, upper-class Jewish scholar and Roman citizen who can rub shoulders at the highest levels of society. That is all the more reason for him to attach himself to a wealthy patron. It would look like this:

Not only does Paul not participate in this patronage system, he does something no Roman elite would do—he works with his hands. Manual labor was beneath the upper classes—remember, the "physical" was considered impure. The Roman orator Cicero (106–43 BC) referred to "craftsmen, petty shopkeepers, and all that filth in the cities," calling their work "degrading." "The very wages of a laborer are the badges of slavery."[2]

So tentmaking isn't just a side job for Paul—by doing it, he de-grades himself. Instead of reaching up for the protection of a wealthy patron, Paul descends into "all that filth." Why? Love. Love for the lost. Love for the *weak*. He explains:

> For though I am free from all, I have made myself a slave to all, that I might win more of them. To the Jews I became as a Jew, in order to win Jews. To those under the law I became as one under the law . . . that I might win those under the law. To those outside the law I became as one outside the law . . . that I might win those outside the law. To the weak I became weak, that I might win the weak. (1 Cor. 9:19–22 AT)

Sitting at the workbench with other tentmakers, repairing sails and sewing awnings, Paul tells these men, whose wages are "the badges of slavery," about the death and resurrection of a Jewish peasant who redeemed them from their sin.

Paul becomes *weak* to win the *weak*. He dies as he shares about a dying Savior. He looks like the gospel he preaches. He reeks of authenticity. So when Paul asks the *strong* Corinthians to love the *weak*, he's

---

2. Cicero, *Pro Flacco*, 18, and *De officiis*, 1.5, quoted in Ramsey MacMullen, *Roman Social Relations: 50 B.C to A.D. 284* (New Haven, CT: Yale University Press, 1974), 114–15. MacMullen explains, "Since the better part of a man was mental and spiritual, whoever depended on mere physical powers for his living lived that much lower." *Roman Social Relations*, 114.

reminding them they've already seen the gospel re-enacted. Paul drives home his point: "Be imitators of me, as I am of Christ" (1 Cor. 11:1).

Figure 33A below captures the immensity of what Paul does in his tentmaking.

Fig. 33A. Paul's Descent

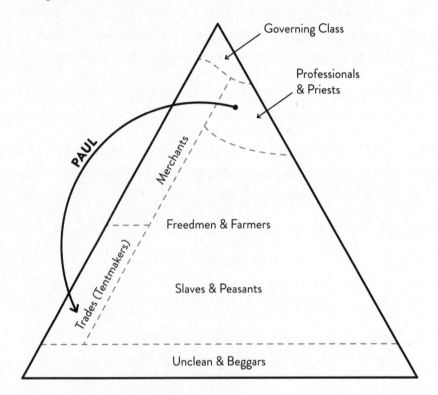

The Cultural Counterattack

Paul debasing himself bothers the Corinthians. In fact, the Judaizers use his tentmaking as evidence that he isn't a true apostle. Paul responds by wondering when humbling himself became a sin:

> Did I commit a sin in humbling myself so that you might be exalted, because I preached God's gospel to you free of charge? (2 Cor. 11:7)

Why are the Corinthians upset?

- They have lost control. They don't have power over Paul because he isn't on the dole. He is free from any obligation to them.
- Paul hasn't joined their in group. His stature would enhance their reputation, but Paul won't help them move up the Failure-Boasting Chart. He doesn't "play their game."
- They are unnerved by Paul's treatment of lowly tentmakers as equals because they've defined themselves by wealth and status.

Figure 33B below captures what the *strong* Corinthians see and what Paul sees:

Fig. 33B. The Corinthians' View vs. Paul's View

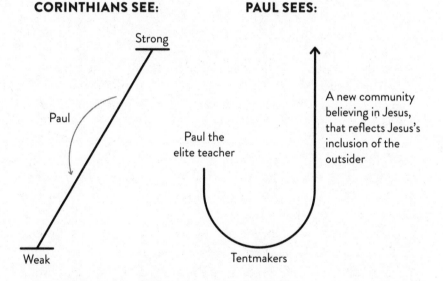

Imagine how baffling this is for the *strong*. They wonder, "Is Paul one of us or one of them? Which group is he in?" He's in Jesus's group, of course. Because he's *in Christ*, he's free of all in groups. He uses his freedom to create a Jesus community that brings together the *strong* and the *weak*, thus making *in Christ* a present reality.

Incarnating with the Weak

Paul goes into some detail describing how he incarnates. He takes on the lifestyle and culture of the people he seeks to win to Christ: "To the Jew, I become a Jew; to the weak, I become weak." He does so to *win some* to the beauty and wonder of Jesus. He enters their worlds so they can enter Jesus's world.

Paul also crosses "the smell line." In the ancient world, most people did not have access to public baths and might wash just once a month—or not at all. I first encountered the smell line in my early thirties when visiting Kiberia outside Nairobi, Kenya, where a million people crowded into a shantytown without sanitation. The smell overwhelmed me. But Paul crosses the smell line because that's what the Son of God did. Jesus almost certainly smelled.

In the West, up until about 1900, smell divided the *weak* from everyone else. In the mid-1930s, George Orwell wrote:

> Here you come to the real secret of class distinctions in the West— the real reason why a European of bourgeois [middle class] up- bringing, even when he calls himself a Communist, cannot without a hard effort think of a working man as his equal. It is summed up in four frightful words which people nowadays are chary [wary] of uttering, but which were bandied about quite freely in my child- hood. The words were: *The lower classes smell.*[3]

Because Paul brings his fellow tentmakers to the house churches, the homes of *strong* Christians reek. Paul introduces the *strong* to the fragrance of Christ. The beauty of the body of Christ brings the washed and the unwashed together.

Because the unwashed were so despised, we know almost nothing about the world of the *weak* from any source in the ancient world. Outside of the Bible, we have no scenes in which slaves are treated as people with any sympathy, let alone dignity. They just don't exist.[4] Our only detailed description of foot washing is Jesus's washing of his disciples' feet (John 13). The reason for washing feet wasn't just dirt; feet smell.

One of the few documents that gives us a glimpse of the *weak* comes from the *Satyricon*, a satire about the Roman upper classes written when Paul was writing. Trimalchio, a newly rich but unrefined merchant, throws a lavish feast. During the feast:

---

3. George Orwell, *The Road to Wigan Pier*, 1937, available at The Complete Works of George Orwell, www.george-orwell.org/The_Road_to_Wigan_Pier/7.html. Emphasis added.
4. Erich Auerbach makes this point in his classic book on the Western mind, *Mimesis: The Representation of Reality in Western Literature* (Princeton, NJ: Princeton University Press, 2003), 21, 43–49.

A small dish happened to fall to the floor . . . and a slave picked it up. Seeing this, Trimalchio ordered that the boy be punished by a box on the ear, and made him throw it down again; a janitor followed with his broom and swept the silver dish away among the litter. Next followed two long-haired Ethiopians . . . and poured wine upon our hands, for no one offered us water. When complimented upon these elegant extras, the host cried out, ". . . I ordered each [guest] a separate table: that way these *stinking* slaves won't make us so hot with their crowding."[5]

In case you missed it, a silver dish falls to the floor during the feast and a slave boy thoughtfully picks it up. To show he is so rich he can throw silver dishes away, Trimalchio shames and abuses this boy. He elevates himself by treating the *weak* cruelly. He also separates the typical U-shaped table into smaller separate tables to disperse the smell of the "stinking slaves." This scene is disgusting, but it gives us a window into how galling Paul's love for the *weak* is to the Corinthians. He wants the *strong* not only to welcome this weak slave boy, but also to give him a seat at their table and serve him! Paul is creating a Jesus community.

We have a snapshot of a Jesus community in action two hundred years later, about 260 AD. During a severe persecution, the head deacon of Rome was given three days to bring all the wealth of the church to the city manager. Three days later, the deacon returned with a large crowd of beggars; he said, "This is the wealth of the church." The deacon was led off to martyrdom.[6]

Secular liberalism has made inclusion into an idol, but inclusion is exactly what Paul is doing. He's including the *weak*. In fact, our cultural elites got the idea of inclusion from Jesus.

Paul's goal is not inclusion for its own sake. He's no Marxist creating solidarity for the poor for its own sake. He never makes love the center. That's what secular liberalism does—it turns compassion and incarnating into a demand. Paul always has Jesus at the center.

---

5. *Satyricon*, chap. 34, https://books.google.com/books?id=TxjazK1dacMC&pg=PT55. Emphasis added. Petronius (AD 27–66), Emperor Nero's director of entertainment, is believed to have been the author of the *Satyricon*.

6. Peter Brown, *Through the Eye of the Needle: Wealth, the Fall of Rome, and the Making of Christianity in the West, 350–550 AD* (Princeton, NJ; Oxford: Princeton University Press, 2012), 77.

A Son-Slave

Paul uses the language of slavery to describe how he loves: "For though I am free from all, I have made myself a slave to all" (1 Cor. 9:19a AT). Like Jesus, he takes "the form of a slave" (Phil. 2:7b AT).[7] Most translations say *servant* instead of *slave*, but that dulls the impact of the descent of love. A servant can exit, but a slave can't.

Many of us are in slave-like situations, where we are trapped, boxed in with a problem or a person we can't escape. Realizing this keeps us from fighting a situation or a relationship in which we might experience ongoing or undeserved shame.

Through Martin Luther, we rediscovered our incredible freedom as sons and daughters of God.[8] The interior of the circle below describes our path from slavery to freedom, but the exterior describes the reverse: our path from freedom to slavery. Paul's death for others is the practice of freedom.

We love the center (believing the gospel), but we are allergic to the outside (becoming like the gospel). Paul can't imagine one without the other. He underlines this in Romans:

> The Spirit himself bears witness with our spirit that we are children of God, and if children, then heirs—heirs of God and fellow heirs with Christ, provided we suffer with him in order that we may also be glorified with him." (8:16–17)

We experience our sonship in our dying ("provided we suffer with him") and rising ("in order that we may be glorified with him"). We experience sonship in a life of suffering love. Reflecting on Romans 8:17, Richard Gaffin asks,

> Will our catechising, including that of our lives, make clear, as Paul does . . . that the comprehensive mode of our enjoying all these privi-

---

7. Most Bible translations use *servant* instead of *slave* because aspects of Roman slavery were better than American slavery. An enterprising slave could buy his way to freedom. Also, Roman slavery was multiethnic, while American slavery was monoethnic (Africans), which birthed a legacy of racism in America. But, in general, Roman slavery was more brutal than American slavery.

8. Martin Luther articulates this idea of son/slave in his book *The Freedom of the Christian Man*. See Carl Trueman, "*Simul peccator et justus*: Martin Luther and Justification," in *Justification in Perspective: Historical Developments and Contemporary Challenges*, ed. Bruce L. McCormack (Grand Rapids, MI: Baker Academic, 2006), 73–97. For additional reflections, see my essay in the Virtual Appendix, "Luther, the Last Medieval Protestant," www.seejesus.net/J-Curvebook.

leges of adopted sons is suffering with him? *There are few truths which the church down through its history has been more inclined to evade;* there are few truths which the church can less afford to evade.[9]

Fig. 33C. Slavery and Freedom

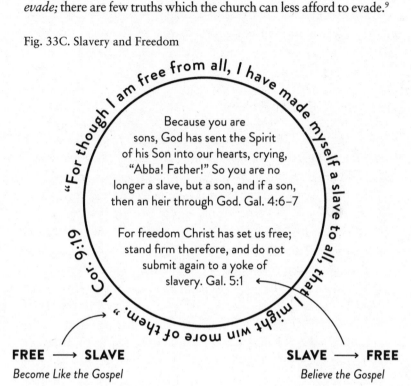

FREE ⟶ SLAVE   SLAVE ⟶ FREE
Become Like the Gospel   *Believe the Gospel*

I used to teach the immensely encouraging truth that we are sons and daughters of God without mentioning *suffering with him*. No longer. I fear it sets people up for thinking that sonship is all about having a good self-image.

Sonship is our interior face; slavery is our exterior face. The feeling of sonship is descending, like Jesus, into the world of tentmakers, living with smell. Only then do we display the fragrance of Christ. That's the normal Christian life.

The feeling of sonship is descending, like Jesus,
into the world of tentmakers, living with smell.

---

9. Richard B. Gaffin Jr., "The Usefulness of the Cross," *Westminster Theological Journal* 41, no. 2 (Spring 1979), 244. Emphasis added.

A Modern Descent to Tentmakers

So what does it look like to descend into the world of tentmakers now? My friend Paula coowns and manages a fast-food restaurant. After going through the J-Curve *Interactive Bible Study*, she told me, "The J-Curve makes sense out of my life—especially my work." She went on to explain:

> My mom started the franchise, so I began working there at fourteen. I resisted working in fast food after college because of the stigma it carries. Choosing to stay was a death to my dignity, but over the years, my work has become a pleasure. I have grown to love my career and even take pride in what people see as low. I am quiet about being the owner, so people judge me and treat me as one of the employees. The beauty of the J-Curve is a big part of my change. It has shown me it is okay to be in a low place. Jesus was. At times I am.
>
> Every time we get hit with a staff shortage, I'm at the window, taking orders. I'm already depersonalized because customers view me as low, but it's even WORSE when someone is ordering into an object (the microphone). Studying the J-Curve has empowered me to see these moments and to live in them instead of getting angry at people or walking away in shame. Jesus washed his disciples' feet, and I'm constantly wiping people's feet. In my twenty-six years in fast food, I've been cussed at, stolen from, verbally abused, threatened, and lied to. When a customer submits a complaint to corporate, we have to follow up by offering that person a free meal. Studying Paul's descent to the tentmakers tells me it's okay to be treated like a slave.
>
> My employees, mostly teenagers and kids in their twenties, see the job as "low." Society tells them this is the worst job, and it affects their performance—even if they enjoy the work. I have to be down low with "the tentmakers" to encourage them.
>
> Being down low has given me the chance to experience many resurrections. Today I can say that many of the best things in my life came from fast food—I met and fell in love with my husband at our restaurant!
>
> In the last couple of weeks, I received several notes from former employees. One of them is now an ER nurse. She said we trained her to multitask, which ultimately helped her be a better ER nurse.

Another former employee texted me:

> 3 years ago I wandered into [name of restaurant] and applied for a job. This might sound silly, but that job changed my life. I don't generally tell people this, but before I started working for you, I was struggling with depression. Silly as it may sound, my job gave me purpose. It was the first thing in years I'd been motivated to do my absolute best at. You have no idea of how much it meant to me getting hired there.

Another employee who just resigned to get a better job wrote me, "The way you are open about your faith is something unique. You have used your store to help so many people." God is using our business to point people to Jesus, even if they can't see it's Jesus we are pointing to.

Paula's business gives away about $100,000 a year to the community and especially to families with medical needs. The J-Curve has shown her that the "low" place is OK, that God is with her in fast food. He is using her to create a small piece of heaven that she can be proud of. And he's using her to point people to Jesus, even if they can't see it's Jesus she is pointing to.

34

Keeping Jesus Pure

The J-Curve Divides the Community

I love doing seeJesus's *Person of Jesus* studies with seekers.[1] It's a real joy to see people discovering truths from the Word and even falling in love with Jesus. I saw that happening with a biker couple, Steven and Elsa. They had come to a Biker Sunday at our church, and he proudly wore his Christian Motorcyclists Association jacket, but you could tell they had a rough background.

Nine months into our study, Steven confided to me that Elsa was pregnant. The rest of the story spilled out: he was still married to another woman, who lived in a nursing home, bedridden with multiple sclerosis. She was filled with hate for him. I asked Steven and Elsa if I could take them to lunch.

At lunch, my first job was to incarnate, to understand their world. I'd checked on his wife, and yes, everything was true. She was an extraordinarily difficult person. Over that meal and a subsequent one, I asked Steven to honor both his wedding vows and Elsa by living celibate, separate from Elsa. I even offered to raise funds to pay for a separate apartment.

[1]. *Person of Jesus* is a series of energetic, interactive Bible studies by Paul Miller designed to help Christians and seekers alike discover the beauty of Jesus. Learn more at seeJesus.net/person-of-jesus.

At lunch, my first job was to incarnate,
to understand their world.

Steven replied that he didn't consider himself married anymore. He had inhaled the therapeutic vision of *the good* that dominates our relational culture: because he didn't feel married, he wasn't. Feelings trumped law.

I asked Steven to help me understand what I should do with what Paul told the Corinthians when he discovered a man was committing incest in their community. I read 1 Corinthians 5 to Steven:

> It is actually reported that there is sexual immorality among you, and of a kind that is not tolerated even among pagans, for a man has his father's wife. And you are arrogant! Ought you not rather to mourn? Let him who has done this be removed from among you. (vv. 1–2)

In order to help Steven understand what Paul says next, I used the example of a prostitute and identified three possible ways the church can welcome her.

- A *practicing prostitute* is warmly welcomed into the church community.
- A *repentant prostitute* who turns away from prostitution is warmly welcomed into full membership, including communion.
- A *repenting prostitute* who falls back into sin, but continues to turn and repent, is welcomed into the community and communion.

Then I said that Paul does not welcome an *unrepentant prostitute* who *claims to be a Christian*:

> I wrote to you in my letter not to associate with sexually immoral people—not at all meaning the sexually immoral of this world, or the greedy and swindlers, or idolaters, since then you would need to go out of the world. But now I am writing to you not to associate with anyone who bears the name of brother if he is guilty of sexual immorality or greed, or is an idolater, reviler, drunkard, or swindler—not even to eat with such a one. (vv. 9–11)

Paul is guarding the integrity of the church community from evil. Since evil has no substance of its own or power to create, it needs a host to corrupt. For example, our body's T-cells struggle to destroy cancer because cancer masks itself as normal cells. Judas masked his betrayal of Jesus with a kiss. Likewise, cloaking incest with Jesus's name brings evil into the heart of the community.

Evil is on Paul's mind as he tells the church to shun this couple. The Israelites at Passover rid their houses of leaven, as a symbol of eliminating evil. Only a tiny amount of leaven makes bread rise. Only a little bit of evil destroys the whole.

> Do you not know that a little leaven leavens the whole lump? Cleanse out the old leaven that you may be a new lump, as you really are unleavened. For Christ, our Passover lamb, has been sacrificed. Let us therefore celebrate the festival, not with the old leaven, the leaven of malice and *evil*, but with the unleavened bread of sincerity and truth. (vv. 6–8)

The Sowing and Reaping Trajectory

Strikingly, Paul doesn't incarnate with either the Corinthians or the couple committing incest. He doesn't try to "understand" this couple's background or empathize about how difficult this must be. That's because the *love* J-Curve sits in a biblical and moral frame. As much as Paul holds up love as a missing value for the Corinthians, he does not, like secular liberalism, make love the center. Love exists in the larger frame of the mind of God, which includes the Old Testament's radical call to sexual and moral purity. Paul isn't singling out sex; he also tells the Corinthians to shun the drunkard and swindler (v. 11).

Keep in mind that every culture shuns. Every culture has taboos that, if broken, will lead to the shunning of the "sinner." In the past, the F-word was taboo. Now it's cool for comedians to use the F-word, but the N-word is taboo. Michael Richards felt angst because he used the N-word in anger with an African-American. Of course, both words are evil. Our taboos are good.

Shunning introduces this Corinthian couple to another thoroughly biblical pattern: sowing and reaping. If you sow or do bad things, you reap bad consequences. Much of evil is focused on overturning this narrative. We saw that an attitude of "What happens in Vegas, stays in Vegas" denies the sowing → reaping cycle. When Satan said to Eve, "You will not surely die" (Gen. 3:4), he was saying that she and Adam could eat the fruit without fear of consequences.

Sowing and reaping is on the father's mind in the parable of the prodigal son (Luke 15:11–32). His greedy, pleasure-seeking son wants his inheritance now because his father is keeping him from having fun. The only thing that will rescue the son is for him to reap what he sows. After receiving his inheritance, the son sows foolishness and reaps poverty. Only when he is finally destitute, down with the pigs, reaping what he's sown, does he realize his foolishness.

The father of the prodigal does not send care packages, money, or help. He lets his son feel the full consequences of his sin by not intervening in the sowing-reaping path. He's aware that life is lived in paths or narratives that are either shaped by God (the J-Curve) or by our flesh.

It's increasingly common for parents, who've put their children at the center, to not let them experience the pain of their own foolishness. The parents think their love will create lasting community with their children, but, in fact, they are keeping their children from maturing. Their desire to prevent pain in their children's lives, to help them avoid the J-Curve, leads them to interrupt the good work of sowing → reaping. Currently, idolizing family and relationships is creating a whole generation of family enablers.

The sowing-reaping path is on Paul's mind here. He wants to save this man:

> When you are assembled in the name of the Lord Jesus and my spirit is present, with the power of our Lord Jesus, you are to deliver this man to Satan for the destruction of the flesh, so that his spirit may be saved in the day of the Lord. (1 Cor. 5:4–5)

Paul wants this man to enter the *repentance* J-Curve. If you recall, in the *repentance* J-Curve, evil is inside of you.

When I continued to pose my suggestion of abstinence and separation to Steven, he finally left. Sadly, he found a church with no moral frame. Because our culture removes Jesus's compassion from its moral frame, even the evangelical church is recoiling from teaching sowing and reaping, and the good work of introducing people to the *repentance* J-Curve. The *love* J-Curve shaped how I approached Steven, but he needed the *repentance* J-Curve. Only in the dying of repentance was there hope that *his spirit might be saved*. You've got to keep your J-Curves straight.

A *fellowship of his sufferings* does not mean rolling over in the face of evil. It means the opposite. Like a Hebrew prophet, Paul boldly confronts evil. Confronting masked evil almost always leads to some kind of dying. Paul's letter of 2 Corinthians is one long death for him as he responds to the Judaizers who are corrupting the Corinthians. My most difficult, most enduring "deaths" have come from confronting Christian leaders who were caught in sin.

Friends of mine, business owners, suspected they were being slandered in their community by one of their managers. They were familiar with the J-Curve and assumed that this was just a *suffering* J-Curve that they had to accept. I said, "No way. This is evil you have to go after." In other words, the sanity of God's law ("Don't bear false witness") helped them see that evil needed to be confronted, not understood. They confronted their manager, and several weeks later, she quit. Dying doesn't mean hiding.

Sometimes creating a Jesus community means *dividing*. If you idolize community, perhaps by putting your children's happiness at the center of your family, then you will eventually destroy community. If you make inclusion and compassion sacred, you'll give way to evil and end up destroying a Jesus community and creating an inclusive tribe. Sometimes, to remove evil, the body of Christ needs surgery.

My most difficult, most enduring "deaths" have come from confronting Christian leaders who were caught in sin. Dying doesn't mean hiding.

35

Jesus

The Ultimate Party Crasher

One of the hardest, most enduring divisions to bridge in any community, let alone a Jesus community, is the rich/poor barrier. Wealth naturally separates. If you add money to any system, it increases the space between people. For instance, if you are limited to $300 for a week's vacation with your family, you can only go camping, jammed together in a tent, sharing public showers. With $2,000, you can rent a condo at the beach, with multiple bedrooms and bathrooms. With $10,000 you can travel to Europe, far away from everyone else. As money increases, distance increases.

When Paul discovers the rich in the Corinthian church treating the poor badly at communion, he is appalled:

> When you come together, it is not the Lord's supper that you eat. For in eating, each one goes ahead with his own meal. One goes hungry, another gets drunk. What! Do you not have houses to eat and drink in? Or do you despise the church of God and humiliate those who have nothing? (1 Cor. 11:20–22a)

To better understand what went on during a celebration of the Lord's Supper, read this description of a typical feast by Pliny the Younger (AD 61–113), a Roman nobleman:

The best dishes were set in front of himself [the host] and a select few, and cheap scraps of food before the rest of the company. He even put the wine into very small flasks, divided into three categories . . . one for himself and us, another for his lesser friends (all his friends are graded) and the third for his and our freed persons.[1]

Notice the triple layer: close friends, lesser friends, and freedmen. Your social ranking determined the quality of your food and wine. Pliny's and Paul's descriptions are similar.

Fig. 35A. Paul and Pliny

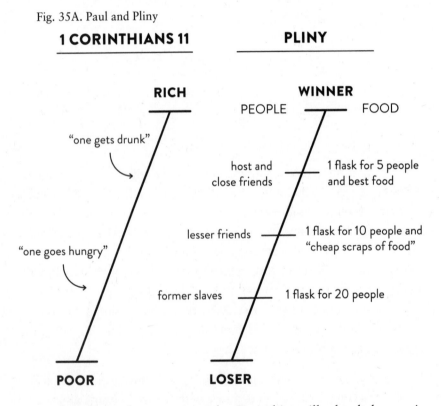

Archaeologists have uncovered a Corinthian villa that helps us visualize what happened during the Lord's Supper, since house churches met in the homes of the wealthy.[2] The house itself reinforced the dis-

---

1. Pliny, *Letters*, 2.6, quoted in Anthony C. Thiselton, *The First Epistle to the Corinthians* (Grand Rapids, MI: Eerdmans, 2000), 861.

2. The floor plan of the Anaploga Villa is in S. G. Miller, "A Mosaic Floor from a Roman Villa at Anaploga," *Hesperia* 41 (1972), 335; and Jerome Murphy-O'Connor, *St. Paul's Corinth: Text and Archaeology* (Collegeville, MN: Liturgical Press, 2003), 179.

tance between the *strong* and the *weak*. The *strong* likely ate in the ornate private dining room, the triclinium. About nine people could recline on couches around a U-shaped table resting on an ornate tile floor. Freedmen and slaves were allowed in the open atrium, which could squeeze in thirty or more.[3] It was like camping!

Imagine a house church gathering. The *strong* arrive first—their shorter working hours allow them the luxury of a visit to the bathhouse prior to the evening gathering. They are relaxed and gleaming with oil from a rubdown. Slaves greet them at the door and usher them into the spacious triclinium, where a feast awaits.

Several hours later, at the end of their twelve-hour day, the *weak* straggle in—the tentmakers, the shopkeepers, and a number of freedmen and slaves. As they crowd into the atrium, the smell noticeably worsens. Most haven't taken a bath in weeks. Some artisans come with half a loaf of bread; others have nothing. The *weak* share their meager fare with one another. They hear the laughter from the dining room as slaves scurry back and forth carrying loaded trays of food for the *strong*.

Just before the service begins, the *strong* join the *weak* in the atrium. Several of the *strong* stagger slightly; they've clearly had too much wine. The *strong* are oblivious as several of the *weak* shake their heads in disgust. Here's the imaginary reaction of a barmaid:

> "Not slave and free, not poor and rich!" That makes me laugh! Clearly the better class gentlemen have been looked after for quite some time in the dining room when our kind comes rushing along. They eat lavishly, drink the finest wines. They mix up the well-laid table of the master of the house with the Lord's table. If we're lucky, all that's left for the shared meal is a bit of bread and a sip of wine. We get the bits.[4]

Paul Goes after the Strong

When Paul confronts these rich Christians—the leaders of the church—he becomes bitingly sarcastic. The *strong* have mocked the *weak*; now Paul mocks their desire for prominence. Here's one scholar's

---

3. Thiselton, *First Corinthians*, 860.
4. Hans Frör, *You Wretched Corinthians!* trans. John Bowden (London: SCM, 1995), 59, quoted in Thiselton, *First Corinthians*, 851.

translation of 1 Corinthians 11:19: "For of course there must be 'discrimination' among you so that it will be clear who among you are the 'distinguished ones.'"[5] When the *strong* eat in the triclinium, they show they are the "distinguished ones," the important ones. It's easy to imagine the impact as Paul's letter is read aloud to this house church. The *strong* look down, ashamed, and smiles spread over the faces of the *weak*.

I love how Paul takes sides. He doesn't remain above the fray or hedge his bets with the *strong*. He unabashedly speaks truth to power. His reaction is shaped by a clear vision of the true and good, the dying love of Jesus that includes the *weak*. We're watching Paul's template, the J-Curve, flatten a community by shaming the *strong* and empowering the *weak*.

I love how Paul takes sides. He doesn't remain above the fray or hedge his bets with the *strong*. He unabashedly speaks truth to power.

When Paul says, "It's not the Lord's supper that you eat" (v. 20), we hear "the Lord's supper" as a single phrase, like "Mother's Day." But Paul means, "It's Jesus's meal; he's the Lord of this feast. But when you mock and exclude the *weak* who are his very body, it is no longer his feast; it's a supper for the *strong*."[6] Pliny is correct—who you eat with at a feast announces your identity. When you include and honor the *weak*, you announce the identity of Jesus, for they are the beauty of his broken and scarred body on earth.

Paul exposes the sins of the leaders because he's a follower of Jesus, the ultimate party crasher. At my favorite Jesus feast (Luke 14), Jesus seems to forget he's a guest, eating another person's food. When he notices other guests jostling for better seats, he tells them that if they want to get noticed, they're better off taking a lower seat; then, when the host corrects the ranking, everyone will see them moving up! By going lower, you actually become more visible.

---

5. Richard A. Horsley, *I Corinthians* (Nashville: Abingdon, 1998), 159, quoted in Thiselton, *First Corinthians*, 859.

6. G. Theissen, *The Social Setting of Pauline Christianity* (Eugene, OR: Wipf & Stock, 1982), 145–74, quoted in Thiselton, *First Corinthians*, 862.

Fig. 35B. A Working Model of the Church

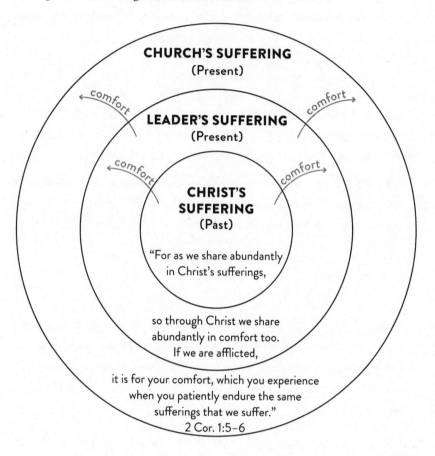

Then Jesus turns to the host and tells him that he appears generous, but he's invited all the wrong people. "Next time you have a feast, go out to the highways and byways, and invite the poor, the blind, and the lame; then you will be loving, because these people can't pay you back, but your heavenly Father will." Isn't it better to be moved up by the "host of the universe" than to promote yourself by trying to appear generous?

Paul envisions a Jesus community with three layers (2 Cor. 1:3–7). As we saw earlier, Christ's dying love is at the core; the next layer is the dying love of the leaders, which invites the whole community into a dying love. In my opinion, the weakest of those three layers in our churches is the middle one—the leaders. For Christ's community to re-flect his beauty, Christian leaders need to constantly re-enact his death.

Death at the Heart of Community

Paul's inclusion of the *weak* as equal partners revolutionized humani-ty.[7] Secular liberalism, which dominates our culture, is a secular ver-sion of Jesus and Paul's theology of compassion and inclusion. But unlike secular liberalism, Paul doesn't put the *weak* or inclusion at the center. He puts Jesus's death at the center of Jesus's meal:

> The Lord Jesus on the night when he was betrayed . . . took the cup, after supper, saying, "This cup is the new covenant in my blood. Do this, as often as you drink it, in remembrance of me." For as often as you eat this bread and drink the cup, you proclaim the Lord's death until he comes. (1 Cor. 11:23, 25–26)

Every culture has death at the center. In the post-Civil War South, the lynchings of black men "protected" white culture. In Communism, the death of the bourgeois (middle class) "freed" the proletariat (the working class). In Nazism, the death of the Jews "preserved" the purity of the Aryan race. In secular liberalism, abortion "protects" a woman's freedom of choice. Someone has to die so others can live. Outside of Jesus, it's always someone else who dies. Someone else is the problem. Our founder's death lies at the center of our faith. Instead of killing our enemies so we can live, he died so that we, his enemies, can live.

Eliminating the High School Lunchroom

To visualize what Paul is doing to form a Jesus community, imagine that most sacred of all high school spaces, the lunchroom, divided up between different tribes: the football players, the nerds, the Goths, the socially awkward, and the disabled—all at their own tables. Each tribe is ranked internally and in relationship to the other tribes. Paul, the football player, leaves his table, sits with the Goths, and then brings them up to the football table. From the culture's perspective,

---

7. Peter Brown, *Through the Eye of the Needle: Wealth, the Fall of Rome, and the Making of Christianity in the West, 350–550 AD* (Princeton, NJ; Oxford: Princeton University Press, 2012), describes how, in the late 300s, the church's love for the poor captured the imagination of the broader culture.

he's destroying the lunchroom. From Paul's perspective, he's creating the body of Christ.

Paul drives home the leveling effect of the body of Christ in his description of the gifts of the Spirit (1 Corinthians 12). Frankly, most of us miss what Paul is doing here. He's only mildly interested in helping us identify our gift. The most striking feature of Paul's description of the gifts is that he doesn't rank them. Like much of the modern church, the Corinthians ranked wealth, eloquence, and leadership high. Not only does Paul flatten the gifts, but he says particular care must be given to honor the *weak*.

Paul is bringing all the tribes (rich and poor, strong and weak, slave and free) into one body—Jesus.

> For just as the body is one and has many members, and all the members of the body, though many, are one body, *so it is with Christ*. (1 Cor. 12:12)

Using *body* as a metaphor for the church, we expect Paul to say "so it is with the church," but instead he says "so it is with Christ." Christ and the church are so fused that Paul substitutes *Christ* for *church*.

Paul's vision of a Jesus community focuses not on community, but on Jesus. So when the Corinthians break up Jesus's body into tribes and factions or when the *strong* run roughshod over the *weak*, Paul is incredulous.

In his next breath, he describes how baptism, following the path of the J-Curve, erases all tribal and class differences:

> For in one Spirit we were all *baptized into one body—Jews or Greeks, slaves or free*—and all were made to drink of one Spirit. (v. 13)

Notice the similar pattern in Galatians:

> For as many of you as were baptized into Christ have put on Christ. *There is neither Jew nor Greek, there is neither slave nor free, there is no male and female*, for you are all one in Christ Jesus. (3:27–28)

Scholars believe that Paul is reciting an early church baptismal formula, "neither Jew nor Greek, . . . neither slave nor free, . . . no male and female," which was spoken as the person was being immersed.

You go down into the water as a wealthy Greek landowner and come up *one in Christ*.[8] You go down as a poor Scythian slave and come up as a son or daughter of God. The slave and landowner are now equals in the *one body* of Jesus. Our former identities have not only been erased, but replaced with his. We are now both *in Christ*. A new *us* has been created in Jesus!

Fig. 35C. Baptism

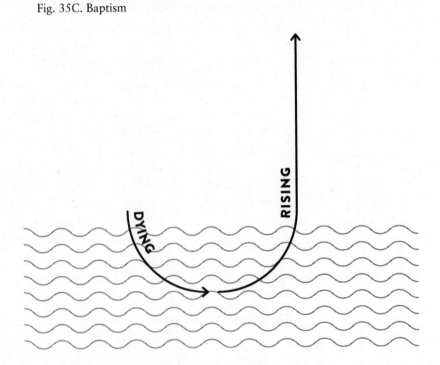

The initiation rite into the world of Jesus, baptism, relives his journey out of the world of Adam by physically acting out his dying and rising, thus placing the J-Curve at the center of a Jesus community.

Quite honestly, this takes my breath away. Don't do anything with this chapter; just let the wonder of what God wants to create in us

---

8. "But whether the person being baptized should be wholly immersed, and whether thrice or once, whether he should only be sprinkled with poured water—these details are of no importance, but ought to be optional to churches according to the diversity of countries. Yet the word 'baptize' means to immerse, and it is clear that the rite of immersion was observed in the ancient church." John Calvin, *Institutes of the Christian Religion*, ed. John T. McNeill, trans. Ford Lewis Battles (Louisville, KY: Westminster, 2006), 4.15.19.

thrill you. I was sharing this with a group of pastors, and one of them interrupted me to say, "Stop, don't say anything more." Of course, I blew it by continuing to talk. But in spite of me, this pastor's imagination was captured by the third of Paul's three visions of *the good*— a unified body of Christ that reflects his beauty.

Don't do anything with this chapter; just let the
wonder of what God wants to create in us thrill you.

36

The Beauty of a Jesus Community

Including the Distant Outsider

It's hard enough to include the poor or disabled who already live in our community, but how do we include the outsider, or worse, the distant outsider? What about the distant, poor Jewish outsider? That's Paul's intention as he invites the Corinthians, in his last letter to them to create a Jesus community at Corinth, to love the poor Jewish believers in Judea. He is attempting something incredibly audacious—to create not just a Jesus community in Corinth, but a global, multinational, and multiclass Jesus community.

Paul's means is generosity, a donation from the wealthy Greek world to the poor Jews in Judea. But the wealthy Corinthians drag their feet. If we take another close look at their culture, we'll see why.

"The Poor Take and Give Nothing In Return"

Don't misunderstand, the Corinthians *were* generous. Almost all of the public buildings and entertainment, including plays and games, were donated by wealthy elites. For example, Paul mentions a leader in the

Corinthian church named Erastus, calling him the city treasurer (Rom. 16:23). Archaeologists have discovered a pavement stone in Corinth with the following inscription honoring Erastus for a multimillion-dollar gift of a city street:

> Erastus in return for his aedileship [director of public buildings] paved it at his own expense.[1]

Fig. 36A. Win-Win vs. Lose-Lose

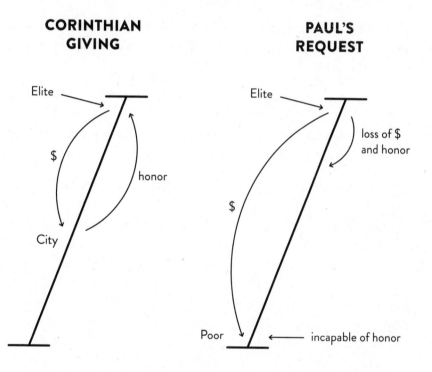

But no one in Corinth gives to the Judean poor. Why? The poor have no value, so their thanks have no weight. The Romans had a saying: "For death is like a beggar, who takes and gives nothing in return."[2] The poor's adulation means nothing to the wealthy

---

1. Quoted in Anthony C. Thiselton, *The First Epistle to the Corinthians* (Grand Rapids, MI: Eerdmans, 2000), 9.

2. Artemidorus, *The Interpretation of Dreams: Oneirocriticon*, 3.53, trans. R. J. White (Park Ridge, NJ: Noyes Press, 1975), 171, quoted in Peter Brown, *Through the Eye of the Needle: Wealth, the Fall of Rome, and the Making of Christianity in the West, 350–550 AD* (Princeton, NJ; Oxford: Princeton University Press, 2012), 76.

Corinthians because the poor are nothing. They are incapable of giving honor to wealthy patrons because they have no honor to give. The left side of the above diagram shows typical Corinthian giving. The elite give to the city. In turn, the citizens elevate the elite by honoring them. It's a win-win proposition. But Paul's request, on the right, is a lose-lose. The Corinthians stand to lose money without gaining honor (see Fig. 36A on p. 299).

Include the Distant Outsider

Paul responds to the Corinthians' balking with a breathtaking masterpiece of incarnational love. First, he shows them how the Philippians embody generosity:

> We want you to know, brothers, about the *grace of God* that has been given among the churches of Macedonia, for in a severe test of affliction, their abundance of joy and their extreme poverty have overflowed in a wealth of generosity on their part. (2 Cor. 8:1–2)

The Philippians' *extreme poverty* (dying) overflowed in a *wealth of generosity* (rising). Their generosity to the unknown, poor outsider follows the path of the J-Curve and resets the Greco-Roman narrative of "What's in it for me?"

Second, Paul redefines the outsider as a saint. In other words, distant, poor Jews are holy, in Christ. Paul renames the *other* by calling him *brother*. Because we are all *in Christ*, you are me. As much as Christ's righteousness becomes mine, so Christ's body, even the poor Jew in Jerusalem, becomes mine. Justification by faith levels the playing ground, destroying the Failure-Boasting Chart with its factions, jealousy, and exclusion.

Justification by faith levels the playing ground,
destroying the Failure-Boasting Chart with
its factions, jealousy, and exclusion.

Philadelphia, where I live, has a reputation for rudeness and abruptness, but a recent survey revealed that it is the highest tipping city in America. I was not surprised. Philly is a very blue-collar city, so the waitperson is "you." He or she is not beneath you, but your friend. You care for your friend.

Third, Paul redefines their gift by repeatedly calling it *an act of grace*:

> Accordingly, we urged Titus that as he had started, so he should complete among you this *act of grace*. But as you excel in everything—in faith, in speech, in knowledge, in all earnestness, and in our love for you—see that you excel in this *act of grace* also. (vv. 6–7)

Because the Corinthians live on the Failure-Boasting Chart, they love receiving grace, but they give it sparingly. Paul's radical idea of grace, based on God's grace to us, is giving without receiving back.[3] It's one-way giving based on one-way love. So Paul not only renames the Judeans as saints, but he also goes on to redefine giving by calling it an *act of grace.*

Fourth, Paul goes out of his way to honor his fellow team member and fundraiser, Titus (vv. 16–23). I've done lots of fundraising, and it can be hard and humbling work. One board member said to me, "I think of fundraisers like undertakers. You know you need them, but you aren't sure you want to shake their hand!" Paul is empowering Titus in an often thankless job.

Fifth, notice how Paul incarnates with the Corinthians. Even though they have used excellence as a way of getting honor, Paul segues from their desire for excellence ("as you excel in everything" v. 7) to calling them to become excellent in extending grace to the distant and despised outsider.

Sixth, Paul roots *grace* in the narrative of Jesus's dying and rising:

> For you know the *grace* of our Lord Jesus Christ, that though he was rich [*life*], yet for your sake he became poor [*death*], so that you by his poverty might become rich [*resurrection*]. (2 Cor. 8:9)

---

3. John Barclay, *Paul and the Gift* (Grand Rapids, MI: Eerdmans, 2017), is an excellent study of this theme in Paul.

One-way generosity re-enacts the dying and rising of Jesus. I die. You live. Here's what that looks like on the familiar *love* J-Curve:

Fig. 36B. One-Way Generosity

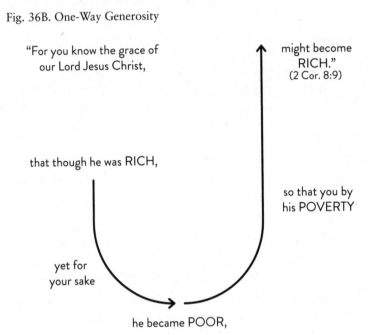

"For you know the grace of our Lord Jesus Christ,

that though he was RICH,

yet for your sake

he became POOR,

might become RICH." (2 Cor. 8:9)

so that you by his POVERTY

Paul doesn't berate the Corinthians for not giving. He points them to a new vision of beauty—the sacrificial death of Jesus. He gives them a new narrative to entice them off the Failure-Boasting Chart and into the J-Curve. Otherwise, no amount of teaching on giving to the poor will make any sense.

Finally, Paul incarnates yet again with the Corinthians by addressing their fear: "Who's going to take care of me?" It's hard for us to fathom that prior to the nineteenth-century agricultural revolution, much of the world teetered on the brink of starvation for part of each year. For example, in Galilee in Jesus's day, a loaf of bread cost one-fourth of a laborer's daily wage. In today's economy, that comes to about $25 for a loaf of bread. Paul addresses the Corinthians' fears by using a positive image of sowing and reaping: if they sow to the poor, they will reap a harvest from God. "God is able to make all grace abound to you" (2 Cor. 9:8a). We do the dying, and God does the rising.

Creating a Jesus Community with the J-Curve

Paul now pulls all his threads together and describes how re-enacting the dying and rising of Christ creates a divine community. In his concluding paragraph of 2 Corinthians 9, he paints a picture of a divine community in which God, the rich Corinthians, and the poor, distant Jews are all moving toward one another. Each arrow represents a movement of love. Love closes the social/class distance and the physical distance.

> For the ministry of this service is not only supplying the needs of the saints [*rich→poor*] but is also overflowing in many thanksgivings to God [*poor→God*]. By their approval of this service [*poor→rich*], they will glorify God [*poor→God*] because of your submission that comes from your confession of the gospel of Christ, and the generosity of your contribution for them [*rich→poor*] and for all others, while they long for you [*poor→rich*] and pray for you [*poor→God*] because of the surpassing grace of God upon you [God→*rich*]. Thanks be to God for his inexpressible gift! (2 Cor. 9:12–15)

The critical hinge is the Corinthians' *submission that comes from their confession of the gospel of Christ.* When they re-enact Jesus's generous dying love, they submit to their confession of the gospel. As they surrender their narrative and take on his narrative, they participate in a virtual Jesus community.

A Jesus Community Snapshot

So, does Paul pull it off? Does his constant modeling and teaching of the J-Curve form a Jesus community at Corinth? Just before he leaves for Jerusalem—and prison—Paul sends greetings to the church in Rome from Corinth, giving us a snapshot of the Corinthian church:

> I *Tertius*, who wrote this letter, greet you in the Lord. *Gaius*, who is host to me and to the whole church, greets you. *Erastus*, the city treasurer, and our brother *Quartus*, greet you. (Rom. 16:22–23)

You'll recall that *Erastus* gifted a street to Corinth. *Gaius* hosts a house church. Both are wealthy, upper-class elites, the *strong*. But who are *Tertius* and *Quartus*? Their names give us a clue. *Tertius* means "third" and *Quartus* means "fourth." What do you name a valueless slave? Why bother with a name? Why not just number slaves with their birth order?[4] But Paul mentions in the same breath the now infinitely valuable slaves and the wealthy aristocrats. They are on equal footing, completely valued in Christ, in his body in a virtual Jesus community. The gospel re-enacted by its leaders has worked.

We don't merely donate to the poor, the outsider, and the *weak*; we enter their world, we befriend them. Only when *the other* becomes *my brother or sister*, only when objects of pity become people—even friends—do we create a divine community. Only then does Jesus's beauty emerge in us.

> Only when *the other* becomes *my brother or sister*,
> only when objects of pity become people—even
> friends—do we create a divine community.

4. F. F. Bruce, "Some Roman Slave-Names," *Proceedings of the Leeds Philosophical Society: Literary and Historical Section* 5 (1938), I:44–60, esp. p. 50.

Conclusion

Not long after the Cell Phone Seminar, I got a chance to briefly embody Jesus at another prayer seminar with three hundred attending. With an audience of that size, we use roving mics so we can still be interactive, but I forgot to tell the mic-holders to guard against returning repeatedly to the same person. One of the mic-holders returned three times to a woman who shared lengthy insights that threatened to derail the seminar. She rambled, and I struggled to pay attention to her. In the smartphone seminar, I was lower than my audience. Here, I was higher. I was *strong*, and she was *weak*.

So what did I do to rescue the seminar? Nothing. I'd immersed myself long enough in the person of Jesus to know that this woman had instantly become more important than the other 299 people.[1] Our prayer seminar had momentarily become a seminar on love. She was my lost sheep. So here I was, caught off guard, in another J-Curve, with 299 sheep watching. It was just her now. She was my equal, deserving of dignity and respect.

During her interruptions, I prayed quietly as I concentrated on what she was saying. I prayed because I was aware of the power of my flesh—nothing in me was naturally disposed to listen to or value her. I can still feel how difficult it was to enter her world, to make sense of her. Her interruptions lasted about ten minutes, and the time passed quietly.

At the break, the associate pastor came up and apologized. "That won't happen again." Evidently, he'd talked with the woman. For a

---

1. Jesus frequently narrows his focus from a large crowd to just one person: the widow of Nain (Luke 7:11–17), the bleeding woman (Matt. 9:20–22), the lame man at Bethesda (John 5:1–9), Jairus's daughter (Matt. 9:18–19, 23–26), and the blind man (John 9:1–7).

second, I was confused—I was so engaged with her, I'd forgotten her impact on the seminar. I thanked him, but said, "You know, it's not the worst thing in the world for people to see me loving her. I get to display the beauty of Jesus to three hundred people." He said, "I've never thought about it that way." It was a new paradigm for him. When I've told this story at pastor training events, the reaction is always the same: "I would have focused on how she was ruining the seminar."

She wasn't ruining my seminar—the seminar just changed its focus; she was drawing me into Christ. I wasn't disoriented by something going badly—I knew my location, *in him*, moving downward for a moment of dying.

I prayed as she was speaking because it's not enough to see I'm on Jesus's path; I need him to guide me. I needed help to love her. The Spirit, who re-enacts resurrection, brought Jesus's presence to my heart and life to give me the grace to love her.

The chain of love worked: she weakened me, so I prayed, which allowed the Spirit to let Christ shine through me ever so briefly. The Spirit not only makes the J-Curve work, but he also shapes its goal: imaging Jesus. So instead of the fleeting glory of a well-run seminar, we get the enduring glory of the cross—where the beauty of Jesus shines. If we embrace the dying of Jesus, the beauty of Jesus emerges in us—and resurrection begins. His beauty is the end product, the goal, *the good*.

We began our journey together on a plane to Florida with Kim having a meltdown. I was confused, vowing to never do that again. Fifteen years later, confronted with a seminar out of control, I was in familiar territory—the path of Jesus. Immersing myself in the *mind of Christ*, the J-Curve, brought clarity, balance, and wisdom to the work of love.

Have I Embraced Christ in Dying *and* Rising?

If you feel stuck at the bottom of a J-Curve and struggle to live in the power of the resurrection, let me encourage you by leaving you with a few reflection questions that recall many of our themes:

1. *Have I shut my heart down?* If we don't embrace Christ's fellowship of suffering, we will often shut down our hearts in

order to survive. Either we stop feeling or we fill our life with the narcotics of busyness, entertainment, or work.

2. *Am I cynical or bitter?* Cynicism means that death, not life, has the last word. We give up hope, because we've lost any sense that our life is a divine story. Bitterness is the final fruit of our refusal to embrace our J-Curve. It is anger at God for designing our life so badly.

3. *Am I able to sing in this prison?* Singing in prison is an early taste of resurrection. That doesn't mean we are always rejoicing, but it should be a regular feature of a Spirit-led life.

4. *Am I aware of and living in the hope of the resurrection?* It is easy to get stuck in death, because death is so real, so binding, so limiting. So meditating on and praying for resurrection feeds hope.

5. *Have I done everything possible to escape this death?* We've seen Paul do this again and again. He is fully alive even in his deaths.

6. *Have I embraced the role of a slave and continued to hunt for new ways to love?* Because we're slaves of Jesus Christ, we're free to love.

7. *Is my life's goal a suffering-free life?* If we want to be free of suffering, our life will be tragic and shallow. If dying and rising with Jesus is our master narrative, then we can look forward to a rich life filled with adventure, hope, and joy.

Whenever I describe the J-Curve to believers who are going through hard times (most everyone), they almost immediately brighten up. Suddenly, they have hope and meaning, even a hint of glory—they sense their story is part of his larger story. That's the way the Christian life is meant to feel. As we participate together in Jesus's dying and rising, his beauty will emerge in us before a watching world. Only then will the bride be prepared for the coming of her lover. Come quickly, Lord Jesus!

Reflections on our Daughter, Ashley Frearson

Several months after I finished this book, our daughter Ashley went to be with her Lord and Savior. Ashley was our family's version of Mother Teresa—she loved freely. When taking Ashley to chemo in Philadelphia, Jill was amazed to watch Ashley hand out homemade "blessing bags" to the homeless. Each bag contained food, a gift card, socks, soap, a Bible verse, and directions to shelters.

The person who first taught Ashley compassion was her sister Kim. When Kim was younger, she would regularly crawl into bed with Ashley at night. Kim is why Ashley became a special-education teacher. Kim's autism forced Ashley to deal with life's difficult questions at an early age.

That came home to me poignantly during a 1990 family camping trip that I mention in the opening to *A Praying Life*. As we were unpacking, I could see Ashley in front of our minivan, frustrated and tense. I asked her, "What's wrong?" She said, "I lost my contact." The forest floor was covered with hundreds of crevices. I said, "Freeze. Let's pray," but she burst into tears and said, "What good does it do? God doesn't answer my prayers for Kim to speak." At age fourteen, she'd poured out her heart to God, but seemingly God hadn't heard. Her heart had shut down to God.

A similar question was on Ashley's heart twenty-eight years later when she and I were watching her son Jack play baseball in May. She was grappling with her cancer and the possibility of her passing. She told me, "Dad, it doesn't make any sense. Why would God do this?" I told her, "Ashley, I don't know what God is doing. It doesn't make any sense to me either."

It's the Saturday between Good Friday and Easter Sunday, that long pause between death and resurrection, that is the hardest. We don't know the "why," and life is pure pain. Everything has gone wrong.

The Saturday before Ashley's passing, when we had a few moments together, I reminded her of the contact story. In front of our minivan, I had prayed with her, "God, help us find this contact." Then I prayed quietly to myself as I bent down, "Lord, this would really be a good time to come through." There on the forest floor, balancing on a leaf, was her contact. I reminded Ashley that God works in stories that are just like the story of Jesus. Like Jesus, we go through death and then resurrection. In death, we don't know how or when a resurrection will occur.

I also reminded her how she had been an answer to her own prayer for Kim by taking Kim to speech computer camp with me, where Kim learned to speak using her computer. God did answer Ashley's heartfelt prayer for Kim. Kim speaks to us all. Resurrection came out of death. It just took time to see the story God was weaving.

I do know that God reveals himself in the wounds of his Son, Jesus. And now, we, his followers, reveal Jesus in the wounds that God permits in our lives. The beauty that all of us saw in Ashley emerged out of a strange wound that God permitted in our family—her sister Kim. Ashley's chemo especially affected her hands and feet, leaving them cracked, raw, and painful. I told her several years ago that she bore the wounds of Christ—only to discover that during chemo, when faced with turning inward or looking to Jesus, she'd meditated on the sufferings of Christ. She told her women's Bible study:

> During chemo I couldn't read. I couldn't watch TV, so my thoughts always had to take a path as they always do, right? Satan or Jesus.

So by God's grace I just sat at the cross and pictured Jesus's face over and over again. One particular night, I felt really nauseous. I looked up from my bed and I saw the most majestic eyes of a lion over my bed, and he roared once and then the image was gone. And I immediately felt the Lion of Judah say to me, "I hate cancer more than you. I love you, Ashley." That's what suffering does. It drags us to the cross again and again.

Faith is at its finest on the long Saturdays when life has lost all meaning. Ashley's "Saturday" of not knowing why is now our "Saturday" of grieving the loss of this fair flower of Jesus. Even here, Ashley still speaks to us. At her women's Bible study in 2015, she recalled Shadrach, Meshach, and Abednego's reply to Nebuchadnezzar's threat:

"Our God whom we serve IS ABLE to deliver us from the fiery furnace, and He will deliver us from your hand. BUT IF NOT, let it be known to you, O king, that we do not serve your gods, nor will we worship the golden image which you have set up."

I was told last September that my colon cancer wanted to wage war again. When my oncologist breathed the words "malignant cells are in your mediastinum," I felt like I was literally walking in the valley with the shadow of death chasing me.

So my prayer is, "My God whom I serve is able to deliver me completely from cancer, BUT IF NOT, let it be known that even if I face a chronic or a short life, you are Lord of my life. I will choose to fight every day and make the choice to worship you with all my heart, soul and mind, by trusting fully in Jesus."

To say, "BUT IF NOT," is the choice to believe when we've lost hope; to continue to show up for life and to worship even in the despair.

During her suffering, Ashley unfailingly displayed and shared Jesus. She never missed an opportunity. She told her Bible study:

I still fall apart in my oncologist's office—the smells and sounds in the hospital dismantle me. My oncologist saw my tears gushing so he referred me to the mental health department. Through tears I said I couldn't figure out mommy tired vs chemo tired vs hormones vs fear—just a few variables going on! A couple days later

I received a phone call from this brand-new, nervous mental-health therapist. He shared his methods of meditation, yoga, positive thinking. I interrupted, "Hold on for a second. If I told you tomorrow that you would be diagnosed with ugly cancer and had to face hard chemo again and again, what would you do?" Silence. Hello? So God gave me another grace opportunity to speak the name of Jesus and to tell him that only Jesus can help me each day fend off fear and feed my faith. Only Jesus knows my cells and gets me. I have sore hands, feet, and difficulty breathing, but knowing Jesus experienced all of these things on the cross is such a mind-boggling comfort to my mind and soul—it is the PEACE THAT BLOWS MY MIND—PASSES UNDERSTANDING.

In reality, we all have stage 4 spiritual cancer flowing through our bodies. Jesus's death on the cross abolished every sinful disease. This is where my healing began when I was nineteen. Each day I need to run to him and be reminded of my eternal, unshakable prognosis. So needless to say, my oncologist said, "I got a call from mental health and they thought our services would not be beneficial." I cannot talk about cancer without talking about Jesus. We attended a family-support cancer group last fall. My daughter Layne labeled the group "Unfortunates" because those in attendance were unfortunate. So at the Unfortunates, I shared that I cannot talk about my trials without Jesus. I equated it to eating a Reese's—Jesus is the chocolate and suffering is the peanut butter—they just go together. Without Jesus in the hard, there is no hope. Only Jesus marries hope with suffering.

Ashley told Jill just before her passing that "she'd lived a long life." Jill was puzzled by her comment (Ashley was forty-two) until the week after Ashley's passing, when Facebook lit up with hundreds of people mentioning Ashley's welcoming smile and thoughtful love. In the greeting line, more than a thousand people waited two hours or more not just to grieve with us but to tell the family some snippet of her love. One couple (Ashley had cared for their severely disabled daughter) described how, when their son committed suicide, Ashley came over and stayed with them, bringing hope in the midst of their pain. In M. Night Shyamalan's movie *The Village*, a town elder says,

"The world moves for love. It kneels before it in awe." In her short life, she'd packed in several lives of love.

Ashley's combination of love for Jesus and love for people broke into people's hearts in multiple ways. Her oncologist posted this on Ashley's Facebook page:

> I remember my nurse meeting her for the 1st time and she couldn't stop talking about how this patient was just . . . different. She just made her feel good. About life, family, love, god. On the latter topic, at best, I have been indifferent to religion, at worst, scorning it often, citing the cop-out mantra, "I'm spiritual but not religious." But I can truly say no one has made me question my cynicism more, without even trying!

Ashley not only embraced the fellowship of Christ's suffering in her life, but in that crucible, she shone with Jesus. She embodied the vision of *the good* that we desperately need to rediscover. Her love for Jesus compelled her into a life of love that stuns all of us and points us to a God who is all love.

If you'd like to glimpse Ashley through the eyes of her husband, Dave, along with her parents, siblings, and friends, go to www.AshleyFrears on.com.

Acknowledgments

My work on the J-Curve began in *The Love Course* (1992–1995), but many scholars, and especially these, were an immense help: Anthony Thiselton (1 Corinthians), Richard B. Gaffin, Jr. (the gospel and resurrection), Simon Gathercole (the theme of boasting), Peter O'Brien (Philippians), Michael Gorman (cruciformity), Robert Tannehill (boasting), William Evans (union with Christ), Carl Trueman (Martin Luther), Jason Hood (imitation), and Peter Brown (Greco-Roman culture). My dad, Jack Miller, first introduced me to the wonder of the gospel—which he now enjoys face to face with Jesus.

I'm especially indebted to these scholars for giving me helpful feedback on the manuscript and/or concepts: Richard B. Gaffin Jr. (Westminster Theological Seminary), Clair Davis (Westminster Theological Seminary), David Powlison (CCEF), John Frame (Reformed Theological Seminary), C. D. "Jimmy" Agan (Covenant Theological Seminary), Robert Yarborough (Covenant Theological Seminary), and Kevin McFadden (Cairn University).

I'm thankful for the immense help provided by my editor, Liz Heaney, in this our fourth book. Liz keeps me clear, focused, and simple. David Powlison's wisdom and encouragement were a real blessing. My son, John Miller, and Rich Cannon encouraged me to use the title J-Curve.

I'm thankful for the churches that participated in the J-Curve Seminar: West End Presbyterian (Richmond, VA), Chelten (Dresher, PA), Westlake (Lausanne, Switzerland), Trinity Presbyterian (Lakeland, FL), Redeemer City (Winter Haven, FL), Redemption (Phoenix, AZ), and New Life Presbyterian (Glenside, PA). These readers also provided helpful feedback and ideas: Sherri Hughes, Katie Sullivan, Dane Ort-lund, Jill Miller, John Miller, Liz Voboril, Corey Widmer, Steve Firmin, Vicki Schwenk, Jon Hori, Carson Adcock, and Michele Walton.

I'm thankful for my friend Tim O. Strawbridge and his development work. Donna Herr, my assistant, managed multiple projects. Michele Walton and Les Swift did the diagrams. Steve Bohannon (bohannonediting.com) did valuable research. The board of seeJesus (Nessa Parks, Bob Loker, Steve Young, Blair Simmons, Carson Adcock, Dwight Smith, and Drew Bennett) provided wisdom and leadership.

At Crossway, I'm thankful for Lane Dennis, Justin Taylor, Dane Ortlund, Anthony Gosling, and David DeWit's encouragement, along with Amy Kruis and Lauren Harvey.

A special thank you to the people who funded the extensive research behind this book: our friends at Trinity Presbyterian, Christ Community Presbyterian, and Redeemer City in Lakeland and Winter Haven, Florida, including Keith and Payton Albritton, Mike Arnett, Howard and Deanna Bayless, Jim and Deena Davie, Jerri and Jill Gable, David and Cynthia Hallock, Jack and Tina Harrell, Shawn and Kelly Jones, Scott and Julie McBride, Richard Nicholson, Joe O'Brien, Dane and Tracy Parker, Frank and Dyeanna Portlock, Sam and Victoria Portlock, Dwight and Jayna Smith, Tim O. and Tina Strawbridge, Mike and Rebecca Wells, and Steve and Kinsey Young, and our friends in Pennsylvania, John and Pam Miller, Michael and Hyelee Yoon, and an anonymous family foundation.

I'm particularly thankful to my wife, Jill, for encouraging me to "get this done"! And last but not least, for my daughter Kim, who prays for my writing every day!

Virtual Appendix

@ seeJesus.net/J-Curvebook

1. "Luther: The Last Medieval Protestant"
2. Bibliography
3. Scripture References to Dying and Rising in 1 and 2 Corinthians
4. Overview Chart of Paul's Suffering
5. Gospel Summaries in Luke and Acts
6. Photos of Corinth: Babbius, Agora
7. *Spirit* and *Spiritual* Texts in Paul
8. Reflections on The New Perspective
9. Usage of "Spiritual" in the apostle Paul's writings
10. Scripture references for parallels between Paul and Jesus's Passion (chap. 29)

General Index

Scripture Index

The J-Curve is a journey.
Take your time.

J-CURVE DISCUSSION GUIDE

J-CURVE BIBLE STUDY SERIES

"Take time with the J-Curve. You will become a deeper, wiser, truer person. You will become more humble, more joyous, more purposeful. And you will walk more steadily in the light."

DAVID POWLISON, Executive Director, Christian Counseling & Educational Foundation

"Get ready to begin perhaps the deepest and most fulfilling Bible adventure you've ever undertaken!"

JONI EARECKSON TADA, Joni and Friends International Disability Center

Learn more at **seeJesus.net**.

Host a J-Curve Seminar
at Your Church

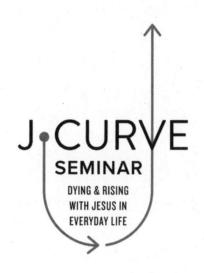

The J-Curve seminar helps your church interact with the
J-Curve map for the Christian life. Explore these simple but
profound truths together and learn to plot life's ups and
downs onto the story of Jesus.

Learn more at **seeJesus.net/events**.

Also Available from Paul Miller

How do you love with no love in return? How do you love when no one notices or cares? Best-selling author Paul Miller tackles these tough questions to offer the help we need to embrace relationships, endure rejection, cultivate community, and reach out to even the most unlovable around us as we discover the power to live a loving life.

"This is the most honest, timely, and helpful book I've ever read about the costly and exhausting demands of loving well."

SCOTTY WARD SMITH, Pastor Emeritus, Christ Community Church, Franklin, Tennessee

"A book that is so profound, so fresh, and so life changing that you can't get it out of your mind or your heart."

STEVE BROWN, Host, *Key Life* radio program; author, *Three Free Sins*

For more information, visit **crossway.org**.